ISLAMIC FINANCE AND BANKING

ISLAMIC FINANCE AND BANKING

AH Mastan

MD PUBLICATIONS PVT LTD
NEW DELHI
www.mdppl.com

Published by:

MD Publications Pvt Ltd
"MD House", 11, Darya Ganj,
New Delhi - 110 002
Phone : +91-11-45355555
E-mail : contact@mdppl.com
website : www.mdppl.com

ISBN: 978-81-7533-305-5

Published and Printed by Mr. Pranav Gupta on behalf of **MD Publications Pvt Ltd** at JJ offset Printers, Delhi.

PREFACE

Islamic banking refers to a system of banking or banking activity that is consistent with the principles of Islamic law (*Sharia*) and its practical application through the development of Islamic economics. Sharia prohibits the payment or acceptance of interest fees for the lending and accepting of money respectively, (Riba, usury) for specific terms, as well as investing in businesses that provide goods or services considered contrary to its principles (Haraam, forbidden). While these principles were used as the basis for a flourishing economy in earlier times, it is only in the late 20th century that a number of Islamic banks were formed to apply these principles to private or semi-private commercial institutions within the Muslim community.

Islamic banking has the same purpose as conventional banking except that it operates in accordance with the rules of Shariah, known as *Fiqh al-Muamalat* (Islamic rules on transactions). The basic principle of Islamic banking is the sharing of profit and loss and the prohibition of *riba* (usury). Common terms used in Islamic banking include profit sharing (*Mudharabah*), safekeeping (*Wadiah*), joint venture (*Musharakah*), cost plus (*Murabahah*), and leasing (*Ijarah*).

The Islamic Banking Act is a unique piece of legislation. It provides for the setting up and licensing of "Islamic banks". It is unique in the sense that probably for the first time an Act of Parliament has been enacted to deal specifically with Islamic banking. The writer is not aware of similar legislation in any other jurisdiction following the common law system. Up to the present only one bank, Bank Islam has been licensed under the Islamic Banking Act. The Islamic Banking Act stipulates that a bank licensed under it Act shall carry on "Islamic banking business".

It must be remembered that the Islamic Banking Act and Islamic law generally are to be applied and implemented within the existing common law system and the regime of all other existing laws. This includes not only the laws but also the courts system and court procedure. Needless to say, that system and those laws and procedure were not drafted or designed with Islamic law in mind or to facilitate the application of Islamic law.

The first modern experiment with Islamic banking was undertaken in Egypt under cover without projecting an Islamic image-for fear of being seen as a manifestation of Islamic fundamentalism that was anathema to the political regime. The pioneering effort, led by Ahmad Elnaggar, took the form of a savings bank based on profit-sharing in the Egyptian town of Mit Ghamr in 1963. This experiment lasted until 1967 (Ready 1981), by which time there were nine such banks in the country.

I am very grateful to Mr. Pranav Gupta, Director of MD Publications Pvt Ltd, New Delhi, for his kind cooperation and support for this book.

AH Mastan

CONTENTS

	Preface	*v*
1.	Introduction to Islamic Banking	1
2.	Conventional Banking	53
3.	Islamic Economic System	103
4.	Commercial Interest and Usury	137
5.	Islamic Financing	191
6.	Concepts in Islamic Banking	215
7.	Issues in Islamic Banking	249
	Bibliography	305
	Index	309

1

Introduction to Islamic Banking

INTRODUCTION

Islam is not only a religion in ordinary sense of the word, but a complete system of life. While other religious codes provide guidance only for the relation between man and his Creator, Islam guides man in his relationship with God, and gives him the norms which govern his temporal existence, since Islam is concerned with the spiritual, political, social economic, moral and all other material aspects of the human being.

Every social system has its own economic system. Islam being a comprehensive and distinct social system possesses a corresponding economic system of its own. Islamic economics is fast developing into a different and distinct paradigm of economics. Therefore, a number of Islamic financial institutions have emerged in various Muslim as well as some non-Muslim countries reaching finally at long last to our country Kenya. Hence the development of Islamic or interest free banks in the region.

DIFFERENCE BETWEEN ISLAMIC AND CONVENTIONAL BANKS

There are a number of key differences between the products and services offered by a conventional bank in comparison to an Islamic financial institution.

First, Islam is the back bone of interest free banking; moral principles and objectives play a more important role in its operations. As such, it is organized on the basis of cooperation with each other as stated in the Quranic injuction, "Help you one another in righteousness and piety but help you not one another in sin and trasgression". The Quran also calls for trade: Eat up not your property among yourselves in vanities but let there be amongst you, traffic by mutual goodwill. Honesty and trustworthiness is so essential in business; thus, the Prophet (Pbuh) had declared that dishonest transactions are illegal.

Second, no gain is accepted without either effort or liability. Islam forbids receiving a monetary advantage without giving a counter value, but is not opposed to profit or financial gain as long as an effort is performed or (partial) liability is accepted for the financial result of a venture.

Third, general conditions of a debtor should be evaluated genuinely. If one is in financial distress, and is not able to pay back the principal, one should be given an extension on humanitarian ground without any penalty.

Fourth, certain business transactions are considered unlawful in Islam and cannot be carried out in an Islamic bank. For example trading in alcohol, intoxicating drugs, gambling or producing pornography are contrary to Islam.

Fifth, Islamic banks offer no interest-bearing products or services, and in its organisational structure and corporate governance, Islamic banks have Shariah board, to ensure that the bank practices are in conformity with the Shariah and do not oppress the disadvantaged client.

RIBA

The word "Riba" means excess, increase or addition which, as correctly interpreted according to Shariah terminology, implies any excess compensation without due consideration (consideration does not include time value of money).This definition of Riba is derived from the Quran and is unanimously accepted by all Islamic scholars. The meaning of Riba has been clarified in the following verses of Quran:

"O those who believe fear Allah and give up what still remains of the Riba if you are believers. But if you do not do so, then be warned of war from Allah and His Messenger. If you repent even now, you have the right of the return of your capital; neither will you do wrong nor will you be wronged."

These verses clearly indicate that the term Riba means any excess compensation over and above the principal which is without due consideration. However, the Quran has not altogether forbidden all types of excess; as it is present in trade as well, which is permissible. The excess that has been rendered haram in Quran is a special type termed as Riba. In the dark ages, the Arabs used to accept Riba as a type of sale, which unfortunately is also being understood at the present times. Islam has categorically made a clear distinction between the excess in capital resulting from sale and excess resulting from interest. The first type of excess is permissible but the second type is forbidden and rendered Haram.

"Seized in this state they say: 'Buying and selling is but a kind of interest', even though Allah has made buying and selling lawful, and interest unlawful."

Riba in Quran

First Revelation (Surah al-Rum, verse 39)

"That which you give as interest to increase the peoples' wealth increases not with God; but that which you give in charity, seeking the goodwill of God, multiplies manifold."

Second Revelation (Surah al-Nisa', verse 161)

"And for their taking interest even though it was forbidden for them, and their wrongful appropriation of other peoples' property. We have prepared for those among them who reject faith a grievous punishment (4: 161)"

Third Revelation (Surah Al 'Imran, verses 130-2)

"O believers, take not doubled and redoubled interest, and fear God so that you may prosper. Fear the fire which has been prepared for those who reject faith, and obey God and the Prophet so that you may receive mercy."

Fourth Revelation (Surah al-Baqarah, verses 275-81)

"Those who benefit from interest shall be raised like those

who have been driven to madness by the touch of the Devil; this is because they say: "Trade is like interest" while God has permitted trade and forbidden interest. Hence those who have received the admonition from their Lord and desist may keep their previous gains, their case being entrusted to God; but those who revert shall be the inhabitants of the fire and abide therein for ever."

"God deprives interest of all blessing but blesses charity; He loves not the ungrateful sinner."

"Those who believe, perform good deeds, establish prayer and pay the zakat, their reward is with their Lord; neither should they have any fear, nor shall they grieve."

"O, believers, fear Allah, and give up what is still due to you from the interest (usury), if you are true believers."

"If you do not do so, then take notice of war from Allah and His Messenger. But, if you repent, you can have your principal. Neither should you commit injustice nor should you be subjected to it."

"If the debtor is in difficulty, let him have respite until it is easier, but if you forego out of charity, it is better for you if you realize."

"And fear the Day when you shall be returned to the Lord and every soul shall be paid in full what it has earned and no one shall be wronged."

Riba in Hadith

From Jabir

The Prophet may curse the receiver and the payer of interest, the one who records it and the two witnesses to the transaction and said: "They are all alike [In guilt]." (Muslim, Kitab al-Musaqat, Bab la'ni akili al-riba wa mu'kilihi; also in Tirmidhi and Musnad Ahmad)

Jabir ibn 'Abdallah, giving a report on the Prophet's Farewell Pilgrimage, said: The Prophet addressed the people and said "All of the riba of Jahiliyyah is annulled. The first riba that I annul is our riba, that accruing to 'Abbas ibn 'Abd al-Muttalib [the Prophet's uncle]; it is being cancelled completely."

From 'Abdallah ibn Hanzalah

The Prophet said: "A dirham of riba which a man receives knowingly is worse than committing adultery thirty-six times" (Mishkat al-Masabih, Kitab al-Buyu', Bab al-riba, on the authority of Ahmad and Daraqutni). Bayhaqi has also reported the above hadith in Shu'ab al-iman with the addition that "Hell befits him whose flesh has been nourished by the unlawful."

From Abu Hurayrah

The Prophet said: "On the night of Ascension I came upon people whose stomachs were like houses with snakes visible from the outside. I asked Gabriel who they were. He replied that they were people who had received interest

From Abu Hurayrah 5

The Prophet said: "Riba has seventy segments, the least serious being equivalent to a man committing adultery with his own mother."

From Abu Hurayrah

The Prophet said: "There will certainly come a time for mankind when everyone will take riba and if he does not do so; its dust will reach him."

From Abu Hurayrah

The Prophet said: "God would be justified in not allowing four persons to enter paradise or to taste its blessings: he who drinks habitually, he who takes riba, he who usurps an orphan's property without right, and he who is undutiful to his parents."

Riba An Nasiyah

From Usamah ibn Zayd

The Prophet said: "There is no riba except in Nasiyah [waiting]." (Bukhari, Kitab al-Buyu', Bab Bay' al-dinari bi aldinar nasa'an; also Muslim and Musnad Ahmad) "There is no riba in hand-to-hand [spot] transactions."

From Ibn Mas'ud

The Prophet said: "Even when interest is much, it is bound to end up into paltriness."

From Anas ibn Malik

The Prophet said: "When one of you grants a loan and the borrower offer him a dish, he should not accept it; and if the borrower offers a ride on an animal, he should not ride, unless the two of them have been previously accustomed to exchanging such favours mutually."

From Anas ibn Malik

The Prophet said: "If a man extends a loan to someone he should not accept a gift."

From Abu Burdah ibn Abi Musa

I came to Madinah and met 'Abdallah ibn Salam who said, "You live in a country where riba is rampant; hence if anyone owes you something and presents you with a load of hay, or a load of barley, or a rope of straw, do not accept it for it is riba."

Fadalah ibn 'Ubayd said that "The benefit derived from any loan is one of the different aspects of riba." (Sunan al-Bayhaqi) This hadith is mawquf implying that it is not necessarily from the Prophet; it could be an explanation provided by Fadalah himself, a companion of the Prophet.

Riba al-Fadl

From 'Umar ibn al-Khattab

The last verse to be revealed was on riba and the Prophet was taken without explaining it to us; so give up not only riba but also raibah [whatever raises doubts in the mind about its rightful-ness].

The Prophet said, "Sell gold in exchange of equivalent gold, sell silver in exchange of equivalent silver, sell dates in exchange of equivalent dates, sell wheat in exchange of equivalent wheat, sell salt in exchange of equivalent salt, sell barley in exchange of equivalent barley, but if a person transacts in excess, it will be usury (riba). However, sell gold for silver anyway you please on the condition it is hand-to-hand (spot) and sell barley for date anyway you please on the condition it is hand-to-hand (spot)."

From Abu Sa'id al-Khudri

The Prophet said: "Do not sell gold for gold except when it is like for like, and do not increase one over the other; do not sell silver for silver except when it is like for like, and do not increase one over the other; and do not sell what is away [from among these] for what is ready."

From 'Ubada ibn al-Samit

The Prophet said: "Gold for gold, silver for silver, wheat for wheat, barley for barley, dates for dates, and salt for salt - like for like, equal for equal, and hand-to-hand; if the commodities differ, then you may sell as you wish, provided that the exchange is hand-to-hand."

From Abu Sa'id al-Khudri

The Prophet said: "Gold for gold, silver for silver, wheat for wheat, barley for barley, dates for dates, and salt for salt - like for like, and hand-to-hand. Whoever pays more or takes more has indulged in riba. The taker and the giver are alike [in guilt]."

From Abu Sa'id and Abu Hurayrah

A man employed by the Prophet in Khaybar brought for him janibs [dates of very fine quality]. Upon the Prophet's asking him whether all the dates of Khaybar were such, the man replied that this was not the case and added that "they exchanged a sa' [a measure] of this kind for two or three [of the other kind]". The Prophet replied, "Do not do so. Sell [the lower quality dates] for dirhams and then use the dirhams to buy janibs. [When dates are exchanged against dates] they should be equal in weight."

From Abu Sa'id

Bilal brought to the Prophet some barni [good quality] dates whereupon the Prophet asked him where these were from. Bilal replied, "I had some inferior dates which I exchanged for these - two sa's for a sa'." The Prophet said, "Oh no, this is exactly riba. Do not do so, but when you wish to buy, sell the inferior dates against something [cash] and then buy the better dates with the price you receive."

From Fadalah ibn 'Ubayd al-Ansari

On the day of Khaybar he bought a necklace of gold and pearls for twelve dinars. On separating the two, he found that the gold itself was equal to more than twelve dinars. So he mentioned this to the Prophet who replied, "It [jewellery] must not be sold until the contents have been valued separately."

From Abu Umamah

The Prophet said: "Whoever makes a recommendation for his brother and accepts a gift offered by him has entered riba through one of its large gates."

From Anas ibn Malik

The Prophet said: "Deceiving a mustarsal [an unknowing entrant into the market] is riba."

From 'Abdallah ibn Abi Awfa

The Prophet said: "A najish [one who serves as an agent to bid up the price in an auction] is a cursed taker of riba."

CLASSIFICATION OF RIBA

The first and primary type is called Riba An Nasiyah or Riba Al Jahiliya and, the second type is called Riba Al Fadl, Riba An Naqd or Riba Al Bai.

Since the first type was specified in the Quranic verses before the sayings of the Holy Prophet, this type was termed as Riba al Quran. However the second type was not understood by the Quranic verses alone but also had to be explained by the Holy Prophet, it is also called Riba al Hadees. During the dark ages, only the first form (Riba An Nasiyah) was considered to be Riba. However the Holy Prophet also classified the second form (Riba Al Fadl) as Riba.

1. Riba An Nasiyah

Riba An Nasiyah' is defined as excess, which results from predetermined interest (sood) which a lender receives over and above the principle (Ras ul Maal).This is the real and primary form of Riba. Since the verses of Quran have directly rendered this type of Riba as haram, it is called Riba Al Quran. Similarly, since only this type was considered Riba in the dark ages, it has earned the name of Riba Al Jahiliya. Imam Abu Bakr Hassas Razi has outlined a complete and prohibiting legal definition of Riba An Nasiyah in the following words:

The kind of loan where specified repayment period and an amount in excess of capital are pre determined.

One of the ahadith quoted by Ali ibn at Talib (RAA) has defined Riba An Nasiyah in similar words. The Holy Prophet said: "Every loan that draws interest is Riba."

The famous Sahabi Fazala Bin Obaid has also defined Riba in similar words: "Every loan that draws profit is one of the forms of Riba."

The famous Arab scholar Abu Ishaq az Zajjaj also defines Riba in the following words: "Every loan that draws more than its actual amount."

Riba An Nasiyah refers to the addition of the premium which is paid to the lender in return for his waiting as a condition for the loan and is technically the same as interest. The prohibition of Riba a Nasiyah is one of those issues which have been confirmed in the revealed laws of all Prophets. Some of the old testaments have rendered Riba as haram. The Quran has also stated the prohibition of Riba in various verses. It has warned those who persist in practicing it of a war which is certain to be declared on them by Allah Himself and His messenger and has seriously threatened those engaged as writer, witness and dealer in Riba transactions. These verses and ahadith will be discussed at length in a separate chapter, "The prohibition of Riba in the light of Quran and hadith".

According to the above definition of Riba An Nasiyah, the giving and taking of any excess amount in exchange of a loan at an agreed rate is included in interest irrespective whether at a high or low rate. It has been proven through ahadith that the Holy Prophet paid excess at the loan repayment time but since this excess was not paid through an agreed rate, it cannot be called interest. This clarifies that the word "draws" in the hadith definition" The loan that draws interest is Riba." has been used to highlight the giving and taking of excess amount through an agreed rate in the loan contract. Due to this, Imam Abu Bakr Hasas has added the word "condition" to the definition.

The fact that Riba An Nasiyah is categorically haram has never been disputed in the Muslim community. In short, the Riba of today which is supposed to be the pivot of human economy and features in discussions on the problem of interest is nothing but this Riba, the unlawfulness of which stands proved on the authority of the seven verses of the Quran, of more than forty ahadith and of the consensus of the Muslim community.

Wisdom behind the prohibition of Riba An Nasiyah is that we should realize that there is nothing in the entire creation of the world, which has no goodness or utility at all. But it is commonly recognized in every religion and community that things which have more benefits and less harms are called beneficial and useful. Conversely, things that cause more harm and less benefit are taken to be harmful and useless. Even the noble Quran, while declaring liquor and gambling to be haram, proclaimed that they do hold some benefits for people but the curse of sins they generate is far greater than the benefits they yield. Therefore, these cannot be called good or useful; on the contrary, taking these to be acutely harmful and destructive, it is necessary that they be avoided.

The case of Riba a Nasiyah is not different. Here the consumer of Riba does have some casual and transitory profits apparently coming to him, but its curse in this world and in the Hereafter is much too severe as compared to this benefit. The Riba consumer suffers such a spiritual and moral loss that it virtually takes away the great quality of being 'human' from him. An intelligent person who compares things in terms of their profit and loss, harm and benefit can hardly include things of casual benefit with an everlasting loss in the list of useful things. Similarly no sane and just person will say that personal and individual gain which causes loss to the whole community or group is useful. In theft and robbery for example, the gain of the gangster and the take of the thief is all too obvious but it is certainly harmful for the entire community since it ruins its peace and sense of security.

2. Riba Al Fadl

The second classification of Riba is Riba Al Fadl. Since the prohibition of this Riba has been established on Sunnah, it is also called Riba Al Hadees and is defined as excess compensation without any consideration resulting from a sale of goods. 'Riba Al Fadl' will be covered in greater detail later.

Riba Al Fadl actually means that excess which is taken in exchange of specific homogenous commodities and encountered in their hand-to-hand purchase & sale as explained in the famous hadith:

The Prophet said, "Sell gold in exchange of equivalent gold, sell silver in exchange of equivalent silver, sell dates in exchange of equivalent dates, sell wheat in exchange of equivalent wheat, sell salt in exchange of equivalent salt, sell barley in exchange of equivalent barley, but if a person transacts in excess, it will be usury (Riba). However, sell gold for silver anyway you please on the condition it is hand-to-hand (spot) and sell barley for date anyway you please on the condition it is hand-to-hand (spot)." This hadith enumerates 6 different commodities namely:

1. Gold, 2. Silver, 3. Dates, 4. Wheat, 5. Salt and 6. Barley

These six commodities can only be bought and sold in equal quantities and on spot. An unequal sale or a deferred sale of these commodities will constitute Riba. These six commodities in fiqh terminology are called "Amwal-e-Ribawiya". Does this hadith apply only to the items mentioned in it? Does it concern sales of barley or wheat and not rice, or, of dates and not raisins? A complete legal definition differs in every fiqh. Scholars such as Taoos and Qatada hold that Riba Al Fadl includes these specified types only, however a majority of Islamic scholars believe that some other commodities should also be included. In order to answer the question, which other commodities should be included, some fiqhs hold that the characteristics which are common amongst these items can be used as basis (illat) for Riba Al Fadl. An illat is the attribute of an event that entails a particular divine ruling in all cases possessing that attribute; it is the basis for applying analogy. Ribawi goods are therefore goods that exhibit one of the efficient causes occasioning application of Riba rules. Various schools define these causes differently:

Imam Abu Hanifa: 1. Weight and 2. Volume

Meaning all these six goods is sold by either weight or volume. Therefore all those commodities, which have weight or volume and are being exchanged, with the same commodity will fall under the rules of Riba Al Fadl.

Imam Shafi: 1. Medium of Exchange, or 2. Eatable

Therefore this law will apply on everything edible or having the natural ability of becoming a medium of exchange (currency).

Imam Maalik: 1. Eatables, and 2. Preservable

Imam Ahmad Bin Hanbal: 1. First citation conforms to the opinion of Imam Abu Hanifa 2. Second citation conforms to the opinion of Imam Shafai and 3. Third citation includes three characteristics at the same time namely edible, weight and volume.

After a detailed study of the above schools of thought, it has been declared by Islamic scholars that if a commodity bears both of the two characteristics namely; it has weight and can be used as a medium of exchange, and then the following two kinds of transactions are not allowed when the same goods are being exchanged:

- A deferred sale of goods (A deferred sale is when the goods are returned/or paid for after some undetermined period).

- A sale of unequal quantities of the same goods.

However, when only one of the two characteristics is present to term the sale as Riba Al Fadl, then exchange of unequal goods are allowed but deferred sale is not allowed. Wisdom behind the prohibition of Riba Al Fadl is that it is intended to ensure justice and remove all forms of exploitation through 'unfair' exchanges and to close all back-doors to Riba An Nasiyah because in the Islamic Shariah, anything that serves as a means to the unlawful is also unlawful.

After closely analyzing the meaning and interpretation of the above ahadith and their explanation in further ahadith along with issues raised in reference work of Hanafi fiqh, the following rules and laws governing Riba Al Fadl are derived:

1. It is evident that the exchange of homogeneous commodities will only be required if they differ in quality and characteristic e.g. different genus of rice and wheat, superior quality gold and inferior quality gold, mineral salt and sea salt etc. The exchange of any of these six commodities with itself, but differing in type/quality (which is called barter in modern terminology) even when considering market rate, is prohibited in unequal amount. The reason being that by exchanging these commodities in unequal amounts there is a fear of developing the rationale in a person eventually leading to interest (sood) based earnings and illegal benefits. Such transactions might also lead to defrauding. For example, a shrewd trader may claim that a kilogram of a specific brand of wheat is equivalent to 3 kilograms of the other kind because of the excellence of its quality, or this unique piece of gold ornament is equivalent in value to twice its weight in gold; in such transactions there undoubtedly is defrauding of people and harm to them.

   As a step to prevent this state, the Shariah has made it a law that exchange of any of these six commodities with itself but differing in quality, is allowed in only one of the following forms:

   a. Any difference in value/quality should be ignored and the commodities should be exchanged in equal amounts (equal weight and volume).

   b. Instead of direct exchange of commodities of the same kind, a person should sell his commodity against cash at the market value and buy someone else's commodity in exchange of cash proceeds at the market value.

2. One of the ways of transacting commodities of the same kind is that a person has a raw material and someone else has a product made of that material and both decide to exchange their product. In this case, one has to see whether:
   a. The characteristics of this product has been totally changed by the industry: For e.g. the remarkable changes that transform raw cotton into cloth or iron into machinery. In this case, it is permissible to transact lesser amount of cloth against greater amount of raw cotton or raw iron having more weight against machinery having lighter weight.
   b. Little difference has been made to its original form after its formulation: For e.g. gold which changes its shape in the form of jewelry. In this case, the Shariah'h holds that such a transaction should not happen in the first place or if it does, the exchange should be in equal weights in order to discourage unfair deals. Another alternative would be to sell gold against cash and the cash proceeds are used to buy the needed jewelry. This is because it is not possible in a barter transaction, except for an expert, to visualize the fair equivalent of one commodity in terms of all other goods. Hence, the equivalent may be established only approximately thus leading to some injustice to one or the other party. The use of money could therefore help reduce the possibility of an unfair exchange.
3. Different commodities can be unequally exchanged but deferred payment is not allowed. E.g., one kg wheat can be sold against 2 kg date or one gram of gold can be exchanged against 4 grams of silver on the condition that they are spot transactions reason being that such a

transaction will surely be carried on the market rate. E.g., a person who wants to exchange silver for gold on spot will only transact as per the market rate. However, if the transaction is on credit, there is a possibility, no matter how minor, of stepping into interest that cannot be ignored. E.g., a buyer who has traded 80 tolas silver on credit today on the understanding that it will be exchanged against 2 tolas gold after a month has in fact no means to find in advance that 40 tolas silver will be equivalent to one tola gold after a month. Therefore this ascertaining of value in advance actually signifies its roots in interest and gambling. Similarly the seller who has accepted credit has in fact yielded to gambling by hoping that the ratio of gold and silver might come down from 1:40 to 1:35. The law of exchanging different commodities only at spot has been established due to this reason.

The general conditions of sale, however, should be borne in mind while making a trade transaction so that the goods are specified in addition to the cash aspect of the transaction. The correct way of specifying is that gold and silver should be under the possession of the sellers or delivered at the place of contract because both goods have the original (natural) price, which cannot be specified until they are delivered.

This rule applies to only exchange of gold and silver. Other goods can be exchanged against each other without delivery and can be specified any other way but will be restricted to cash transaction.

E.g., Zaid made a spot sale of one kg wheat to Bakar with 2 kg salt against future delivery after having identified their goods, this transaction is allowed in Shariah since it meets both conditions:

i. The transaction is on spot, and ii. It is also specified.

However, if Zaid was selling one tola gold to Bakar against 40 tola silver, then it is necessary that both take delivery of their purchased goods at the place of contract because without delivery, goods cannot be specified.

To sum up, the Hanafi jurists maintain that in case of commodities that weigh or measure, it is illegal to transact unequally or on credit. But in case of different commodities unequal exchange is legal but credit remains illegal; the transaction in this case too should be spot.

PROHIBITION OF RIBA IN THE QURAN AND SUNNAH

It is the addition of premium paid to the lender in return for the waiting period as a condition for the loan. Riba has the same meaning and import as interest in accordance with the consensus of all fuqaha (jurists) and is haram. The following are the steps on Riba prohibition:

First stage of prohibition of Riba

Says God: "That which you give as interest to increase the peoples wealth increases not with God; but that which you give in charity, seeking the pleasure of God, multiplies manifold".

Second stage of prohibition

Say God: "For the wrong doing of Jews, we made unlawful for them certain good foods which had been lawful for them - and for their hindering many from God's way. And their taking of Riba"(usury) though they were forbidden from taking it. (Quran, 4:160-161)

Third stage of prohibition

Says God: "O you who believe: Eat not Riba (usury) doubled and multiplied, and fear God that you may be successful.

Fourth and final stage of prohibition

Says God: "O you who believe! Be conscious of Allah and give up what remains (due to you) from Riba (usury) (from now onward), if you are (really) believers. And if you do not do it, then take a notice of war from Allah and his Messenger, but if you repent you shall have your capital sums. Deal not unjustly (by asking more than your capital sums) and you shall not be dealt unjustly (by receiving less than your capital sums).

Prohibition of Riba in the Sunnah

Reported by Jabir bin Abdullah that the Prophet (Pbuh) said: "Cursed is the receiver and the payer of interest, the one who records it and the two witnesses to the transaction". And he said: "They are all alike".

EVOLUTION AND FEATURES OF ISLAMIC BANKING

EVOLUTION OF ISLAMIC BANKING

The first modern experiment with Islamic banking was undertaken in Egypt under cover, without projecting an Islamic image, for fear of being seen as a manifestation of Islamic fundamentalism which was anathema to the political regime. The pioneering effort, led by Ahmad El Najjar, took the form of a savings bank based on profit-sharing in the Egyptian town of Mit Ghamr in 1963. This experiment lasted until 1967 (Ready 1981), by which time there were nine such banks in the country. These banks which neither charged nor paid interest invested mostly by engaging in trade and industry, directly or in partnership with others, and shared the profits with their depositors. Thus, they functioned essentially as saving investment institutions rather than as commercial banks. The Nasir Social Bank, established in Egypt in 1971, was declared an interest-free commercial bank, although its charter made no reference to Islam or *Shariah* (Islamic law).

The IDB was established in 1974 by the Organization of Islamic Countries (OIC), but it was primarily an intergovernmental bank aimed at providing funds for development projects in member countries. The IDB provides fee based financial services and profit-sharing financial assistance to member countries. The IDB operations are free of interest and are explicitly based on *Shariah* principles.

In the seventies, changes took place in the political climate of many Muslim countries so that there was no longer any strong need to establish Islamic financial institutions under cover. A number of Islamic banks, both in letter and spirit, came into existence in the Middle East, e.g., the Dubai Islamic Bank (1975), the Faisal Islamic Bank of Sudan (1977), the Faisal Islamic Bank of Egypt (1977), and the Bahrain Islamic Bank (1979), to mention a few.

The Asia-Pacific region was not oblivious to the winds of change. The Philippine Amanah Bank (PAB) was established in 1973 by Presidential Decree as a specialized banking institution without reference to its Islamic character in the bank's charter. The establishment of the PAB was a response by the. Philippines Government to the Muslim rebellion in the south, designed to serve the special banking needs of the Muslim community. However, the primary task of the PAB was to assist rehabilitation and reconstruction in Mindanao, Sulu and Palawan in the south (Mastura 1988). The PAB has eight branches located in the major cities of the southern Muslim provinces, including one in Makati (Metro Manila), in addition to the head office located at Zamboanga City in Mindanao. The PAB, however, is not strictly an Islamic bank, since interest-based operations continue to coexist with the Islamic modes of financing. It is indeed fascinating to observe that the PAB operates two 'windows' for deposit transactions, i.e., conventional and Islamic. Nevertheless, efforts are underway to convert the PAB into a full-fledged Islamic bank (Mastura 1988).

Islamic banking made its debut in Malaysia in 1983, but not without antecedents. The first Islamic financial institution in Malaysia was the Muslim Pilgrims Savings Corporation set up in 1963 to help people save for performing *hajj* (pilgrimage to Mecca and Medina). In 1969, this body evolved into the Pilgrims Management and Fund Board or the Tabung Haji as it is now popularly known. The Tabung Haji has been acting as a finance company that invests the savings of would-be pilgrims in accordance with Shariah, but its role is rather limited, as it is a non-bank financial institution. The success of the Tabung Haji, however, provided the main impetus for establishing Bank Islam Malaysia Berhad (BIMB) which represents a full fledged Islamic commercial bank in Malaysia.

The Tabung Haji also contributed 12.5 per cent of BIMB's initial capital of M$80 million. BIMB has a complement of fourteen branches in several parts of the country. Plans are afoot to open six new branches a year so that by 1990 the branch network of BIMB will total thirty-three (Man 1988).

Reference should also be made to some Islamic financial institutions established in countries where Muslims are a minority. There was a proliferation of interest-free savings and loan societies in India during the seventies (Siddiqi 1988). The Islamic Banking System (now called Islamic Finance House), established in Luxembourg in 1978, represents the first attempt at Islamic banking in the Western world. There is also an Islamic Bank International of Denmark, in Copenhagen, and the Islamic Investment Company has been set up in Melbourne, Australia.

FEATURES OF ISLAMIC BANKING

Rationale

The essential feature of Islamic banking is that it is interest-free. Although it is often claimed that there is more to Islamic banking, such as contributions towards a more equitable distribution of income and wealth, and increased equity participation in the economy (Chapra 1982), it nevertheless derives its specific rationale from the fact that there is no place for the institution of interest in the Islamic order.

Islam prohibits Muslims from taking or giving interest (*riba)* regardless of the purpose for which such loans are made and regardless of the rates at which interest is charged. To be sure, there have been attempts to distinguish between usury and interest and between loans for consumption and for production. It has also been argued that riba refers to usury practised by petty moneylenders and not to interest charged by modern banks and that no riba is involved when interest is imposed on productive loans, but these arguments have not won acceptance. Apart from a few dissenting opinions, the general consensus among Muslim scholars clearly is that there is no difference between riba and interest. In what follows, these two terms are used interchangeably.

The prohibition of riba is mentioned in four different revelations in the Qur'an. The first revelation emphasizes that interest deprives wealth of God's blessings. The second revelation condemns it, placing interest in juxtaposition with wrongful appropriation of property belonging to others. The third revelation enjoins Muslims to stay clear of interest for the sake of their own welfare. The fourth revelation establishes a clear distinction between interest and trade, urging Muslims to take only the principal sum and to forgo even this sum if the borrower is unable to repay. It is further declared in the Qur'an that those who disregard the prohibition of interest are at war with God and His Prophet. The prohibition of interest is also cited in no uncertain terms in the Hadith (sayings of the Prophet). The Prophet condemned not only those who take interest but also those who give interest and those who record or witness the transaction, saying that they are all alike in guilt.

It may be mentioned in passing that similar prohibitions are to be found in the preQur'anic scriptures, although the 'People of the Book', as the Qur'an refers to them, had chosen to rationalize them. It is amazing that Islam has successfully warded off various subsequent rationalization attempts aimed at legitimizing the institution of interest.

Some scholars have put forward economic reasons to explain why interest is banned in Islam. It has been argued, for instance, that interest, being a pre determined cost of production, tends to prevent full employment (Khan 1968; Ahmad n.d.; Mannan 1970). In the same vein, it has been contended that international monetary crises are largely due to the institution of interest (Khan, n.d), and that trade cycles are in no small measure attributable to the phenomenon of interest (Ahmad 1952; Su'ud n.d.). None of these studies, however, has really succeeded in establishing a causal link between interest, on the one hand, and employment and trade cycles, on the other. Others, anxious to vindicate the Islamic position on interest, have argued that interest is not very effective as a monetary policy instrument even in capitalist economies and have questioned the efficacy of the rate of interest as a determinant of saving and investment (Ariff 1982).

A common thread running through all these discussions is the exploitative character of the institution of interest, although some have pointed out that profit (which is lawful in Islam) can also be exploitative. One response to this is that one must distinguish between profit and profiteering, and Islam has prohibited the latter as well.

Some writings have alluded to the 'unearned income' aspect of interest payments as a possible explanation for the Islamic doctrine. The objection that rent on property is considered halal (lawful) is then answered by rejecting the analogy between rent on property and interest on loans, since the benefit to the tenant is certain, while the productivity of the borrowed capital is uncertain. Besides, property rented out is subject to physical wear and tear, while money lent out is not. The question of erosion in the value of money and hence the need for indexation is an interesting one. But the Islamic jurists have ruled out compensation for erosion in the value of money, or, according to Hadith, a fungible good must be returned by its like *(mithl)*: 'gold for gold, silver for silver, wheat for wheat, barley for barley, dates for dates, salt for salt, like for like, equal for equal, and hand to hand ...' .

The bottom line is that Muslims need no 'proofs' before they reject the institution of interest: no human explanation for a divine injunction is necessary for them to accept a dictum, as they recognize the limits to human reasoning. No human mind can fathom a divine order; therefore it is a matter of faith *(iman)*.

The Islamic ban on interest does not mean that capital is costless in an Islamic system. Islam recognizes capital as a factor of production but it does not allow the factor to make a prior or predetermined claim on the productive surplus in the form of interest. This obviously poses the question as to what will then replace the interest rate mechanism in an Islamic framework. There have been suggestions that profit-sharing can be a viable alternative (Kahf 1982a and 1982b). In Islam, the owner of capital can legitimately share the profits made by the entrepreneur. What makes profit sharing permissible in Islam, while interest is not, is that in the case of the former it is only the profit-sharing *ratio*, not the rate of return itself that is predetermined.

It has been argued that profit-sharing can help allocate resources efficiently, as the profit-sharing ratio can be influenced by market forces so that capital will flow into those sectors which offer the highest profit sharing ratio to the investor, other things being equal. One dissenting view is that the substitution of profit-sharing for interest as a resource allocating mechanism is crude and imperfect and that the institution of interest should therefore be retained as a necessary evil (Naqvi 1982). However, mainstream Islamic thinking on this subject clearly points to the need to replace interest with something else, although there is no clear consensus on what form the alternative to the interest rate mechanism should take. The issue is not resolved and the search for an alternative continues, but it has not detracted from efforts to experiment with Islamic banking without interest.

Anatomy

Islam does not deny that capital, as a factor of production, deserves to be rewarded. Islam allows the owners of capital a share in a surplus which is uncertain. To put it differently, investors in the Islamic order have no right to demand a fixed rate of return. No one is entitled to any addition to the principal sum if he does not share in the risks involved. The owner of capital (rabbul-mal) may 'invest' by allowing an entrepreneur with ideas and expertise to use the capital for productive purposes and he may share the profits, if any, with the entrepreneur borrower (mudarib); losses, if any, however, will be borne wholly by the rabbulmal. This mode of financing, termed as Mudaraba in the Islamic literature, was in practice even in the pre Qur'anic days and, according to jurists, it was approved by the Prophet.

Another legitimate mode of financing recognized in Islam is one based on equity participation (musharaka); in which the partners use their capital jointly to generate a surplus. Profits or losses will be shared between the partners according to some agreed formula depending on the equity ratio.

Mudaraba and musharaka constitute, at least in principle if not in practice, the twin pillars of Islamic banking. The musharaka principle is invoked in the equity structure of Islamic banks and is similar to the modern concepts of partnership and joint stock ownership. In so far as the depositors are concerned, an Islamic bank acts as a mudarib which manages the funds of the depositors to generate profits subject to the rules of Mudaraba as outlined above. The bank may in turn use the depositors' funds on a Mudaraba basis in addition to other lawful modes of financing. In other words, the bank operates a two-tier Mudaraba system in which it acts both as the mudarib on the saving side of the equation and as the *rabbulmal* on the investment portfolio side. The bank may also enter into musharaka contracts with the users of the funds, sharing profits and losses, as mentioned above.

At the deposit end of the scale, Islamic banks normally operate three broad categories of account, mainly current, savings, and investment accounts. The current account, as in the case of conventional banks, gives no return to the depositors. It is essentially a safekeeping *(alwadiah)* arrangement between the depositors and the bank, which allows the depositors to withdraw their money at any time and permits the bank to use the depositors' money. As in the case of conventional banks, cheque books are issued to the current ac count deposit holders and the Islamic banks provide the broad range of payment facilities clearing mechanisms, bank drafts, bills of exchange, travellers cheques, etc. (but not yet, it seems, credit cards or bank cards). More often than not, no service charges are made by the banks in this regard.

The savings account is also operated on an *al-wadiah* basis, but the bank may at its absolute discretion pay the depositors a *positive* return periodically, depending on its own profitability. Such payment is considered lawful in Islam since it is not a condition for lending by the depositors to the bank, nor is it predetermined. The savings account holders are issued with savings books and are allowed to withdraw their money as and when they please.

The investment account is based on the Mudaraba principle, and the deposits are term deposits which cannot be withdrawn before maturity. The profit-sharing ratio varies from bank to bank and from time to time depending on supply and demand conditions. In theory, the rate of return could be positive or negative, but in practice the returns have always been positive and quite comparable to rates conventional banks offer on their term deposits.

At the investment portfolio end of the scale, Islamic banks employ a variety of instruments. The Mudaraba and musharaka modes, referred to earlier, are supposedly the main conduits for the outflow of funds from the banks. In practice, however, Islamic banks have shown a strong preference for other modes which are less risky. The most commonly used mode of financing seems to be the 'mark-up' device which is termed murabaha . In a murabaha transaction, the bank finances the purchase of a good or asset by buying it on behalf of its client and adding a mark-up before reselling it to the client on a 'cost-plus' basis. It may appear at first glance that the mark-up is just another term for interest as charged by conventional banks, interest thus being admitted through the back door. What makes the murabaha transaction islamically legitimate is that the bank first acquires the asset and in the process it assumes certain risks between purchase and resale. The bank takes responsibility for the good before it is safely delivered to the client. The services rendered by the Islamic bank are therefore regarded as quite different from those of a conventional bank which simply lends money to the client to buy the good.

Islamic banks have also been resorting to purchase and resale of properties on a deferred payment basis, which is termed *bai' muajjal*. It is considered lawful in fiqh (jurisprudence) to charge a higher price for a good if payments are to be made at a later date. According to *fiqh*, this does not amount to charging interest, since it is not a lending transaction but a trading one.

Leasing or ijara is also frequently practised by Islamic banks. Under this mode, the banks would buy the equipment or machinery and lease it out to their clients who may opt to buy the items eventually, in which case the monthly payments will consist of two components, i.e., rental for the use of the equipment and instalment towards the purchase price.

Reference must also be made to pre-paid purchase of goods, which is termed *bai'salam*, as a means used by Islamic banks to finance production. Here the price is paid at the time of the contract but the delivery would take place at a future date. This mode enables an entrepreneur to sell his output to the bank at a price determined in advance. Islamic banks, in keeping with modern times, have extended this facility to manufactures as well.

It is clear from the above sketch that Islamic banking goes beyond the pure financing activities of conventional banks. Islamic banks engage in equity financing and trade financing. By its very nature, Islamic banking is a risky business compared with conventional banking, for risk-sharing forms the very basis of all Islamic financial transactions. To minimize risks, however, Islamic banks have taken pains to distribute the eggs over many baskets and have established reserve funds out of past profits which they can fall back on in the event of any major loss.

Theory

It is not possible to cover in this survey all the publications which have appeared on Islamic banking. There are numerous publications in Arabic and Urdu which have made significant contributions to the theoretical discussion. A brief description of these in English can be found in the appendix to Siddiqi's book on *Banking without Interest* (Siddiqi 1983a).

The early contributions on the subject of Islamic banking were somewhat casual in the sense that only passing references were made to it in the discussion of wider issues relating to the Islamic economic system as a whole. In other words, the early writers had been simply thinking aloud rather than presenting well-thought-out ideas. Thus, for example, the book by Qureshi on *Islam and the Theory of Interest* (Qureshi 1946) looked upon banking as a social service that should be sponsored by the government like public health and education. Qureshi took this point of view since the bank could neither pay any interest to account holders nor charge any interest on loans advanced. Qureshi also spoke of partnerships between banks and businessmen as a possible alternative, sharing losses if any. No mention was made of profit-sharing.

Ahmad, in Chapter VII of his book *Economics of Islam* (Ahmad 1952), envisaged the establishment of Islamic banks on the basis of a joint stock company with limited liability. In his scheme, in addition to current accounts, on which no dividend or interest should be paid, there was an account in which people could deposit their capital on the basis of partnership, with shareholders receiving higher dividends than the account holders from the profits made. Like Qureshi, above, Ahmad also spoke of possible partnership arrangements with the businessmen who seek capital from the banks. However, the partnership principle was not left undefined, nor was it clear who would bear the loss, if any. It was suggested that banks should cash bills of trade without charging interest, using the current account funds.

The principle of Mudaraba based on *Shariah* was invoked systematically by Uzair (1955). His principal contribution lay in suggesting Mudaraba as the main premise for 'interestless banking'. However, his argument that the bank should not make any capital investment with its own deposits rendered his analysis somewhat impractical.

Al-Arabi (1966) envisaged a banking system with Mudaraba as the main pivot. He was actually advancing the idea of a two-tier Mudaraba which would enable the bank to mobilize savings on a Mudaraba basis, allocating the funds so mobilized also on a Mudaraba basis. In other words the bank would act as a mudarib in so far as the depositors were concerned, while the 'borrowers' would act as mudaribs in so far as the bank was concerned. In his scheme, the bank could advance not only the capital procured through deposits but also the capital of its own shareholders. It is also of interest to note that his position with regard to the distribution of profits and the responsibility for losses was strictly in accordance with the *Shariah*.

Irshad (1964) also spoke of Mudaraba as the basis of Islamic banking, but his concept of Mudaraba was quite different from the traditional one in that he thought of capital and labour (including entrepreneurship) as having equal shares in output, thus sharing the losses and profits equally. This actually means that the owner of capital and the entrepreneur have a fifty-fifty share in the profit or loss as the case may be, which runs counter to the *Shariah* position. Irshad envisaged two kinds of deposit accounts. The first sounded like current deposits in the sense that it would be payable on demand, but the money kept in this deposit would be used for social welfare projects, as the depositors would get zero return. The second one amounted to term deposits which would entitle the depositors to a share in the profits at the end of the year proportionately to the size and duration of the deposits. He recommended the setting up of a Reserve Fund which would absorb all losses so that no depositor would have to bear any loss. According to Irshad, all losses would be either recovered from the Reserve Fund or borne by the shareholders of the bank.

A pioneering attempt at providing a fairly detailed outline of Islamic banking was made in Urdu by Siddiqi in 1968 (The English version was not published until 1983). His Islamic banking model was based on Mudaraba and shirka (partnership or musharaka as it is now usually called). His model was essentially one based on a two-tier Mudaraba financier-entrepreneur relationship, but he took pains to describe the mechanics of such transactions in considerable detail with numerous hypothetical and arithmetic examples. He classified the operations of an Islamic bank into three categories: services based on fees, commissions or other fixed charges; financing on the basis of Mudaraba and partnership; and services provided free of charge. His thesis was that such interest-free banks could be a viable alternative to interest-based conventional banks.

The issue of loans for consumption clearly presents a problem, as there is no profit to be shared. Siddiqi addressed this problem, but he managed only to scratch the surface. While recognizing the need for such interest-free loans *(qard hasan)*, especially for meeting basic needs, he seemed to think it was the duty of the community and the State (through its *baitul mal* or treasury) to cater to those needs; the Islamic bank's primary objective, like that of any other business unit, is to earn profit. He therefore tended to downplay the role of Islamic banks in providing consumption loans, but he suggested limited overdraft facilities without interest. He even considered a portion of the fund being set aside for consumption loans, repayment being guaranteed by the State. He also suggested that consumers buying durables on credit would issue 'certificates of sale' which could be encashed by the seller at the bank for a fee. It was then the seller not the buyer who would be liable as far as the bank was concerned. However, the principles of murabaha and *bai' muajjal* were not invoked.

Strangely, Siddiqi favoured keeping the number of shareholders to the minimum, without advancing any strong reasons. This is contrary to the general consensus which now seems to have emerged with reference to Islamic banks operating on a joint stock company basis, a consensus which incidentally is also in line with the Islamic value attached to a broad equity base as against heavy concentration of equity and wealth. Ironically, Siddiqi thought that interest-free banking could operate successfully 'only in a country where interest is legally prohibited and any transaction based upon interest is declared a punishable offence' (1983b:13). He also thought it important to have Islamic laws enforced before interest-free banking could operate well. This view has not gained acceptance, as demonstrated by the many Islamic banks which operate profitably in 'hostile' environments, as noted earlier.

Chapra's model of Islamic banking (Chapra 1982), like Siddiqi's, was based on the Mudaraba principle. His main concern, however, centred on the role of artificial purchasing power through credit creation. He even suggested that 'seigniorage' resulting from it should be transferred to the public exchequer, for the sake of equity and justice. Al-Jarhi (1983) went so far as to favour the imposition of a 100 per cent reserve requirement on commercial banks. Chapra was also much concerned about the concentration of economic power private banks might enjoy in a system based on equity financing. He therefore preferred mediumsized banks which are neither so large as to wield excessive power nor so small as to be uneconomical. Chapra's scheme also contained proposals for loss-compensating reserves and loss-absorbing insurance facilities. He also spoke of non-bank financial institutions, which specialize in bringing financiers and entrepreneurs together and act as investment trusts.

Mohsin (1982) has presented a detailed and elaborate framework of Islamic banking in a modern setting. His model incorporates the characteristics of commercial, merchant, and development banks, blending them in novel fashion. It adds various non-banking services such as trust business, factoring, real estate, and consultancy, as though interest-free banks could not survive by banking business alone. Many of the activities listed certainly go beyond the realm of commercial banking and are of so sophisticated and specialized a nature that they may be thought irrelevant to most Muslim countries at their present stage of development. Mohsin's model clearly was designed to fit into a capitalist environment; indeed he explicitly stated that riba-free banks could coexist with interest-based banks.

The point that there is more to Islamic banking than mere abolition of interest was driven home strongly by Chapra (1985). He envisaged Islamic banks whose nature, outlook and operations could be distinctly different from those of conventional banks. Besides the outlawing of riba, he considered it essential that Islamic banks should, since they handle public funds, serve the public interest rather than individual or group interests. In other words, they should play a social-welfare-oriented rather than a profit-maximizing role. He conceived of Islamic banks as a crossbreed of commercial and merchant banks, investment trusts and investment-management institutions that would offer a wide spectrum of services to their customers. Unlike conventional banks which depend heavily on the 'crutches of collateral and of non-participation in risk' (p. 155), Islamic banks would have to rely heavily on project evaluation, especially for equity-oriented financing. Thanks to the profit-and-loss sharing nature of the operations, bank-customer relations would be much closer and more cordial than is possible under conventional banking. Finally, the problems of liquidity shortage or surplus would have to be handled differently in Islamic banking, since the ban on interest rules out resort to the money market and the central bank. Chapra suggested alternatives such as reciprocal accommodation among banks without interest payments and creation of a common fund at the central bank into which surpluses would flow and from which shortages could be met without any interest charges.

The literature also discusses the question of central banking in an Islamic framework. The general opinion seems to be that the basic functions of a modern central bank are relevant also for an Islamic monetary system, although the mechanisms may have to be different. Thus, for example, the bank rate instrument cannot be used as it entails interest. Uzair (1982) has suggested adjustments in profit-sharing ratios as a substitute for bank rate manipulations by the central bank. Thus, credit can be tightened by reducing the share accruing to the businessmen and eased by increasing it. Siddiqi (1982) has suggested that variations in the so-called 'refinance ratio' (which refers to the central bank refinancing of a part of the interest-free loans provided by the commercial banks) would influence the quantum of short-term credit extended. Siddiqi has also proposed a prescribed 'lending ratio' (i.e., the proportion of demand deposits that commercial banks are obliged to lend out as interest-free loans) that can be adjusted by the central bank according to changing circumstances. In this context, reference may also be made to a proposal by Uzair (1982) that the central bank should acquire an equity stake in commercial banking by holding, say, 25 per cent of the capital stock of the commercial banks. The rationale behind this proposal was that it would give the central bank access to a permanent source of income so that it could effectively act as lender of last resort.

The discussion of central banking in an Islamic context is somewhat scanty, presumably because Islamic central banking is viewed as too farfetched an idea, except in Iran and Pakistan.

It emerges from all this that Islamic banking has three distinguishing features: (a) it is interest-free, (b) it is multi-purpose and not purely commercial, and (c) it is strongly equity-oriented. The literature contains hardly any serious criticism of the interest-free character of the operation, since this is taken for granted, although concerns have been expressed about the lack of adequate interest-free instruments. There is a near-consensus that Islamic banks can function well without interest. A recent International Monetary Fund study by Iqbal and Mirakhor (1987) has found Islamic banking to be a viable proposition that can result in efficient resource allocation. The study suggests that banks in an Islamic system face fewer solvency and liquidity risks than their conventional counterparts.

The multi-purpose and extra-commercial nature of the Islamic banking operation does not seem to pose intractable problems. The abolition of interest makes it imperative for Islamic banks to look for other instruments, which renders operations outside the periphery of commercial banking unavoidable. Such operations may yield economies of scope. But it is undeniable that the multipurpose character of Islamic banking poses serious practical problems, especially in relation to the skills needed to handle such diverse and complex transactions (Iqbal and Mirakhor 1987).

The stress on equity-oriented transactions in Islamic banking, especially the Mudaraba mode, has been criticized. It has been argued that the replacement of predetermined interest by uncertain profits is not enough to render a transaction Islamic, since profit can be just as exploitative as interest is, if it is 'excessive' (Naqvi 1981). Naqvi has also pointed out that there is nothing sacrosanct about the institution of Mudaraba in Islam. Naqvi maintains that Mudaraba is not based on the Qur'an or the Hadith but was a custom of the preIslamic Arabs. Historically, Mudaraba, he contends, enabled the aged, women, and children with capital to engage in trade through merchants for a share in the profit, all losses being borne by the owners of capital, and therefore it cannot claim any sanctity. The fact remains that the Prophet raised no objection to Mudaraba, so that it was at least not considered un-Islamic.

The distribution of profit in Mudaraba transactions presents practical difficulties, especially where there are multiple providers of capital, but these difficulties are not regarded as insurmountable. The Report of Pakistan's Council of Islamic Ideology (CII 1983) has suggested that the respective capital contributions of parties can be converted to a common denominator by multiplying the amounts provided with the number of days during which each component, such as the firm's own equity capital, its current cash surplus and suppliers' credit was actually deployed in the business, i.e., on a daily product basis. As for deposits, profits (net of administrative expenses, taxes, and appropriation for reserves) would be divided between the shareholders of the bank and the holders of deposits, again on a daily product basis.

Practicality

Recent years have brought an increasing flow of empirical studies of Islamic banking. The earliest systematic empirical work was undertaken by Khan (1983). His observations covered Islamic banks operating in Sudan, United Arab Emirates, Kuwait, Bahrain, Jordan, and Egypt. Khan's study showed that these banks had little difficulty in devising practices in comformity with *Shariah*. He identified two types of investment accounts: one where the depositor authorized the banks to invest the money in *any* project and the other where the depositor had a say in the choice of project to be financed. On the asset side, the banks under investigation had been resorting to Mudaraba, musharaka and murabaha modes. Khan's study reported profit rates ranging from 9 to 20 per cent which were competitive with conventional banks in the corresponding areas. The rates of return to depositors varied between 8 and 15 per cent, which were quite comparable with the rates of return offered by conventional banks.

Khan's study revealed that Islamic banks had a preference for trade finance and real estate investments. The study also revealed a strong preference for quick returns, which is understandable in view of the fact that these newly established institutions were anxious to report positive results even in the early years of operation. Nienhaus (1988) suggests that the relative profitability of Islamic banks, especially in the Middle East in recent years, was to a large extent due to the property (real estate) boom. He has cited cases of heavy losses which came with the crash of the property sector.

The IMF study referred to earlier by Iqbal and Mirakhor (1987) also contains extremely interesting empirical observations, although these are confined to the experience of Iran and Pakistan, both of which have attempted to islamize the entire banking system on a comprehensive basis.

Iran switched to Islamic banking in August 1983 with a three-year transition period. The Iranian system allows banks to accept current and savings deposits without having to pay any return, but it permits the banks to offer incentives such as variable prizes or bonuses in cash or kind on these deposits. Term deposits (both short-term and longterm) earn a rate of return based on the bank's profits and on the deposit maturity. No empirical evidence is as yet available on the interesting question as to whether interest or a profit-share provides the more effective incentive to depositors for the mobilization of private saving. Where Islamic and conventional banks exist side by side, the Central Bank control of the bank interest rates is liable to be circumvented by shifts of funds to the Islamic banks.

Iqbal and Mirakhor have noted that the conversion to Islamic modes has been much slower on the asset than on the deposit side. It appears that the Islamic banking system in Iran was able to use less than half of its resources for credit to the private sector, mostly in the form of short-term facilities, i.e., commercial and trade transactions. The slower pace of conversion on the asset side was attributed by the authors to the inadequate supply of personnel trained in long-term financing. The authors, however, found no evidence to show that the effectiveness of monetary policy in Iran, broadly speaking, was altered by the conversion.

The Pakistani experience differs from the Iranian one in that Pakistan had opted for a gradual islamization process which began in 1979. In the first phase, which ended on 1 January 1985, domestic banks operated both interest-free and interest-based 'windows'. In the second phase of the transformation process, the banking system was geared to operate all transactions on the basis of no interest, the only exceptions being foreign currency deposits, foreign loans and government debts. The Pakistani model took care to ensure that the new modes of financing did not upset the basic functioning and structure of the banking system. This and the gradual pace of transition, according to the authors, made it easier for the Pakistani banks to adapt to the new system. The rate of return on profit-and-loss sharing (PLS) deposits appears not only to have been in general higher than the interest rate before islamization but also to have varied between banks, the differential indicating the degree of competition in the banking industry. The authors noted that the PLS system and the new modes of financing had accorded considerable flexibility to banks and their clients. Once again the study concluded that the effectiveness of monetary policy in Pakistan was not impaired by the changeover.

The IMF study, however, expressed considerable uneasiness about the concentration of bank assets on short-term trade credits rather than on long-term financing. This the authors found undesirable, not only because it is inconsistent with the intentions of the new system, but also because the heavy concentration on a few assets might increase risks and destabilize the asset portfolios. The study also drew attention to the difficulty experienced in both Iran and Pakistan in financing budget deficits under a non-interest system and underscored the urgent need to devise suitable interest-free instruments. Iran has, however, decreed that government borrowing on the basis of a fixed rate of return from the nationalized banking system would not amount to interest and would hence be permissible. The official rationalization is that, since all banks are nationalized, interest rates and payments among banks will cancel out in the consolidated accounts. (This, of course, abstracts from the banks' business with non-bank customers.)

There are also some small case studies of Islamic banks operating in Bangladesh (Huq 1986), Egypt (Mohammad 1986), Malaysia (Halim 1988b), Pakistan (Khan 1986), and Sudan (Salama 1988b). These studies reveal interesting similarities and differences. The current accounts in all cases are operated on the principles of *alwadiah*. Savings deposits, too, are accepted on the basis of *alwadiah*, but 'gifts' to depositors are given entirely at the discretion of the Islamic banks on the minimum balance, so that the depositors also share in profits. Investment deposits are invariably based on the Mudaraba principle, but there are considerable variations. Thus, for example, the Islamic Bank of Bangladesh has been offering PLS Deposit Accounts, PLS Special Notice Deposit Accounts, and PLS Term Deposit Accounts, while Bank Islam Malaysia has been operating two kinds of investment deposits, one for the general public and the other for institutional clients.

The studies also show that the profit-sharing ratios and the modes of payment vary from place to place and from time to time. Thus, for example, profits are provisionally declared on a monthly basis in Malaysia, on a quarterly basis in Egypt, on a half-yearly basis in Bangladesh and Pakistan, and on an annual basis in Sudan. A striking common feature of all these banks is that even their investment deposits are mostly short-term, reflecting the depositors' preference for assets in as liquid a form as possible. Even in Malaysia, where investment deposits have accounted for a much larger proportion of the total, the bulk of them were made for a period of less than two years. By contrast, in Sudan most of the deposits have consisted of current and savings deposits, apparently because of the ceiling imposed by the Sudanese monetary authorities on investment deposits which in turn was influenced by limited investment opportunities in the domestic economy.

There are also interesting variations in the pattern of resource utilization by the Islamic banks. For example, musharaka has been far more important than murabaha as an investment mode in Sudan, while the reverse has been the case in Malaysia. On the average, however, murabaha, *bai'muajjal* and ijara, rather than musharaka represent the most commonly used modes of financing. The case studies also show that the structure of the clientele has been skewed in favour of the more affluent segment of society, no doubt because the banks are located mainly in metropolitan centres with small branch networks.

The two main problems identified by the case studies are the absence of suitable non-interest-based financial instruments for money and capital market transactions and the high rate of borrower delinquency. The former problem has been partially redressed by Islamic banks resorting to mutual interbank arrangements and central bank cooperation, as mentioned earlier. The Bank Islam Malaysia, for instance, has been placing its excess liquidity with the central bank which usually exercises its discretionary powers to give some returns. The delinquency problem appears to be real and serious. Murabaha payments have often been held up because late payments cannot be penalized, in contrast to the interest system in which delayed payments would automatically mean increased interest payments. To overcome this problem, the Pakistani banks have resorted to what is called 'mark-down' which is the opposite of 'mark-up' (i.e., the profit margin in the cost-plus approach of murabaha transactions). 'Mark-down' amounts to giving rebates as an incentive for early payments. But the legitimacy of this 'mark-down' practice is questionable on *Shariah* grounds, since it is time based and therefore smacks of interest.

In the Southeast Asian context, two recent studies on the Bank Islam Malaysia by Man (1988) and the Philippine Amanah Bank by Mastura (1988) deserve special mention. The

Malaysian experience in Islamic banking has been encouraging. Man's study shows that the average return to depositors has been quite competitive with that offered by conventional banks. By the end of 1986, after three years of operation, the bank had a network of fourteen branches. However, 90 per cent of its deposits had maturities of two years or less, and non-Muslim depositors accounted for only 2 per cent of the total. Man is particularly critical of the fact that the Mudaraba and musharaka modes of operation, which are considered most meaningful by Islamic scholars, accounted for a very small proportion of the total investment port folio, while *bai'muajjal* and ijara formed the bulk of the total.

It is evident from Mastura's analysis that the Philippine Amanah Bank is, strictly speaking, not an Islamic bank, as interest-based operations continue to coexist with Islamic modes of financing. Thus, the PAB has been operating both interest and Islamic 'windows' for deposits. Mastura's study has produced evidence to show that the PAB has been concentrating on murabaha transactions, paying hardly any attention to the Mudaraba and musharaka means of financing. The PAB has also been adopting unorthodox approaches in dealing with excess liquidity by making use of interest bearing treasury bills. Nonetheless, the PAB has also been invoking some Islamic modes in several major investment activities. Mastura has made special references to the *qirad* principle adopted by the PAB in the Kilusang Kabuhayan at Kaunlaran (KKK) movement launched under Marcos and to the ijara financing for the acquisition of farm implements and supplies in the Quedon food production program undertaken by the present regime.

So far, no reference has been made to Indonesia, the largest Muslim country in the world with Muslims accounting for 90 per cent of a population of some 165 million. The explanation is that a substantial proportion, especially in Java, are arguably nominal Muslims. Indonesians by and large subscribe to the Pancasila ideology which is essentially secular in character. The present regime seems to associate Islamic banking with Islamic fundamentalism to which the regime is not at all sympathetic. Besides, the intellectual tradition in Indonesia in modern times has not been conducive to the idea of interest-free banking. There were several well respected Indonesian intellectuals including Hatta (the former Vice President) who had argued that riba prohibited in Islam was not the same as interest charged or offered by modern commercial banks, although Islamic jurists in Indonesia hold the opposite view. The Muslim public seems somewhat indifferent to all this. This, however, does not mean that there are no interest-free financial institutions operating in Indonesia. One form of traditional interest-free borrowing is the still widely prevalent form of informal rural credit known as *ijon* (green) because the loan is secured on the standing crop as described by Partadireja (1974). Another is the *arisan* system practised among consumers and small craftsmen and traders. In this system, each member contributes regularly a certain sum and obtains interest-free loans from the pool by drawing lots. The chances of an Islamic bank being established in Indonesia seem at present remote (cf. Rahardjo 1988).

Finally, in the most recent contribution to the growing Islamic banking literature, Nienhaus (1988) concludes that Islamic banking is viable at the microeconomic level but dismisses the proponents' ideological claims for superiority of Islamic banking as 'unfounded'. Nienhaus points out that there are some failure stories. Examples cited include the Kuwait Finance House which had its fingers burned by investing heavily in the Kuwaiti real estate and construction sector in 1984, and the Islamic Bank International of Denmark which suffered heavy losses in 1985 and 1986 to the tune of more than 30 per cent of its paid-up capital. But then, as Nienhaus himself has noted, the quoted troubles of individual banks had specific causes and it would be inappropriate to draw general conclusions from particular cases.

Nienhaus notes that the high growth rates of the initial years have been falling off, but he rejects the thesis that the Islamic banks have reached their 'limits of growth' after filling a market gap. The falling growth rates might well be due to the bigger base values, and the growth performance of Islamic banks has been relatively better in most cases than that of conventional banks in recent years.

According to Nienhaus, the market shares of many Islamic banks have increased over time, notwithstanding the deceleration in the growth of deposits. The only exception was the Faisal Islamic Bank of Sudan (FIBS) whose market share had shrunk from 15 per cent in 1982 to 7 per cent in 1986, but Nienhaus claims that the market shares lost by FIBS were won not by conventional banks but by newer Islamic banks in Sudan.

Short-term trade financing has clearly been dominant in most Islamic banks regardless of size. This is contrary to the expectation that the Islamic banks would be active mainly in the field of corporate financing on a participation basis. Nienhaus attributes this not only to insufficient supply by the banks but also to weak demand by entrepreneurs who may prefer fixed interest cost to sharing their profits with the banks.

The preceding discussion makes it clear that Islamic banking is not a negligible or merely temporary phenomenon. Islamic banks are here to stay and there are signs that they will continue to grow and expand. Even if one does not subscribe to the Islamic injunction against the institution of interest, one may find in Islamic banking some innovative ideas which could add more variety to the existing financial network.

One of the main selling points of Islamic banking, at least in theory, is that, unlike conventional banking, it is concerned about the viability of the project and the profitability of the operation but not the size of the collateral. Good projects which might be turned down by conventional banks for lack of collateral would be financed by Islamic banks on a profit-sharing basis. It is especially in this sense that Islamic banks can play a catalytic role in stimulating economic development. In many developing countries, of course, development banks are supposed to perform this function. Islamic banks are expected to be more enterprising than their conventional counterparts. In practice, however, Islamic banks have been concentrating on short-term trade finance which is the least risky.

Part of the explanation is that long-term financing requires expertise which is not always available. Another reason is that there are no backup institutional structures such as secondary capital markets for Islamic financial instruments. It is possible also that the tendency to concentrate on short-term financing reflects the early years of operation: it is easier to administer, less risky, and the returns are quicker. The banks may learn to pay more attention to equity financing as they grow older.

It is sometimes suggested that Islamic banks are rather complacent. They tend to behave as though they had a captive market in the Muslim masses that will come to them on religious grounds. This complacency seems more pronounced in countries with only one Islamic bank. Many Muslims find it more convenient to deal with conventional banks and have no qualms about shifting their deposits between Islamic banks and conventional ones depending on which bank offers a better return. This might suggest a case for more Islamic banks in those countries as it would force the banks to be more innovative and competitive. Another solution would be to allow the conventional banks to undertake equity financing and/or to operate Islamic 'counters' or 'windows', subject to strict compliance with the *Shariah* rules. It is perhaps not too wild a proposition to suggest that there is a need for specialized Islamic financial institutions such as Mudaraba banks, murabaha banks and musharaka banks which would compete with one another to provide the best possible services.

ISLAMIC BANKING IN PRACTICE

Islamic banking and finance are a part of Islamic economic system, the basis of which revolves around justice and morality. It is a very young concept in modern times yet it is emerging as one of the fastest growing areas of international finance. It facilitates the uplifting of economic standards of its clients by providing various types of lending contracts. Above all it is Shari'ah compliant, hence protects a Muslim from dealing with Riba, thus avoiding Allah's wrath and war. Islamic banks operate various types of transactions the most important of which are:

Collection of Deposit

Since interest bearing deposits entail Riba, the Islamic banks offer two different kinds of deposits mentioned as below:

Current account

The deposited capital is guaranteed and made available to the client on demand. No reward is paid on the deposit but is mainly used for transactions and safety keeping.

Investment account

Deposits remain with the bank for a certain previously agreed period. Customers open investment account to yield financial return based on trust financing. The depositor is the financing partner, while the managing partner is the bank.

FINANCING CONTRACTS

Murabaha (mark-up sale)

It comes from the Arabic word 'ribh' which means profit (short –term trade financing). Murabaha is selling a commodity as per the purchasing price with a defined and agreed profit mark-up. This mark-up may be a percentage of the selling price or a lump sum. Murabaha financing differs from a conventional financing, as it involves the financing of physical assets. The bank shares in the risk of ownership. Rather than simply advancing money to a client, the bank itself buys the goods from a third party on request of a customer. The bank then sells it to the customer for a pre-agreed price through a deferred payment scheme, usually in the form of installments.

Musharaka (profits and loss sharing system)

It is an agreement between two persons or more (bank and customer) sharing both profits and losses. It is joint enterprises where all the partners contribute capital and the client bring in know how. Profit/losses are shared on agreed ratios.

ISLAMIC BANK VS. CONVENTIONAL BANK

Conventional banks have fixed rate of returns; while Musharaka, base their returns on the actual profits made. Conventional banks as opposed to Islamic ones do not share losses nor do they take such risks. Conventional banks have no interest on how the business is run; while in Musharaka the Islamic bank is directly involved in the proper functioning of the business.

TYPES OF MUSHARAKA PARTNERSHIPS

There are many types of Musharaka ranging from traditional types of partnerships to modern corporations. Musharaka could be either of the two types:

a. Permanent Musharaka - An Islamic bank participates in the equity of a project and receives a share of the profit on a prorata basis. The time length of the contract is specified, making it suitable for financing projects where funds are committed over a long period.

b. Diminishing Musharaka- This allows equity participation and sharing of profits on a prorata basis, and provides a method through which the bank keeps on reducing its equity in the project, ultimately transferring ownership of the asset to the customer. The contract provides for payment over and above the bank's share in the profit for the equity held by the bank. Simultaneously the entrepreneur purchases some of the banks equity, progressively reducing it until the bank has no equity and thus ceases to be a partner.

MUDHARABA

It is a partnership in profit whereby one party provides capital (rab al-maal-the bank) and the other party provides the know how/labour (Mudharib). The bank contributes 100% of the capital. Profits are shared on an agreed ratio. If there is any loss the bank takes 100% responsibility unless there was a case of misconduct, negligence or breech of contract on the part of Mudharib.

IJARA CONTRACT (LEASING) OR IJARA MUNTAHIA BI AT-TAMLEEK

Ijara (leasing)

It is the same as leasing thus leasing practised in interest – free banks are similar to its conventional practice. During the life of the asset, the risk of ownership remains with the bank, while the lessee is liable for misuse of the asset.

Ijara Muntahia bi at-tamleek (lease ending in property ownership)

This is a form of leasing contract, which includes a promise by the lesser to transfer the ownership of the leased property to the lessee. Example, the bank purchases the asset say a house. The client rents it from the bank, as he enters into an agreement to buy the shares from the bank over an agreed time frame. He then buys out small shares from the bank from time to time ending up with 100% ownership.

Bay'us-Salam (Advance purchase)

Advance payment for goods which are to be delivered at a specified future date. Under normal circumstances, a sale cannot be affected unless the goods are in existence at the time of the bargain. However, this type of sale is an exception, provided the goods are defined and the date of delivery is fixed. The objects of sale must be tangible goods that can be defined as to the quantity, quality and workmanship.

MODERN ISLAMIC BANKING

Modern banking system was introduced into the Muslim countries in the late 19th century at a time when they were politically and economically at low ebb. The main banks in the home countries of the imperial powers established local branches in the capitals of the subject countries and they catered mainly to the import export requirements of the foreign businesses. The banks were generally confined to the capital cities and the local population remained largely untouched by the banking system. The local trading community avoided the "foreign" banks both for nationalistic as well as religious reasons. However, as time went on it became difficult to engage in trade and other activities without making use of commercial banks. Even then many confined their involvement to transaction activities such as current accounts and money transfers. Borrowing from the banks and depositing their savings with the bank were strictly avoided in order to keep away from dealing in interest which is prohibited by religion.

With the passage of time, however, and other socio-economic forces demanding more involvement in national economic and financial activities, avoiding the interaction with the banks became impossible. Local banks were established on the same lines as the interest-based foreign banks for want of another system and they began to expand within the country bringing the banking system to more local people. As countries became independent the need to engage in banking activities became unavoidable and urgent. Governments, businesses and individuals began to transact business with the banks, with or without liking it. This state of affairs drew the attention and concern of Muslim intellectuals. The story of interest-free or Islamic banking begins here. In the following paragraphs we will trace this story to date and examine how far and how sucessfully their concerns have been addressed.

HISTORICAL DEVELOPMENT

It seems that the history of interest-free banking could be divided into two parts. First, when it still remained an idea; second, when it became a reality - by private initiative in some countries and by law in others. We will discuss the two periods separately. The last decade has seen a marked decline in the establishment of new Islamic banks and the established banks seem to have failed to live up to the expectations. The literature of the period begins with evaluations and ends with attempts at finding ways and means of correcting and overcoming the problems encountered by the existing banks.

INTEREST-FREE BANKING AS AN IDEA

Interest-free banking seems to be of very recent origin. The earliest references to the reorganisation of banking on the basis of profit sharing rather than interest are found in Anwar Qureshi (1946), Naiem Siddiqi (1948) and Mahmud Ahmad (1952) in the late forties, followed by a more elabourate exposition by Mawdudi in 1950 (1961). Muhammad Hamidullah's 1944, 1955, 1957 and 1962 writings too should be included in this category. They have all recognised the need for commercial banks and the evil of interest in that enterprise, and have proposed a banking system based on the concept of *Mudarabha* - profit and loss sharing.

In the next two decades interest-free banking attracted more attention, partly because of the political interest it created in Pakistan and partly because of the emergence of young Muslim economists. Works specifically devoted to this subject began to appear in this period. The first such work is that of Muhammad Uzair (1955). Another set of works emerged in the late sixties and early seventies. Abdullah al-Araby (1967), Nejatullah Siddiqi (1961, 1969), al-Najjar (1971) and Baqir al-Sadr (1961, 1974) were the main contributors.

Early seventies saw the institutional involvement. Conference of the Finance Ministers of the Islamic Countries held in Karachi in 1970, the Egyptian study in 1972, First International Conference on Islamic Economics in Mecca in 1976, International Economic Conference in London in 1977 were the result of such involvement. The involvement of institutions and governments led to the application of theory to practice and resulted in the establishment of the first interest-free banks. The Islamic Development Bank, an inter-governmental bank established in 1975, was born of this process.

THE COMING INTO BEING OF INTEREST-FREE BANKS

The first private interest-free bank, the Dubai Islamic Bank, was also set up in 1975 by a group of Muslim businessmen from several countries. Two more private banks were founded in 1977 under the name of Faisal Islamic Bank in Egypt and the Sudan. In the same year the Kuwaiti government set up the Kuwait Finance House.

However, small scale limited scope interest-free banks have been tried earlier, one in Malaysia in the mid-forties and another in Pakistan in the late-fifties and neither survived. In 1962 the Malaysian government set up the "Pilgrim's Management Fund" to help prospective pilgrims to save and profit. The savings bank established in 1963 at Mit-Ghamr in Egypt was very popular and prospered initially and then closed down for various reasons. However this experiment led to the creation of the Nasser Social Bank in 1972. Though the bank is still active, its objectives are more social than commercial.

In the ten years since the establishment of the first private commercial bank in Dubai, more than 50 interest-free banks have come into being. Though nearly all of them are in Muslim countries, there are some in Western Europe as well: in Denmark, Luxembourg, Switzerland and the UK. Many banks were established in 1983 and 1984. The numbers have declined considerably in the following years.

In most of the countries, establishment of interest-free banking had been by private initiative and were confined to that bank. In Iran and Pakistan, however, it was by government initiative and covered all banks in the country. The governments in both these countries took steps in 1981 to introduce interest-free banking. In Pakistan, effective 1 January,1981 all domestic commercial banks were permitted to accept deposits on the basis of profit-and-loss sharing (PLS). New steps were introduced on 1 January 1985 to formally transform the banking system over the next six months to one based on no interest. From 1 July 1985 no banks could accept any interest bearing deposits, and all existing deposits became subject to PLS rules. Yet some operations were still allowed to continue on the old basis. In Iran, certain administrative steps were taken in February 1981 to eliminate interest from banking operations. Interest on all assets was replaced by a 4 per cent maximum service charge and by a 4 to 8 per cent 'profit' rate depending on the type of economic activity. Interest on deposits was also converted into a 'guaranteed minimum profit.' In August 1983 the Usury-free Banking Law was introduced and a fourteen-month change over period began in January 1984. The whole system was converted to an interest-free one in March 1985.

THE LAST DECADE

The subject matter of writings and conferences in the eighties have changed from the concepts and possibilities of interest-free banking to the evaluation of their performance and their impact on the rest of the economy and the world. Their very titles bear testimony to this and the places indicate the world-wide interest in the subject. Conference on Islamic Banking: Its impact on world financial and commercial practices held in London in September 1984, Workshop on Industrial Financing Activities of Islamic Banks held in Vienna in June 1986, International Conference on Islamic Banking held in Tehran in June 1986, International Conference on Islamic Banking and Finance: Current issues and future prospects held in Washington, D.C. in September 1986, Islamic Banking Conference held in Geneva in October 1986, and Conference 'Into the 1990's with Islamic Banking' held in London in 1988 belong to this category. The most recent one is the Workshop on the Elimination of Riba from the Economy held in Islamabad in April 1992.

Several articles, books and PhD theses have been written on Islamic Banking during this period. Special mention must be made of the work by M. Akram Khan in preparing annotated bibliographies of all published (and some unpublished) works on Islamic Economics (including Islamic Banking) from 1940 and before. It is very useful to students of Islamic Economics and Banking, especially since both English and Urdu works are included (1983, 1991, and 1992). M.N. Siddiqi's bibliographies include early works in Arabic, English and Urdu (1980, 1988). Turkish literature is found in Sabahuddin Zaim (1980).

CURRENT PRACTICES

Generally speaking, all interest-free banks agree on the basic principles. However, individual banks differ in their application. These differences are due to several reasons including the laws of the country, objectives of the different banks, individual bank's circumstances and experiences, the need to interact with other interest-based banks, etc. In the following paragraphs, we will describe the salient features common to all banks.

Deposit accounts

All the Islamic banks have three kinds of deposit accounts: current, savings and investment.

Current account

Current or demand deposit accounts are virtually the same as in all conventional banks. Deposit is guaranteed.

Savings accounts

Savings deposit accounts operate in different ways. In some banks, the depositors allow the banks to use their money but they obtain a guarantee of getting the full amount back from the bank. Banks adopt several methods of inducing their clients to deposit with them, but no profit is promised. In others, savings accounts are treated as investment accounts but with less stringent conditions as to withdrawals and minimum balance. Capital is not guaranteed but the banks take care to invest money from such accounts in relatively risk-free short-term projects. As such lower profit rates are expected and that too only on a portion of the average minimum balance on the ground that a high level of reserves needs to be kept at all times to meet withdrawal demands.

Investment account

Investment deposits are accepted for a fixed or unlimited period of time and the investors agree in advance to share the profit (or loss) in a given proportion with the bank. Capital is not guaranteed.

MODES OF FINANCING

Banks adopt several modes of acquiring assets or financing projects. But they can be broadly categorised into three areas: investment, trade and lending.

Investment financing

This is done in three main ways: a) Musharaka where a bank may join another entity to set up a joint venture, both parties participating in the various aspects of the project in varying degrees. Profit and loss are shared in a pre-arranged fashion. This is not very different from the joint venture concept. The venture is an independent legal entity and the bank may withdraw gradually after an initial period. b) Mudarabha where the bank contributes the finance and the client provides the expertise, management and labour. Profits are shared by both the partners in a pre-arranged proportion, but when a loss occurs the total loss is borne by the bank. c) Financing on the basis of an estimated rate of return. Under this scheme, the bank estimates the expected rate of return on the specific project it is asked to finance and provides financing on the understanding that at least that rate is payable to the bank. (Perhaps this rate is negotiable.) If the project ends up in a profit more than the estimated rate the excess goes to the client. If the profit is less than the estimate the bank will accept the lower rate. In case a loss is suffered the bank will take a share in it.

Trade financing

This is also done in several ways. The main ones are: a) Mark-up where the bank buys an item for a client and the client agrees to repay the bank the price and an agreed profit later on. b) Leasing where the bank buys an item for a client and leases it to him for an agreed period and at the end of that period the lessee pays the balance on the price agreed at the beginning an becomes the owner of the item. c) Hire-purchase where the bank buys an item for the client and hires it to him for an agreed rent and period, and at the end of that period the client automatically becomes the owner of the item. d) Sell-

and-buy-back where a client sells one of his properties to the bank for an agreed price payable now on condition that he will buy the property back after certain time for an agreed price. e) Letters of credit where the bank guarantees the import of an item using its own funds for a client, on the basis of sharing the profit from the sale of this item or on a mark-up basis.

Lending

Main forms of Lending are: a) Loans with a service charge where the bank lends money without interest but they cover their expenses by levying a service charge. This charge may be subject to a maximum set by the authorities. b) No-cost loans where each bank is expected to set aside a part of their funds to grant no-cost loans to needy persons such as small farmers, entrepreneurs, producers, etc. and to needy consumers. c) Overdrafts also are to be provided, subject to a certain maximum, free of charge.

Services

Other banking services such as money transfers, bill collections, trade in foreign currencies at spot rate etc. where the bank's own money is not involved are provided on a commission or charges basis.

SHORTCOMINGS IN CURRENT PRACTICE

In the previous section we listed the current practices under three categories: deposits, modes of financing (or acquiring assets) and services. There seems to be no problems as far as banking services are concerned. Islamic banks are able to provide nearly all the services that are available in the conventional banks. The only exception seems to be in the case of letters of credit where there is a possibility for interest involvement. However some solutions have been found for this problem - mainly by having excess liquidity with the foreign bank. On the deposit side, judging by the volume of deposits both in the countries where both systems are available and in countries where law prohibits any dealing in interest, the non-payment of interest on deposit accounts seems to be no serious problem. Customers still seem to deposit their money with interest-free banks.

The main problem, both for the banks and for the customers, seems to be in the area of financing. Bank lending is still practised but that is limited to either no-cost loans (mainly consumer loans) including overdrafts, or loans with service charges only. Both these types of loans bring no income to the banks and therefore naturally they are not that keen to engage in this activity much. That leaves us with investment financing and trade financing. Islamic banks are expected to engage in these activities only on a profit and loss sharing (PLS) basis. This is where the banks' main income is to come from and this is also from where the investment account holders are expected to derive their profits from. And the latter is supposed to be the incentive for people to deposit their money with the Islamic banks. And, it is precisely in this PLS scheme that the main problems of the Islamic banks lay. Therefore we will look at this system more carefully in the following section.

PROBLEMS IN IMPLEMENTING THE PLS SCHEME

Several writers have attempted to show, with varying degrees of success, that Islamic Banking based on the concept of profit and loss sharing (PLS) is theoretically superior to conventional banking from different angles. See, for example, Khan and Mirakhor (1987). However from the practical point of view things do not seem that rosy. Our concern here is this latter aspect. In the over half-a-decade of full-scale experience in implementing the PLS scheme, the problems have begun to show up. If one goes by the experience of Pakistan as portrayed in the papers presented at the conference held in Islamabad in 1992, the situation is very serious and no satisfactory remedy seems to emerge.

2

Conventional Banking

FEATURES OF CONVENTIONAL BANKING

The conventional banking, which is interest based, performs the following major activities and would like to make a comparison of these activities with Islamic concept of banking.

1. Deposits (The liability side)

Deposit-qard (loan) not amanah (trust)

The common misconception regarding "deposit" is that it is a form of amanah (security or trust). However, according to Shariah definition, deposit has more resemblance to qard (loan) than amanah. This conclusion is based on the fact that in Islam an item is termed as amanah, if it bears all the features of amanah. Deposits cannot be termed amanah, as they do not have two of its special features, i.e., Amanah cannot be used by the bank for its business or benefit. The bank cannot be liable in case of any damage or loss to the amanah resulting from circumstances beyond its control.

On the other hand, in banks, deposits are primarily placed to earn profit, which is only possible when the bank uses these deposits to invest in other business. Hence, deposits do not fulfill the first condition of amanah, which says that it should not be used by the caretaker for his own business or benefit.

Secondly, the bank is held 100% responsible for these deposits in all circumstances even in case of loss or damage to the bank. This feature releases deposits from the ruling of amanah where the assets will not be returned in case of any damage to the asset resulting from circumstances beyond caretaker's control. According to this justification, all three kinds of deposit namely current accounts, fixed deposits and saving accounts are not amanah. They are all governed by qard.

One school of thought says that only fixed deposit and saving accounts fall under the laws of qard but current account is governed by amanah. However, this is also not correct because the bank is as much liable to current account holders as its PLS account holders and is called the "guarantor" in fiqh terminology. Due to this feature, current account is also governed by qard.

The depositors are not interested in terminology but the end-result of holding an account. Therefore if a bank does not offer security to the assets, the depositors under normal circumstance will never keep their assets at such a bank. Similarly if the depositors are told that the status of their account will that be of amanah and in case of any loss to the assets, without any negligence of the bank, will not be returned to them, not a single person would put his asset in the bank. Therefore the bank provides the security to the assets, which the depositors themselves want.

We therefore conclude that the main intention of the depositors is not to put the assets in banks as amanah; rather as qard by having collateral security by appointing the bank as guarantor.

Example of Syedna Zubair bin Awwam (RA): Hazrat Zubair bin Awwam (RA) was famous for his honesty and trustworthiness. Prominent people used to leave with him their properties in trust. Based on their needs they would also withdraw all or part of their properties. It has been reported in Al Bukhari and Tabaqaat-e-Ibn-e-Saad in respect of Hazrat Zubair bin Awwam (RA) that he would decline to accept such property as amanah (trust) but rather accepted them as qard (loan).

The reason for this action on his part was his fear that the property may be lost and it may be suspected that he was neglectful in its safekeeping. As such, he decided to consider it a loan so that the depositor felt more comfortable and his reputation remained intact. Another reason for it was that it could become possible for him to employ these funds for trading and earn profit out of them. The loan amount calculated at 2.2 million at the time of his death by his son Syedna Abdullah bin Zubair was specified as qard not amanah. He also used the term loan while instructing his son before his death "Son, dispose off my property to settle the loans".

From the above discussion, we come to the conclusion that all three forms of bank deposits are governed by the law of qard as a consequence of which the account holder may withdraw only the assets deposited. Any increase on it will be interest. If the purpose of the lender is business or security and not providing financial assistance, then to get an excess amount is also interest, which is prohibited in Islam just like usury.

It is also clear that there is a consensus of Muslim scholars on the point that the transactions in Fixed Deposit and Savings Account is prohibited because the bank pays excess to their account holders over their actual capital, which is interest. The Islamic Fiqh Academy Jeddah in their 2nd session has further endorsed such transactions as interest based transaction. Therefore it is illegal for a Muslim to keep their deposits in such accounts. As far as the current account is concerned, the bank does not pay any excess (interest) over the actual capital, therefore holding such an account is allowed.

To sum up, profit given on fixed deposit and savings accounts is interest and therefore prohibited. However if the banking system is based on Islamic principles, Musharakah can play a very important role. Therefore we will now discuss how the banks can operate on Musharakah basis. As we already know a bank has two sides, one where it receives deposits from customers which is called the liability side and the other where it advances finance to investors and businessmen which is called the asset side. Both sides can operate on Musharakah basis. As far as deposits are concerned, Musharakah is the only instrument in which money can be received from customers meaning that every depositor will become a partner in bank's business through their deposited money. However, for the asset or finance side, there are other instruments apart from Musharakah but since those instruments are not covered in our subject, we will stick to the operation of Musharakah. We will begin by the role of Musharakah in the deposits and its relevant laws and will then discuss the procedure of Musharakah in the finance side.

2. Role of the Bank as an Agent

A bank under Islamic Shariah can act as an agent (on Al-Wakalah basis) of the customer and can carry out the transaction on his behalf. Moreover it can charge agency fee for the services. The agency fee can be charged in the following cases:

Payment /Receipt of cash on behalf of the customer

Inward bill of collection

Outward bill of collection

LC opening and acceptance

Collection of export bills / bills of exchange. In this case the undertaking or guarantee commission and take-up commission can be Islamized. Bank will charge an agency fee for accepting the bills, which is bought at face value.

3. Underwriting and IPO services

4. Role of the Bank as Guarantor

The bank or financial institute gives a guarantee on behalf of its customer but according to Shariah, guarantee fee cannot be charged. Normally conventional banks charge fee for following guarantees:

- Letter of guarantee and
- Shipping guarantee

5. Advisory Services

Most of the advisory services provided by the financial institutes can be carried out easily in compliance with Shariah as long as the nature of business is halal:

- Financial advisory services
- Privatization advisory services
- Equity placement
- Merger & acquisition advice
- Venture capital
- Trading (Capital market operations)
- Cash & portfolio management advice

Brokerage services (Purchase & buying of share of companies involved in halal business, a fee could be charged for it).

6. Other allowed Islamic financial services and products

- Remittance
- Zakat deduction
- Sale & purchase of foreign currency
- Sale & purchase of travelers checks (local foreign currency)
- ATM services
- Electronic online transfer
- Telegraphic transfer (of cash)
- Demand draft
- Pay order
- Lockers and custodial services
- Syndicate funds arrangements services (non-interest or markup based) for some fee.
- Opening of bank account (current & non-interest or no-markup) Clearing facility
- Sales & purchase of shares/stock (of companies involved in halal activities)
- Collection of dividends
- Electronic banking windowTelephone banking

MUSHARAKAH IN BANK DEPOSIT

An important value of an Islamic society is mutual dealing. It also refers to deposits in banks. The operation of fixed deposits and savings account in Islamic banks will be different from conventional banks because the Islamic banks will be based on Musharakah (combination of Shirkah & Mudarabah) in which like conventional banks, people will invest in two ways:

1. Participation in setting up the bank like any other company by joint investment and the participants will be called the "shareholders". They will have a partnership (Shirkah) effected by a mutual contract since they have used their capital and deed on the bank; and
2. Participation by opening their account in fixed deposit and savings account and participants will be called the "account holders". These will not be the actual owner or shareholders of the bank - rather partners in profit only, meaning that they will have a contract of Mudarabah.

The status of the bank or the shareholders will be that of a Mudarib and the account holders will be Rubb-ul-mal. The contract known as Musharakah will be a combination of Shirkah and Mudarabah. This is the reason why the profit ratio of depositors is less than the actual shareholders and the depositors will not have any voting power or the right of management because they are not involved in the deed but has only supplied the capital. This kind of dual relationship is not uncommon in Islamic Fiqh. Therefore, if the Mudarib (Bank or the shareholders) wants to merge his assets with the assets of depositor, it is allowed in which case he will be regarded as owner of half the assets and Mudarib of the other half.

The actual status of deposits is debt and not amanah. The excess paid on loan is interest, not profit. If a bank is operating on Islamic principles, the bank and the depositor will have a partnership through a contract of Shirkah or Mudarabah in which case the depositor's capital will not be regarded as loan. The shareholders will act as Rubb-ul-mal as well as Mudarib . The depositors will only act as Rubb-ul-mal.

Fixed deposit and saving account will be converted into Mudarabah account where the distribution of profit for each partner will be determined in proportion to the actual profit accrued to the business and not according to a fixed ratio or in proportion to the capital invested by him. Fixing lump sum amount is not allowed or any rate of profit tied up with any investment.

The entire set up of the bank is on Musharakah basis where the relationship of the bank and shareholders is through partnership agreement (Shirkah) because they are participating in labour as well as investment and the relationship between the bank and depositors is only that of Mudarabah because they have only invested without participating in labour. Therefore this combination of Shirkah and Mudarabah is called Musharakah in modern terminology.

DISTRIBUTION OF PROFIT UNDER MUSHARAKAH AGREEMENT

The distribution of profit will be done according to the rules of Musharakah. Before we begin the summary of the distribution of profit, it is found appropriate to mention here that the conventional banks do not pay interest to current account holders. Therefore there is no need to convert the operation of current account into any Islamic mode of financing. However the distribution of profit to the rest of the partners and account holders will be made on the following rules governing Musharakah:

It is not a condition for the final distribution of profit that all assets are liquid - rather the profit and loss is calculated on the basis of evaluation of assets. In case of loss, each partner shall suffer the loss exactly according to the ratio of his investment and in case of profit; the profit will be distributed according to the agreed ratio between the partners. It should be taken into account that both parties are free to determine any ratio of profit of the bank as the manager (Mudarib), therefore it can be agreed mutually that Rubb-ul-mal will have a higher profit margin and Mudarib lower. However as a shareholding partner, the share of profit of the Mudarib cannot be less than the ratio of his investment since he is the sole provider of labour. Same rule will apply on the operation of Islamic Banks on the basis of Musharakah. The actual shareholders apart from being the manager are also shareholding partners; their ratio of profit cannot be less than their ratio of investment. However their ratio of profit as Mudarib can be determined at whatever rate they please.

The above may be explained in the following illustration:

Suppose the total investment of the bank is Rs.15 million in which the depositors have invested Rs.10 million on Mudarabah basis and the shareholders as Mudarib have invested Rs.5 million. This means that one third share of the total capital belongs to the shareholders and two third to the depositors. The role of Mudarib in the 2/3rd capital raised by depositors is played by the shareholders, therefore their ratio of profit as manager (Mudarib) can be agreed between themselves through mutual consent but their ratio of profit, as shareholders cannot be less than one third. If their share is agreed at less than 1/3rd, it would mean that the depositors' share has exceeded 2/3rd although it has been established that they will not be managing the bank and their share of profit will not exceed their ratio of investment.

If it has been agreed in the above example that the shareholders as managing partners will get 1/3rd of the profit and the rest 2/3rd will be distributed equally between depositors and shareholders as per the Mudarabah contract between them, then if for eg. the profit amount is Rs.15 lacs then the shareholders will get its one third, i.e., Rs.5 lacs as the investor (Rubb-ul-mal) and half of the two third profit, i.e., Rs.5 lacs as the manager (Mudarib) whereas the other half of the two third profit will go to the depositor as Rubb-ul-mal.

RUNNING MUSHARAKAH ACCOUNT ON THE BASIS OF DAILY PRODUCTS

Many financial institutions finance the working capital of an enterprise by opening a running account for them from where the clients draw different amounts at different intervals, but at the same time, they keep returning their surplus amounts. Thus the process of debit and credit goes on upto the date of maturity and the interest is calculated on the basis of daily products.

Can such an arrangement be possible under the Musharakah or Mudarabah modes of financing? Obviously, being a new phenomenon, no express answer to this question can be found in the classical works of Islamic Fiqh.

A certain percentage of the actual profit must be allocated for the management. The remaining percentage of the profit must be allocated for the investors. The loss, if any, should be borne by the investors only in exact proportion of their respective investments.

The average balance of the contributions made to the Musharakah account calculated on the basis of daily products shall be treated as the share capital of the financier. The profit accruing at the end of the term shall be calculated on daily product basis, and shall be distributed accordingly.

If such an arrangement is agreed upon between the parties, it does not seem to violate any basic principle of the Musharakah. However, this suggestion needs further consideration and research by the experts of Islamic jurisprudence. Practically, it means that the parties have agreed to the principle that the profit accrued to the Musharakah portfolio at the end of the term will be divided based on the average capital utilized per day, which will lead to the average of the profit earned by each rupee per day. The amount of this average profit per rupee per day will be multiplied by the number of the days each investor has put his money into the business, which will determine his profit entitlement on daily product basis.

Some contemporary scholars do not allow this method of calculating profits on the ground that it is just a conjectural method, which does not reflect the actual profits really earned by a partner of the Musharakah. Because the business may have earned huge profits during a period when a particular investor had no money invested in the business at all, or had a very insignificant amount invested, still, he will be treated at par with other investors who had huge amounts invested in the business during that period. Conversely, the business may have suffered a great loss during a period when a particular investor had huge amounts invested in it. Still, he will pass on some of his loss to other investors who had no investment in that period or their size of investment was insignificant.

This argument can be refuted on the ground that it is not necessary in a Musharakah that a partner should earn profit on his own money only. Once a Musharakah pool comes into existence, all the participants, regardless of whether their money is or is not utilized in a particular transaction earn the profits accruing to the joint pool. This is particularly true of the Hanafi School, which does not deem it necessary for a valid Musharakah that the monetary contributions of the partners are mixed up together. It means that if 'A' has entered into a Musharakah contract with 'B', but has not yet disbursed his money into the joint pool, he will be still entitled to a share in the profit of the transactions effected by 'B' for the Musharakah through his own money. Although his entitlement to a share in the profit will be subject to the disbursement of money undertaken by him, yet the fact remains that the profit of this particular transaction did not accrue to his money, because the money disbursed by him at a later stage may be used for another transaction.

Suppose 'A' and 'B' entered into a Musharakah to conduct a business of Rs. 100,000/- They agreed that each one of them shall contribute Rs. 50,000/- and the profits will be distributed by them equally. 'A' did not yet invest his Rs. 50,000/- into the joint pool. 'B' found a profitable deal and purchased two air conditioners for the Musharakah for Rs. 50,000/- contributed by himself and sold them for Rs. 60,000/-, thus earning a profit of Rs. 10,000/-. 'A' contributed his share of Rs. 50,000/- after this deal. The partners purchased two refrigerators through this contribution which could not be sold at a greater price than Rs. 48000/- meaning thereby that this deal resulted in a loss of Rs. 2000/- Although the transaction effected by 'A's money brought loss of Rs. 2000/- while the profitable deal of air conditioners was financed entirely by 'B's money in which 'A' had no contribution, yet 'A' will be entitled to a share in the profit of the first deal. The loss of Rs. 2000/- in the second deal will be set off from the profit of the first deal reducing the aggregate profit to Rs. 8000/-. This profit of Rs. 8000/- will be shared by both partners equally. It means that 'A' will get Rs. 4000/-, even though the transaction effected by his money has suffered a loss.

The reason is that once the parties enter into a Musharakah contract, all the subsequent transactions effected for Musharakah belong to the joint pool, regardless of whose individual money is utilized in them. Each partner is a party to each transaction by virtue of his entering into the contract of Musharakah.

A possible objection to the above explanation may be that in the above example, 'A' had undertaken to pay Rs. 50,000/- and it was known before hand that he would contribute a specified amount to the Musharakah. But in the proposed running account of Musharakah where the partners are coming in and going out every day, nobody has undertaken to contribute any specific amount. Therefore, the capital contributed by each partner is unknown at the time of entering into Musharakah, which should render the Musharakah invalid.

The answer to the above objection is that the classical scholars of Islamic Fiqh have different views about whether it is necessary for a valid Musharakah that the capital is pre-known to the partners. The Hanafi scholars are unanimous on the point that it is not a pre-condition. Al-Kasani, the famous Hanafi jurist, writes:

According to our Hanafi School, it is not a condition for the validity of Musharakah that the amount of capital is known, while it is a condition according to Imam Shafi'i. Our argument is that Jahalah (uncertainty) in itself does not render a contract invalid, unless it leads to disputes. And the uncertainty in the capital at the time of Musharakah does not lead to disputes, because it is generally known when the commodities are purchased for the Musharakah, therefore it does not lead to uncertainty in the profit at the time of distribution." (Badai-us-sanai v.6 p.63)

It is, therefore, clear from the above that even if the amount of the capital is not known at the time of Musharakah, the contract is valid. The only condition is that it should not lead to the uncertainty in the profit at the time of distribution. Distribution of profit on daily product basis fulfills this condition.

It is true that the concept of a running Musharakah where the partners at times draw some amounts and at other times inject new money and the profits are calculated on daily products basis is not found in the classical books of Islamic Fiqh. But merely this fact cannot render a new arrangement invalid in Shariah, so far as it does not violate any basic principle of Musharakah. In the proposed system, all the partners are treated at par. The profit of each partner is calculated on the basis of the period for which his money remained in the joint pool. There is no doubt in the fact that the aggregate profit accrued to the pool is generated by the joint utilization of different amounts contributed by the participants at different times. Therefore, if all of them agree with mutual consent to distribute the profits on daily products basis, there is no injunction of Shari'ah which makes it impermissible; rather, it is covered under the general guidelines given by the Holy Prophet in his famous hadith, as follows: "Muslims are bound by their mutual agreements unless they hold a permissible thing as prohibited or a prohibited thing as permissible."

If distribution on daily products basis is not accepted, it will mean that no partner can draw any amount nor can he inject new amounts to the joint pool. Similarly, nobody will be able to subscribe to the joint pool except at the particular dates of the commencement of a new term. This arrangement is totally impracticable on the deposit side of the banks and financial institutions where the accounts are debited and credited by the depositors many times a day. The rejection of the concept of the daily products will compel them to wait for months before they deposit their surplus money in a profitable account. This will hinder the utilization of savings for development of industry and trade, and will keep the wheel of financial activities jammed for long periods. There is no other solution for this problem except to apply the method of daily products for the calculation of profits, and since there is no specific injunction of Shari'ah against it, there is no reason why this method should not be adopted.

PROJECT FINANCING

The concept of Musharakah and Mudarabah is based on some basic principles. As long as these principles are fully complied with, the details of their application may vary from time to time. Let us have a look at these basic principles before touching the details:

- Financing through Musharakah and Mudarabah does never mean the advancing of money. It means participation in the business and in the case of Musharakah, sharing in the assets of the business to the extent of the ratio of financing.
- An investor/financier must share the loss incurred by the business to the extent of his financing.
- The partners are at liberty to determine, with mutual consent, the ratio of profit allocated to each one of them, which may differ from the ratio of investment. However, the partner who has expressly excluded himself from the responsibility of work for the business cannot claim more than the ratio of his investment.

– The loss suffered by each partner must be exactly in the proportion of his investment.

Keeping in view these basic principles project financing is discussed below:

In the case of project financing, the traditional method of Musharakah or Mudarabah can be easily adopted. If the financier wants to finance the whole project, the form of Mudarabah can come into operation. If investment comes from both sides, the form of Musharakah can be adopted. In this case, if the management is the sole responsibility of one party, while the investment comes from both, a combination of Musharakah and Mudarabah can be brought into play according to the rules already discussed.

Since Musharakah or Mudarabah would have been affected from the very inception of the project, no problem with regard to the valuation of capital should arise. Similarly, the distribution of profits according to the normal accounting standards should not be difficult. However, if the financier wants to withdraw from the Musharakah, while the other party wants to continue the business, the latter can purchase the share of the former at an agreed price. In this way the financier may get back the amount he has invested along with a profit, if the business has earned a profit. The basis for determining the price of his share shall be discussed in detail later on (while discussing the financing of working capital).

On the other hand, the businessman can continue with his project, either on his own or by selling the first financier's share to some other person who can substitute the financier. Since financial institutions do not normally want to remain partner of a specific project for good, they can sell their share to other partners of the project as aforesaid. If the sale of the share on one time basis is not feasible for the lack of liquidity in the project, the share of the financier can be divided into smaller units and each unit can be sold after a suitable interval. Whenever a unit is sold, the share of the financier in the project is reduced to that extent, and when all the units are sold, the financier totally comes out of the project.

FINANCING OF A SINGLE TRANSACTION

Musharakah and Mudarabah can be used more easily for financing a single transaction. Apart from fulfilling the day to day needs of small traders, these instruments can be employed for financing imports and exports. An importer can approach a financier to finance him for that single transaction of import alone on the basis of Musharakah or Mudarabah. The banks can also use these instruments for import financing. If the letter of credit has been opened without any margin, the form of Mudarabah can be adopted, and if the L/C is opened with some margin, the form of Musharakah or a combination of both will be relevant. After the imported goods are cleared from the port, their sale proceeds may be shared by the importer and the financier according to a pre-agreed ratio.

In this case, the ownership of the imported goods shall remain with the financier to the extent of the ratio of his investment. This Musharakah can be restricted to an agreed term, and if the imported goods are not sold in the market up to the expiry of the term, the importer may himself purchase the share of the financier, making himself the sole owner of the goods. However, the sale in this case should take place at the market rate or at a price agreed between the parties on the date of sale, and not at pre-agreed price at the time of entering into Musharakah. If the price is pre-agreed, the financier cannot compel the client / importer to purchase it.

Similarly, Musharakah will be even easier in the case of export financing. The exporter has a specific order from abroad. The price on which the goods will be exported is well known before hand, and the financier can easily calculate the expected profit. He may finance him on the basis of Musharakah or Mudarabah, and may share the amount of export bill on a pre-agreed percentage. In order to secure himself from any negligence on the part of the exporter, the financier may put a condition that it will be the responsibility of the exporter to export the goods in full conformity with the conditions of the L/C. In this case, if some discrepancies are found, the exporter alone shall be responsible, and the financier shall be immune from any loss due to such discrepancies, because it is caused by the negligence of the exporter. However, being a partner of the exporter, the financier will be liable to bear any loss, which may be caused due to any reason other than the negligence or misconduct of the exporter.

WORKING CAPITAL FINANCING

Where finances are required for the working capital of a running business, the instrument of Musharakah may be used in the following manner:

1. The capital of the running business may be evaluated with mutual consent: The value of the business can be treated as the investment of the person who seeks finance, while the amount given by the financier can be treated as his share of investment. The Musharakah may be affected for a particular period, like one year or six months or less. Both the parties agree on a certain percentage of the profit to be given to the financier, which should not exceed the percentage of his investment, because he shall not work for the business. On the expiry of the term, all liquid and non-liquid assets of the business are again evaluated, and the profit may be distributed on the basis of this evaluation.

   Although, according to the traditional concept, the profit cannot be determined unless all the assets of the business are liquidated, yet the valuation of the assets can be treated as "constructive liquidation" with mutual consent of the parties, because there is no specific prohibition in Shariah against it. It can also mean that the working partner has purchased the share of the financier in the assets of the business, and the price of his share has been determined on the basis of valuation, keeping in view the ratio of profit allocated for him according to the terms of Musharakah.

   For example, the total value of the business of 'A' is 30 units. 'B' finances another 20 units, raising the total worth to 50 units; 40% having been contributed by 'B', and 60%

by 'A'. It is agreed that 'B' shall get 20% of the actual profit. At the end of the term, the total worth of the business has increased to 100 units. Now, if the share of 'B' is purchased by 'A', he should have paid to him 40 units, because he owns 40% of the assets of the business. But in order to reflect the agreed ratio of profit in the price of his share, the formula of pricing will be different. Any increase in the value of the business shall be divided between the parties in the ratio of 20% and 80%, because this ratio was determined in the contract for the purpose of distribution of profit.

Since the increase in the value of the business is 50 units, these 50 units are divided at the ratio of 20:80, meaning thereby that 'B' will have earned 10 units. These 10 units will be added to his original 20 units, and the price of his share will be 30 units.

In the case of loss, however, any decrease in the total value of the assets should be divided between them exactly in the ratio of their investment, i.e., in the ratio of 40/60. Therefore, if the value of the business has decreased, in the above example, by 10 units reducing the total number of units to 40, the loss of 4 units shall be borne by 'B' (being 40% of the loss). These 4 units shall be deducted from his original 20 units, and the price of his share shall be determined as 16 units.

2. Sharing in the gross profit only: Financing on the basis of Musharakah according to the above procedure may be difficult in a business having a large number of fixed assets, particularly in a running industry, because the valuation of all its assets and their depreciation or appreciation may create accounting problems giving rise to disputes. In such cases, Musharakah may be applied in another way.

   The major difficulties in these cases arise in the calculation of indirect expenses, like depreciation of the machinery, salaries of the staff etc. In order to solve this problem, the parties may agree on the principle that, instead of net profit, the gross profit will be distributed between the parties, that is, the indirect expenses shall not be deducted from the distributable profit. It will mean that all the indirect expenses shall be borne by the industrialist voluntarily, and only direct expenses (like those of raw material, direct labour, electricity etc.) shall be borne by the Musharakah. But since the industrialist is offering his machinery, building and staff to the Musharakah voluntarily, the percentage of his profit may be increased to compensate him to some extent.

This arrangement may be justified on the ground that the clients of financial institutions do not restrict themselves to the operations for which they seek finance from the financial institutions. Their machinery and staff etc. is, therefore, engaged in some other business also which may not be subject to Musharakah, and in such a case the whole cost of these expenses cannot be imposed on the Musharakah.

Let us take a practical example. Suppose a ginning factory has a building worth Rs. 22 million, plant and machinery valuing Rs. 2 million and the staff is paid Rs. 50,000/- per month. The factory sought finance of Rs. 5,000,000/- from a bank on the basis of Musharakah for a term of one year. It means that after one year the Musharakah will be terminated, and the profits accrued up to that point will be distributed between the parties according to the agreed ratio. While determining the profit, all direct expenses will be deducted from the income. The direct expenses may include the following:

The amount spent in purchasing raw material. The wages of the labour directly involved in processing the raw material. The expenses for electricity consumed in the process of ginning. The bills for other services directly rendered for the Musharakah. So far as the building, the machinery and the salary of other staff is concerned, it is obvious that they are not meant for the business of the Musharakah alone, because the Musharakah will terminate within one year, while the building and the machinery are purchased for a much longer term in which the ginning factory will use them for its own business which is not subject to this one-year Musharakah. Therefore, the whole cost of the building and the machinery cannot be borne by this short-term Musharakah. What can be done at the most is that the depreciation caused to the building and the machinery during the term of the Musharakah is included in its expenses.

But in practical terms, it will be very difficult to determine the cost of depreciation, and it may cause disputes also. Therefore, there are two practical ways to solve this problem.

In the first instance, the parties may agree that the Musharakah portfolio will pay an agreed rent to the client for the use of the machinery and the building owned by him. This rent will be paid to him from the Musharakah fund irrespective of profit or loss accruing to the business.

The second option is that, instead of paying rent to the client, the ratio of his profit is increased.

3. Running Musharakah Account on the Basis of Daily Products: Many financial institutions finance the working capital of an enterprise by opening a running account for them from where the clients draw different amounts at different intervals, but at the same time, they keep returning their surplus amounts. Thus the process of debit and credit goes on up to the date of maturity, and the interest is calculated on the basis of daily products.

   Keeping in view the basic principles of Musharakah the following procedure may be suggested for this purpose:

   a. A certain percentage of the actual profit must be allocated for the management.

   b. The remaining percentage of the profit must be allocated for the investors.

   c. The loss, if any, should be borne by the investors only in exact proportion of their respective investments.

   d. The average balance of the contributions made to the Musharakah account calculated on the basis of daily products shall be treated as the share capital of the financier.

The profit accruing at the end of the term shall be calculated on daily product basis, and shall be distributed accordingly. If such an arrangement is agreed upon between the parties, it does not seem to violate any basic principle of the Musharakah. However, this suggestion needs further consideration and research by the experts of Islamic jurisprudence. Practically, it means that the parties have agreed to the principle that the profit accrued to the Musharakah portfolio at the end of the term will be divided on the capital utilized per day, which will lead to the average of the profit earned by each rupee per day. The amount of this average profit per rupee per day will be multiplied by the number of the days each investor has put his money into the business, which will determine his profit entitlement on daily product basis.

IMPORT FINANCING

Musharakah can be used for Import Financing as well. There are two types of bank charges on the letter of credit provided to the importer:

Service charges for opening an LC Interest charged on LCs, which are not opened on full margin. Collecting service charges for this purpose is allowed, but as interest cannot be charged in any case, experts have proposed two methods for financing LCs:

a. Based on Musharakah / Mudarabah
b. Based on Murabahah

Musharakah /Mudarabah

This is the best substitute for opening the LC. The bank and the importer can make an agreement of Mudarabah or Musharakah before opening the LC.

If the LC is being opened at zero margins, an agreement of Mudarabah can be made, in which the bank will become Rqb-ul-Maal and the importer Mudarib . The bank will own the goods that are being imported and the profit will be distributed according to the agreement.

If the LC is being opened with a margin then a Musharakah agreement can be made. The bank will pay the remaining amount and the goods that are being imported will be owned by both of them according to their share of investment.

The bank and the importer, with their mutual consent can also include a condition in the agreement, whereby; Musharakah or Mudarabah will end after a certain time period even if the goods are not sold. In such a case, the importer will purchase the bank's share at the market price.

Murabahah

At present Islamic banks are using Murabahah , to finance LC. These banks themselves import the required goods and then sell these goods to the importer on Murabahah agreement.

Murabahah financing requires the bank and the importer to sign at least two agreements separately; one for the purchase of the goods, and the other for appointing the importer as the agent of the bank (agency agreement). Once these two agreements are signed, the importer can negotiate and finalize all terms and conditions with the exporter on behalf of the bank.

EXPORT FINANCING

A bank plays two very important roles in Exports. It acts as a negotiating bank and charges a fee for this purpose, which is allowed in Shariah. Secondly it provides export-financing facility to the exporters and charge interest on this service. These services are of two types and interest cannot be charged in any case, experts have proposed certain methods for financing exports.

i. Pre Shipment Financing- It needs can be fulfilled by two methods:

   a. Musharakah/Mudarabah

The most appropriate method for financing exports is Musharakah or Mudarbah. Bank and exporter can make an agreement of Mudarabah provided that the exporter is not investing; other wise Musharakah agreement can be made. Agreement in such case will be easy, as cost and expected profit is known. The exporter will manufacture or purchase goods and the profit obtained by exporting it will be distributed between them according to the predefined ratio.

A problem that can be encountered by the bank is that if the exporter is not able to deliver the goods according to the terms and conditions of the importer, then the importer can refuse to accept the goods, and in this case exporter's bank will ultimately suffer. This problem can be rectified by including a condition in Mudarabah or Musharakah agreement that, if exporter violates the terms and conditions of import agreement then the Bank will not be responsible for any loss which arises due to this negligence. This condition is allowed in Shariah as the Rabb-ul-mal is not responsible for any loss that arises due to the negligence of Mudarib .

b. Murabahah

Murabahah is being used in many Islamic Banks for export financing. Banks purchases goods that are to be exported at price that is less than the price agreed between the exporter and the importer. It then exports goods at the original price and thus earns profit.

Murabahah financing requires bank and exporter to sign at least two agreements separately, one for the purchase of goods and the other for appointing the exporter as the agent of the bank (that is agency agreement). Once these two agreements are signed, the exporter can negotiate and finalize all the terms and conditions with the importer on behalf of the bank.

ii. Post Shipment Financing

Post shipment finance is similar to the discounting of the bill of exchange. Its alternate Shariah compliant procedure is discussed below:

The exporter with the bill of exchange can appoint the bank as his agent to collect receivable on his behalf. The bank can charge a fee for this service and can provide interest free loan to the exporter, which is equal to the amount of the bill, and the exporter will give his consent to the bank that it can keep the amount received from the bill as a payment of the loan.

Here two processes are separated, and thus two agreements will be made. One will authorize the bank to collect the loan on his behalf as an agent, for which he will charge a particular fee. The second agreement will provide interest free loan to the exporter, and authorize the bank for keeping the amount received through bill as a payment for loan. These agreements are correct and allowed according to Shariah because collecting fee for service and giving interest free loan is permissible.

SECURITIZATION

Securitization means issuing certificates of ownership against an investment pool or business enterprise. This chapter discusses the issues, problems and rules in issuing such certificates with respect to the "nature" of investment pool. Basic guidelines are also provided on the negotiability and sale of these certificates in the secondary markets.

Securitization of Musharakah

Musharakah is a mode of financing which can be securitized easily, especially, in the case of big projects where huge amounts are required which a limited number of people cannot afford to subscribe. Every subscriber can be given a Musharakah certificate, which represents his proportionate ownership in the assets of the Musharakah, and after the project is started by acquiring substantial non-liquid assets, these Musharakah certificates can be treated as negotiable instruments and can be bought and sold in the secondary market. However, trading in these certificates is not allowed when all the assets of the Musharakah are still in liquid form (i.e. in the shape of cash or receivables or advances due from others).

For proper understanding of this point, it must be noted that subscribing to a Musharakah is different from advancing a loan. A bond issued to evidence a loan has nothing to do with the actual business undertaken with the borrowed money. The bond stands for a loan repayable to the holder in any case, and mostly with interest. The Musharakah certificate, on the contrary, represents the direct pro rata ownership of the holder in the assets of the project. If all the assets of the joint project are in liquid form, the certificate will represent a certain proportion of money owned by the project. For example, one hundred certificates, having a value of Rs. one million each, have been issued. It means that the total worth of the project is Rs. 100 million. If nothing has been purchased by this money, every certificate will represent Rupees one million. In this case, this certificate cannot be sold in the market except at par value, because if one certificate is sold for more than Rs.one million, it will mean that Rupees one million are being sold in exchange for more than Rupees one million, which is not allowed in Shariah, because where money is exchanged for money, both must be equal. Any excess at either side is Riba.

However, when the subscribed money is employed in purchasing non-liquid assets like land, building, machinery, raw material, furniture etc. the Musharakah certificates will represent the holders' proportionate ownership in these assets. Thus, in the above example, one certificate will stand for one hundredth share in these assets. In this case it will be allowed by the Shariah to sell these certificates in the secondary market for any price agreed upon between the parties which may be more than the face value of the certificate. Since the subject matter of the sale is a share in the tangible assets and not in money alone, therefore the certificate may be taken as any other commodity which can be sold with profit or at a loss.

In most cases, the assets of the project are a mixture of liquid and non-liquid assets. This comes to happen when the working partner has converted a part of the subscribed money into fixed assets or raw material, while rest of the money is still liquid. Or, the project, after converting all its money into non-liquid assets may have sold some of them and has acquired their sale proceeds in the form of money. In some cases the price of its sales may have become due on its customers but may have not yet been received. These receivable amounts, being a debt, are also treated as liquid money. The question arises about the rule of Shariah in a situation where the assets of the project are a mixture of liquid and non-liquid assets, whether the Musharakah certificates of such a project can be traded in? The opinions of the contemporary Muslim jurists are different on this point. According to the traditional Shafi School, this type of certificate cannot be sold. Their classic view is that whenever there is a combination of liquid and non-liquid assets, it cannot be sold unless the non-liquid part of the business is separated and sold independently.

The Hanafi school, however, is of the opinion that whenever there is a combination of liquid and non-liquid assets, it can be sold and purchased for an amount greater than the amount of liquid assets in combination, in which case money will be taken as sold at an equal amount and the excess will be taken as the price of the non-liquid assets owned by the business.

Suppose the Musharakah project contains 40% non-liquid assets i.e. machinery, fixtures etc. and 60% liquid assets, i.e. cash and receivables. Now, each Musharakah certificate with the face value of Rs.100/- represents liquid assets worth Rs. 60/-, and non-liquid assets worth Rs. 40/-. This certificate may be sold at any price more than Rs.60. If it is sold at Rs. 110/- it will mean that Rs. 60 of the price are against Rs. 60/- contained in the certificate and Rs.50/- is against the proportionate share in the non-liquid assets. But it will never be allowed to sell the certificate for a price of Rs.60/- or less, because in the case of Rs. 60/- it will not set off the amount of Rs. 60, let alone the other assets.

According to the Hanafi view, no specific proportion of non-liquid assets in the whole is prescribed. Therefore, even if the non-liquid assets represent less than 50% in the whole, its trading according to the above formula is allowed.

However, most of the contemporary scholars, including those of Shafi school, have allowed trading in the units of the whole only if the non-liquid assets of the business are more than

50%.

Therefore, for a valid trading of the Musharakah certificates acceptable to all schools, it is necessary that the portfolio of Musharakah consists of non-liquid assets valuing more than 50% of its total worth. However, if Hanafi view is adopted, trading will be allowed even if the non-liquid assets are less than 50% but the size of the non-liquid assets should not be negligible.

Securitization of Murabahah

Murabahah is a transaction, which cannot be securitized for creating a negotiable instrument to be sold and purchased in secondary market. The reason is obvious. If the purchaser/ client in a Murabahah transaction signs a paper to evidence his indebtedness towards the seller/financier, the paper will represent a monetary debt receivable from him. In other words, it represents money payable by him. Therefore transfer of this paper to a third party will mean transfer of money. It has already been explained that where money is exchanged for money (in the same currency) the transfer must be at par value. It cannot be sold or purchased at a lower or a higher price. Therefore, the paper representing a monetary obligation arising out of a Murabahah transaction cannot create a negotiable instrument. If the paper is transferred, it must be at par value. However, if there is a mixed portfolio consisting of a number of transactions like Musharakah, leasing and Murabahah , then this portfolio may issue negotiable certificates subject to certain conditions.

Securitization of Ijarah

The arrangement of Ijarah has a good potential of securitization, which may help create a secondary market for the financiers on the basis of Ijarah . Since the lessor in Ijarah owns the leased assets, he can sell the asset, in whole or in part, to a third party who may purchase it and may replace the seller in the rights and obligations of the lessor with regard to the purchased part of the asset.

Therefore, if the lessor, after entering into Ijarah , wishes to recover his cost of purchase of the asset with a profit thereon, he can sell the leased asset wholly or partly either to one party or to a number of individuals. In the latter case, the purchase of a proportion of the asset by each individual may be evidenced by a certificate, which may be called 'Ijarah certificate'. This certificate will represent the holder's proportionate ownership in the leased asset and he will assume the rights and obligations of the owner/lessor to that extent. Since the assets is already leased to the lessee, lease will continue with the new owners, each one of the holders of this certificate will have the right to enjoy a part of the rent according to his proportion of ownership in the asset. Similarly he will also assume the obligations of the lessor to the extent of his ownership. Therefore, in the case of total destruction of the asset, he will suffer the loss to the extent of his ownership. These certificates, being an evidence of proportionate ownership in a tangible asset, can be negotiated and traded freely in the market and can serve as an instrument easily convertible into cash. Thus they may help in solving the problems of liquidity management faced by the Islamic banks and financial institutions.

It should be remembered, however, that the certificate must represent ownership of an undivided part of the asset with all its rights and obligations. Misunderstanding this basic concept, some quarters tried to issue Ijarah certificates representing the holder's right to claim certain amount of the rental only without assigning to him any kind of ownership in the asset. It means that the holder of such a certificate has no relation with the leased asset at all. His only right is to share the rentals received from the lessee. This type of securitization is not allowed in Shariah. As explained earlier in this chapter, the rent after being due is a debt payable by the lessee. The debt or any security representing debt only is not a negotiable instrument in Shariah, because trading in such an instrument amounts to trade in money or in monetary obligation which is not allowed, except on the basis of equality, and if the equality of value is observed while trading in such instruments, the very purpose of securitization is defeated. Therefore, this type of Ijarah certificates cannot serve the purpose of creating a secondary market.

It is, therefore, necessary that the Ijarah certificates are designed to represent real ownership of the leased assets, and not only a right to receive rent.

ISLAMIC INVESTMENT FUNDS

The term 'Islamic Investment Fund' means a joint pool wherein the investors contribute their surplus money for the purpose of its investment to earn halal profit in strict conformity with the precepts of Islamic Shariah. The subscribers of the Fund may receive a document certifying their subscription and entitling them to the pro-rata profit actually earned by the Fund. These documents may be called 'certificates', 'units', 'shares' or may be given any other name, but their validity in terms of Shariah, will always be subject to two basic conditions:

1. Instead of a fixed return tied up with their face value, they must carry a pro-rata profit actually earned by the Fund. Therefore, neither the principal nor a rate of profit (tied up with the principal) can be guaranteed. The subscribers must enter into the fund with a clear understanding that the return on their subscription is tied up with the actual profit earned or loss suffered by the Fund. If the Fund earns huge profits, the return on their subscription will increase to that proportion. However, in case the Fund suffers loss, they will have to share it also, unless the loss is caused by the negligence or mismanagement, in which case the management, and not the Fund, will be liable to compensate it.
2. The amounts so pooled together must be invested in a business acceptable to Shariah. It means that not only the channels of investment, but also the terms agreed with them must conform to the Islamic principles.

   Keeping these basic requisites in view, the Islamic Investment Funds may accommodate a variety of modes of investment, which are discussed here briefly.

Equity Fund

In an equity or mutual fund (unit trust) the amounts are invested in the shares of joint stock companies. The profits are mainly derived through the capital gains by purchasing the shares and selling them when their prices are increased. Profits are also earned through dividends distributed by the relevant companies.

From this angle, dealing in equity shares can be acceptable in Shari'ah subject to the following conditions:

1. The main business of the company does not violate Shariah. Therefore, it is not permissible to acquire the shares of the companies providing financial services on interest, like conventional banks, insurance companies, or the companies involved in some other business not approved by the Shariah, eg. companies manufacturing, selling or offering liquor, pork, haram meat, or involved in gambling, night club activities, pornography, prostitution, or involved in the business of hire purchase or interest etc.
2. If the main business of these companies is halal, like automobiles, textile, etc. but they deposit their surplus amounts in an interest-bearing account or borrow money on interest, the share holder must express his disapproval against such dealings, preferably by raising his voice against such activities in the annual general meeting of the company.
3. If some income from interest-bearing accounts or non-Halal activities is included in the income of the company, the proportion of such income should not exceed 5% of the total income. If it exceeds 5%, it is not permissible to invest in that company. However, if it does not exceed 5%, it must be given in charity, and must not be retained by him. For example, if 5% of the whole income of a company has come out of interest-bearing deposits, 5% of the dividend must be given in charity. Moreover, the company's total short term and long term investment in non-permissible business should not exceed 30% of the company's total market capitalization.

   It may be questioned, "What is the basic rationale of this limitation of 5%?" Infact, there is no specific basis derived from the Holy Quran or Sunnah for the 5% rule of non halal (impermissible) income. However, this is only the collective outcome (consensus) or ijtihad of contemporary Shariah Scholars. To explain this consensus of their ruling, we shall have to go back to the origin or basis of company on Shariah perspective. As mentioned in the books and research papers of Islamic jurists, companies come under the ruling of Shirkatul Ainan. But if the rule of partnership is truly applied in a company, there is no possibility for any kind of impermissible activity or income. Because every shareholder of a company is a sharik (partner) of the company, and every sharik, according to the Islamic jurisprudence, is an agent of the other partners in matters of joint business. Therefore, the mere purchase of a share of a company embodies an authorization from the shareholder to the company to carry on its business in whatever manner the management deems fit. If it is known to the shareholder that the company is involved in an un-Islamic transaction, and he continues to hold the shares of that company, it means that he has authorized the management to proceed with that un-Islamic transaction. In this case, he will not only be responsible for giving his consent to an un-Islamic transaction, but that transaction will also be rightfully attributed to himself, because the management of the company is working under his tacit authorization.

However, a large number of Shariah Scholars say that Joint Stock Company is basically different from a simple partnership. In partnership, all the policy decisions are taken through the consensus of all partners, and each one of them has a veto power with regard to the policy of the business. Therefore, all the actions of a partnership are rightfully attributed to each partner. Conversely, the majority takes the policy decisions in a joint stock company. Being composed of a large number of shareholders, a company cannot give a veto power to each shareholder. The opinions of individual shareholders can be overruled by a majority decision. Therefore, each and every action taken by the company cannot be attributed to every shareholder in his individual capacity. If a shareholder raises an objection against a particular transaction in an Annual General Meeting, but his objection is overruled by the majority, it will not be fair to conclude that he has given his consent to that transaction in his individual capacity, especially when he intends to refrain from the income resulting from that transaction.

Therefore, if a company is engaged in a halal (permissible) business, but also keeps its surplus money in an interest-bearing account, wherefrom a small incidental income of interest is received, it does not render all the business of the company unlawful. Now, if a person acquires the shares of such a company with clear intention that he will oppose this incidental transaction also, and will not use that proportion of the dividend for his own benefit, then it cannot be said that he has approved the transaction of interest and hence that transaction should not be attributed to him.

In short, the matter of traditional partnership is different from the partnership of company in this aspect. Therefore if a very small amount of income is earned through these means despite of his disapproval, then his trade in shares would be permissible with the condition that, he shall have to purify that proportion of income by giving it to charity. Now a question could be raised as to what extent or what limit that income would be forgone. Definitely, this matter could not be left on decisions or opinions of lay men, therefore, it was resolved through the consensus of proficient Shariah Scholars that the limit of impermissible income should not exceed 5% of the total income.

4. The leverage or debt to equity ratio of the company should not exceed 30%. To explain the rationale behind this condition, it should be kept in mind that, such companies sometimes borrow money from financial institutions that are mostly based on interest. Here again the aforementioned principle applies i.e. if a shareholder is not personally agreeable to such borrowings, but has been overruled by the majority, these borrowing transactions

cannot be attributed to him.

Moreover, even though according to the principles of Islamic jurisprudence, borrowing on interest is a grave and sinful act, for which the borrower is responsible in the Hereafter; but, this sinful act does not render the whole business of the borrower as Haram (impermissible). It is explained in the conventional books of Islamic jurisprudence that the contract of loan is among those that are called "Uqood Ghair Muawadha" (Non compensatory contracts), therefore, no void condition such as condition of interest can be stipulated. However, if such a condition has been stipulated, the condition itself is void, but it will not invalidate the contract. Since, the contract remains valid despite of void condition, the borrowed amount would be permissible to use and it would be recognized as owned by the borrower. Hence, anything purchased in exchange for that money would not be unlawful.

However, the responsibility of committing the sinful act of borrowing on interest rests on the person who willfully indulges in such a transaction but this does not render his entire business as unlawful. But it should also be remembered that the extent of investment in shares of companies, that involve borrowing should be limited. Can this limit be the same as the 5% limit that is applied to interest income? No, because in this case this activity does not affect the income of the company, it is less severe than interest based income. Therefore, Shariah scholars and Islamic jurists extended the limit (from 5% which is limit of interest/impermissible income) to 30%. The basis of 30% is that the 30% is less than one third (1/3) of the total asset of the company and one third has been considered abundant by the following Hadith of the Holy prophet (SAW) "One third is big or abundant" (Tirmizy). Hence, whatever is less than one third would be insignificant. Therefore to avoid the majority or abundance specified in the hadith, such limit is fixed at less than one third of the total asset of the company.

5. The shares of a company are negotiable only if the company owns some illiquid assets. If all the assets of a company are in liquid form, i.e. in the form of money they cannot be purchased or sold except at par value, because in this case the share represents money only and the money cannot be traded in except at par.

   What should be the exact proportion of illiquid assets of a company for warranting the negotiability of its shares? The contemporary scholars have different views about this question. Some scholars are of the view that the ratio of illiquid assets must be 51% in the least. They argue that if such assets are less than 50%, then most of the assets are in liquid form, and therefore, all its assets should be treated as liquid on the basis of the juristic principle:

   The majority deserves to be treated as the whole thing. Some other scholars are of the view that even if the illiquid asset of a company is 33%, its shares can be treated as negotiable. The basis of this view is a well-known Hadith that means "One third is big or abundant" (Tirmizy).

   They say that according to the Hadith one-third illiquid assets will be considered as sufficient or abundant for this purpose.

   The third view (of the scholars of the sub continent of Pakistan and India) is based on the Hanafi jurisprudence. The principle of the Hanafi School is that whenever an asset is a combination of liquid and illiquid assets, it can be negotiable irrespective of the proportion of its liquid part. However, this principle is subject to two conditions:

   1. The illiquid part of the combination must not be in insignificant quantity. It means that it should be in a considerable proportion.
   2. The price of the combination should be more than the value of the liquid amount contained therein. For example, if a share of 100 dollars represents 75 dollars, plus some fixed assets, the price of the share

must be more than 75 dollars. In this case, if the price of the share is fixed at 105, it will mean that 75 dollars are in exchange of 75 dollars owned by the share and the balance of 30 dollars is in exchange of the fixed assets. Conversely, if the price of that share is fixed at 70 dollars, it will not be allowed, because the 75 dollars owned by the share are in this case against an amount which is less than 75. This kind of exchange falls within the definition of 'riba' and is not allowed. Similarly, if the price of the share, in the above example, is fixed at 75 dollars, it will not be permissible, because if we presume that 75 dollars of the price are against 75 dollars owned by the share, no part of the price can be attributed to the fixed assets owned by the share. Therefore, some part of the price (75 dollars) must be presumed to be in exchange of the fixed assets of the share. In this case, the remaining amount will not be adequate for being the price of 75 dollars. For this reason the transaction will not be valid. However, in practical terms, this is merely a theoretical possibility, because it is difficult to imagine a situation where the price of a share goes lower than its liquid assets.

Among the three different views mentioned above, the most conservative view is the first one. Therefore, nowadays that has been adopted by the majority of Shariah boards of Islamic mutual funds or in screening of the Islamic stocks methodology.

Subject to aforesaid conditions, the purchase and sale of shares is permissible in Shariah. An Islamic Equity Fund can be established on this basis. The subscribers to the Fund will be treated in shari'ah as partners inter se. All the subscription amounts will form a joint pool and will be invested in purchasing the shares of different companies. The profits can accrue either through dividend distributed by the relevant companies or through appreciation in the prices of the shares. In the first case i.e. where the profits are earned through dividends, a certain proportion of the dividend, which corresponds to the proportion of interest earned by the company, must be given in charity. The contemporary Islamic Funds have termed this process as 'purification'.

Some scholars are of the view that even in the case of capital gains, the process of 'purification' is necessary, because the market price of the share may reflect an element of interest included in the assets of the company. The method of purification adopted by Dow Jones Islamic market Index and Islmiqstocks.com are in favor of this view.

It is essential for the share or securities that they represent more than 55% illiquid assets. If a mutual fund has 10% cash and 90% shares, we shall have to see how much of these shares represent fixed assets. Fixed assets include land, equipment, machinery, and leased assets. If these shares represent more than 55% of fixed or illiquid assets, such shares or Musharkah certificates of mutual fund can be negotiated at other than par value as well.

Sale of option short sale, future sale and forward sale where some principles of Shariah are lacking are not permissible.

Management of the fund

The management of the fund may be carried out in two alternative ways.

The managers of the Fund may act as mudarib s for the subscribers. In this case, a certain percentage of the annual profit accrued to the Fund may be determined as the reward of the management, meaning thereby that the management will get its share only if the fund has earned some profit. If there is no profit in the fund, the management will deserve nothing. The share of the management will increase with the increase of profits.

The second option for the management is to act as an agent for the subscribers. In this case, the management may be given a pre-agreed fee for its services. This fee may be fixed in lump sum or as a monthly or annual remuneration.

According to the contemporary Shariah scholars, the fee can also be based on a percentage of the net asset value of the fund. For example, it may be agreed that the management will get 2% or 3% of the net asset value of the fund at the end of every financial year.

However, it is necessary in Shariah to determine any one of the aforesaid methods before the launch of the fund. The practical way for this would be to disclose in the prospectus of the fund the basis on which the fees of the management will be paid. It is generally presumed that whoever subscribes to the fund agrees with the terms mentioned in the prospectus. Therefore, the manner of paying the management will be taken as agreed upon by all the subscribers.

Ijarah Fund

Another type of Islamic Fund may be an Ijarah fund. Ijarah means leasing the detailed rules of which have already been discussed in chapter 23 this book. In this fund the subscription amounts are used to purchase assets like real estate, motor vehicles or other equipment for the purpose of leasing them out to their ultimate users. The ownership of these assets remains with the Fund and the rentals are charged from the users. These rentals are the source of income for the fund, which is distributed pro rata to the subscribers. Each subscriber is given a certificate to evidence his proportionate ownership in the leased assets and to ensure his entitlement to the pro rata share in the income. These certificates may preferably be called 'sukuk' - a term recognized in the traditional Islamic jurisprudence. Since these sukuk represent the pro rata ownership of their holders in the tangible assets of the fund, and not the liquid amounts or debts, they are fully negotiable and can be sold and purchased in the secondary market. Anyone who purchases these sukuk replaces the sellers in the pro rata ownership of the relevant assets and all the rights and obligations of the original subscriber are passed on to him. The price of these sukuk certificates will be determined on the basis of market forces, and are normally based on their profitability.

However, it should be kept in mind that the contracts of leasing must conform to the principles of Shariah which substantially differ from the terms and conditions used in the agreements of conventional financial leases. The points of difference are explained in detail in the third chapter of this book. However, some basic principles are summarized here:

The leased assets must have some usufruct, and the rental must be charged only from that point of time when the usufruct is handed over to the lessee.

The leased assets must be of a nature that their halal (permissible) use is possible.

The lessor must undertake all the responsibilities consequent to the ownership of the assets.

The rental must be fixed and known to the party right at the beginning of the contract.

In this type of the fund, the management should act as an agent of the subscribers and should be paid a fee for its services. The management fee may be a fixed amount or a proportion of the rentals received. Most of the Muslim jurists are of the view that such a fund cannot be created on the basis of Mudarabah, because Mudarabah, according to them, is restricted to the sale of commodities and does not extend to the business of services and leases. However, in the Hanbali School, Mudarabah can be affected in services and leases also. This view has been preferred by a number of contemporary scholars.

Commodity Fund

Another possible type of Islamic Funds may be a commodity fund. In the fund of this type the subscription amounts are used in purchasing different commodities for the purpose of their resale. The profits generated by the sales are the income of the fund, which is distributed pro rata among the subscribers.

In order to make this fund acceptable to Shariah, it is necessary that all the rules governing the transactions of sale are fully complied with. For example,

The seller must own the commodity at the time of sale,

because short sales in which a person sells a commodity before he owns it are not allowed in Shariah.

Forward sales are not allowed except in the case of Salam and Istisna.

The commodities must be halal. Therefore, it is not allowed to deal in wines, pork or other prohibited materials. The seller must have physical or constructive possession over the commodity he wants to sell. (Constructive possession includes any act by which the risk of the commodity is passed on to the purchaser). The price of the commodity must be fixed and known to the parties. Any price, which is uncertain or is tied up with an uncertain event, renders the sale invalid.

In view of the above and similar other conditions, it may easily be understood that the transactions prevalent in the contemporary commodity markets, especially in the futures commodity markets do not comply with these conditions. Therefore, an Islamic Commodity Fund cannot enter into such transactions. However, if there are genuine commodity transactions observing all the requirements of Shariah, including the above conditions, a commodity fund may well be established. The units of such a fund can also be traded in with the condition that the portfolio owns some commodities at all times.

Murabaha Fund

Murabaha is a specific kind of sale where the commodities are sold on a cost-plus basis. The contemporary Islamic banks and financial institutions as a mode of financing have adopted this kind of sale. They purchase the commodity for the benefit of their clients, and then sell it to them on the basis of deferred payment at an agreed margin of profit added to the cost. If a fund is created to undertake this kind of sale, it should be a closed-end fund and its units cannot be negotiable in a secondary market. The reason is that in the case of murabaha, as undertaken by the present financial institutions, the commodities are sold to the clients immediately after their purchase from the original supplier, while the price being on deferred payment basis becomes a debt payable by the client. Therefore, the portfolio of murabaha does not own any tangible assets. It comprises either cash or the receivable debts. Therefore, the units of the fund represent either the money or the receivable debts, and both these things are not negotiable, as explained earlier. If they are exchanged for money, it must be at par value.

Bai-Al-Dain

Here comes the question as to whether or not bai-al-dain is allowed in Shariah. Dain means 'debt' and Bai means sale. Bai-al-dain, therefore, connotes the sale of debt. If a person has a debt receivable from a person and he wants to sell it at a discount, as normally happens in the bills of exchange, it is termed in Shariah as Bai-al-dain. The traditional Muslim jurists (fuqah) are unanimous on the point that bai-al-dain with discount is not allowed in Shariah. The overwhelming majority of the contemporary Muslim scholars are of the same view. However, some scholars of Malaysia have allowed this kind of sale. They normally refer to the ruling of Shafai School wherein it is held that the sale of debt is allowed, but they did not pay attention to the fact that the Shafai jurists have allowed it only in a case where a debt is sold at its par value.

In fact, the prohibition of bai-al-dain is a logical consequence of the prohibition of 'riba' or interest. A 'debt' receivable in monetary terms corresponds to money, and every transaction where money is exchanged for the same denomination of money, the price must be at par value. Any increase or decrease from one side is tantamount to 'riba' and can never be allowed in Shariah.

Some scholars argue that the permissibility of bai-al-dain is restricted to a case where the debt is created through the sale of a commodity. In this case, they say, the debt represents the sold commodity and its sale may be taken as the sale of a commodity. The argument, however, is devoid of force. For, once the commodity is sold, its ownership is passed on to the purchaser and it is no longer owned by the seller. What the seller owns is nothing other than money. Therefore if he sells the debt, it is no more than the sale of money and it cannot be termed by any stretch of imagination as the sale of the commodity.

That is why the overwhelming majority of the contemporary scholars have not accepted this view. The Islamic Fiqh Academy of Jeddah, which is the largest representative body of the Shariah scholars and has the representation of all the Muslim countries, including Malaysia, has approved the prohibition of bai-al-dain unanimously without a single dissent.

Mixed Fund

Another type of Islamic Fund may be of a nature where the subscription amounts are employed in different types of investments, like equities, leasing, commodities etc. This may be called a Mixed Islamic Fund. In this case if the tangible assets of the Fund are more than 51% while the liquidity and debts are less than 50% the units of the fund may be negotiable. However, if the proportion of liquidity and debts exceeds 50%, its units cannot be traded according to the majority of the contemporary scholars. In this case the Fund must be a closed-end Fund.

THE PRINCIPLE OF LIMITED LIABILITY

The concept of 'limited liability' has now become an inseparable ingredient of the large-scale enterprises of trade and industry throughout the modern world, including the Muslim countries. The present chapter aims to explain this concept and evaluate it from the Shariah point of view in order to know whether or not this principle is acceptable in a pure Islamic economy.

The limited liability in the modern economic and legal terminology is a condition under which a partner or a shareholder of a business secures himself from bearing a loss greater than the amount he has invested in a company or partnership with limited liability. If the business incurs a loss, the maximum a shareholder can suffer is that he may lose his entire original investment. But the loss cannot extend to his personal assets, and if the assets of the company are not sufficient to discharge all its liabilities, the creditors cannot claim the remaining part of their receivables from the personal assets of the shareholders.

Although the concept of 'limited liability' was, in some countries applied to the partnership also, yet, it was most commonly applied to the companies and corporate bodies. Rather, it will be truer, perhaps, to say that the concept of 'limited liability' originally emerged with the emergence of the corporate bodies and joint stock companies. The basic purpose of the introduction of this principle was to attract the maximum number of investors to the large-scale joint ventures and to assure them that their personal fortunes will not be at stake if they wish to invest their savings in such a joint enterprise. In the practice of modern trade, the concept proved itself to be a vital force to mobilize large amounts of capital from a wide range of investors.

No doubt, the concept of 'limited liability' is beneficial to the shareholders of a company. But, at the same time, it may be injurious to its creditors. If the liabilities of a limited company exceed its assets, the company becomes insolvent and is consequently liquidated; the creditors may lose a considerable amount of their claims, because they can only receive the liquidated value of the assets of the company, and have no recourse to its shareholders for the rest of their claims. Even the directors of the company who may be responsible for such an unfortunate situation cannot be held responsible for satisfying the claims of the creditors. It is this aspect of the concept of 'limited liability' which requires consideration and research from the Shariah viewpoint.

Although the concept of 'limited liability' in the context of the modern commercial practice is a new concept and finds no express mention as such in the original sources of Islamic Fiqh, yet the Shariah viewpoint about it can be sought in the principles laid down by the Holy Quran, the Sunnah of the Holy Prophet and the Islamic jurisprudence. This exercise requires some sort of ijtihad carried out by the persons qualified for it. This ijtihad should preferably be undertaken by the Shariah scholars at a collective level, yet, as a pre-requisite, there should be some individual effort, which may serve as a basis for the collective exercise.

As a humble student of Shariah, this author have been considering the issue since long, and what is going to be presented in this article should not be treated as a final verdict on this subject, nor an absolute opinion on the point. It is the outcome of initial thinking on the subject, and the purpose of this article is to provide a foundation for further research.

The question of 'limited liability' it can be said, is closely related to the concept of juridical personality of the modern corporate bodies. According to this concept, a joint-stock company in itself enjoys the status of a separate entity as distinguished from the individual entities of its shareholders. The separate entity as a fictive person has legal personality and may thus sue and be sued, may make contracts, may hold property in its name, and has the legal status of a natural person in all its transactions entered into in the capacity of a juridical person.

The basic question, it is believed, is whether the concept of a 'juridical person' is acceptable in Shariah or not. Once the concept of 'juridical person' is accepted and it is admitted that, despite its fictive nature, a juridical person can be treated as a natural person in respect of the legal consequences of the transactions made in its name, we will have to accept the concept of 'limited liability' which will follow as a logical result of the former concept. The reason is obvious. If a real person i.e. a human being dies insolvent, his creditors have no claim except to the extent of the assets he has left behind. If his liabilities exceed his assets, the creditors will certainly suffer, no remedy being left for them after the death of the indebted person.

Now, if we accept that a company, in its capacity of a juridical person, has the rights and obligations similar to those of a natural person, the same principle will apply to an insolvent company. A company, after becoming insolvent, is bound to be liquidated: and the liquidation of a company corresponds to the death of a person, because a company after its liquidation cannot exist any more. If the creditors of a real person can suffer, when he dies insolvent, the creditors of a juridical person may suffer too, when its legal life comes to an end by its liquidation.

Therefore, the basic question is whether or not the concept of 'juridical person' is acceptable to Shariah.

Although the idea of a juridical person, as envisaged by the modern economic and legal systems has not been dealt with in the Islamic Fiqh, yet there are certain precedents wherefrom the basic concept of a juridical person may be derived by inference. These are discussed as below:

Waqf

The first precedent is that of a Waqf. A Waqf is a legal and religious institution wherein a person dedicates some of his properties for a religious or a charitable purpose. The properties, after being declared as Waqf, no longer remain in the ownership of the donor. The beneficiaries of a Waqf can benefit from the corpus or the proceeds of the dedicated property, but they are not its owners. Its ownership vests in Allah Almighty alone.

It seems that the Muslim jurists have treated the Waqf as a separate legal entity and have ascribed to it some characteristics similar to those of a natural person. This will be clear from two rulings given by the fuqaha (Muslim jurists) in respect of Waqf.

Firstly, if a property is purchased with the income of a Waqf, the purchased property cannot become a part of the Waqf automatically. Rather, the jurists say, the property so purchased shall be treated, as a property owned by the Waqf. It clearly means that a Waqf, like a natural person, can own a property.

Secondly, the jurists have clearly mentioned that the money given to a mosque as donation does not form part of the Waqf, but it passes to the ownership of the mosque.

Here again the mosque is accepted to be an owner of money. Some jurists of the Maliki School have expressly mentioned this principle also. They have stated that a mosque is capable of being the owner of something. This capability of the mosque, according to them, is constructive, while the capability enjoyed by a human being is physical.

Another renowned Maliki jurist, namely, Ahmad Al-Dardir, validates a bequest made in favor of a mosque, and gives the reason that a mosque can own properties. Not only this, he extends the principle to an inn and a bridge also, provided that they are Waqf.

It is clear from these examples that the Muslim jurists have accepted that a Waqf can own properties. Obviously, a Waqf is not a human being, yet they have treated it as a human being in the matter of ownership. Once its ownership is established, it will logically follow that it can sell and purchase, may become a debtor and a creditor and can sue and be sued, and thus all the characteristics of a 'juridical person' can be attributed to it.

Baitul-Mal

Another example of 'juridical person' found in our classic literature of Fiqh is that of the Baitul-mal (the exchequer of an Islamic state). Being public property, all the citizens of an Islamic state have some beneficial right over the Baitul-mal. Yet, nobody can claim to be its owner. Still, the Baitul-mal has some rights and obligations. Imam Al-Sarakhsi, the well-known Hanafi jurist, says in his work "Al-Mabsut": "The Baitul-mal has some rights and obligations, which may possibly be undetermined."

At another place the same author says: "If the head of an Islamic state needs money to give salaries to his army, but he finds no money in the Kharaj department of the Baitul-mal (wherefrom the salaries are generally given) he can give salaries from the sadaqah (Zakah) department, but the amount so taken from the sadaqah department shall be deemed to be a debt on the Kharaj department".

It follows from this that not only the Baitul-mal, but also the different departments therein can borrow and advance loans to each other. The liability of these loans does not lie on the head of state, but on the concerned department of Baitul-mal. It means that each department of Baitul-mal is a separate entity and in that capacity it can advance and borrow money, may be treated a debtor or a creditor, and thus can sue and be sued in the same manner as a juridical person does. It means that the Fuqaha of Islam have accepted the concept of juridical person in respect of Baitul-mal.

Joint Stock

Another example very much close to the concept of 'juridical person' in a joint stock company is found in the Fiqh of Imam Shafai. According to a settled principle of Shafai School, if more than one person run their business in partnership, where their assets are mixed with each other, the Zakah will be levied on each of them individually, but it will be payable on their joint-stock as a whole, so much so that even if one of them does not own the amount of the nisab, but the combined value of the total assets exceeds the prescribed limit of the nisab, zakah will be payable on the whole joint-stock including the share of the former, and thus the person whose share is less than the nisab shall also contribute to the levy in proportion to his ownership in the total assets, whereas he was not subject to the levy of zakah, had it been levied on each person in his individual capacity.

The same principle is called the principle of 'Khultah-al-Shuyu' is more forcefully applied to the levy of Zakah on the livestock. Consequently, a person sometimes has to pay more Zakah than he was liable to in his individual capacity, and sometimes he has to pay less than that. That is why the Holy Prophet has said: 'The separate assets should not be joined together nor the joint assets should be separated in order to reduce the amount of Zakah levied on them'.

This principle of 'Khultah-al-Shuyu' which is also accepted to some extent by the Maliki and Hanbali schools with some variance in details has a basic concept of a juridical person underlying it. It is not the individual, according to this principle, who is liable to Zakah. It is the 'joint-stock' that has been made subject to the levy. It means that the 'joint-stock' has been treated a separate entity, and the obligation of Zakah has been diverted towards this entity which is very close to the concept of a 'juridical person', though it is not exactly the same.

Inheritance under Debt

The fourth example is the property left by a deceased person whose liabilities exceed the value of all the property left by him. For the purpose of brevity we can refer to it as 'inheritance under debt'.

According to the jurists, this property is neither owned by the deceased, because he is no more alive, nor is it owned by his heirs, for the debts on the deceased have a preferential right over the property as compared to the rights of the heirs. It is not even owned by the creditors, because the settlement has not yet taken place. They have their claims over it, but it is not their property unless it is actually divided between them. Being property of nobody, it has its own existence and it can be termed a legal entity. The heirs of the deceased or his nominated executor will look after the property as managers, but they are not the owners. If the process of the settlement of debt requires some expenses, the same will be met by the property itself.

Looked at from this angle, this 'inheritance under debt' has its own entity which may sell and purchase, becomes debtor and creditor, and has the characteristics very much similar to those of a 'juridical person.' Not only this, the liability of this 'juridical person' is certainly limited to its existing assets. If the assets do not suffice to settle all the debts, there is no remedy left with its creditors to sue anybody, including the heirs of the deceased, for the rest of their claims.

These are some instances where the Muslim jurists have affirmed a legal entity, similar to that of a juridical person. These examples would show that the concept of 'juridical person' is not totally foreign to the Islamic jurisprudence, and if the juridical entity of a joint-stock company is accepted on the basis of these precedents, no serious objection is likely to be raised against it.

As mentioned earlier, the question of limited liability of a company is closely related to the concept of a 'juridical person'. If a 'juridical person' can be treated a natural person in its rights and obligations, then, every person is liable only to the limit of the assets he owns, and in case he dies insolvent no other person can bear the burden of his remaining liabilities, however closely related to him he may be. On this analogy the limited liability of a joint-stock company may be justified.

THE LIMITED LIABILITY OF THE MASTER OF A SLAVE

The example relates to a period of our past history when slavery was in vogue, and the slaves were treated as the property of their masters and were freely traded in. Although the institution of slavery with reference to our age is something past and closed, yet the legal principles laid down by our jurists while dealing with various questions pertaining to the trade of slaves are still beneficial to a student of Islamic jurisprudence, and we can avail of those principles while seeking solutions to our modern problems and in this respect, it is believed that this example is the most relevant to the question at issue.

The slaves in those days were of two kinds. The first kind was of those who were not permitted by their masters to enter into any commercial transaction. A slave of this kind was called 'Qinn'. But there was another kind of slaves who were allowed by their masters to trade. A slave of this kind was called Abde Mazoon in Arabic. The initial capital for the purpose of trade was given to such a slave by his master, but he was free to enter into all the commercial transactions. The capital invested by him totally belonged to his master. The income would also vest in him, and whatever the slave earned would go to the master as his exclusive property. If in the course of trade, the slave incurred debts, the same would be set off by the cash and the stock present in the hands of the slave. But if the amount of such cash and stock would not be sufficient to set off the debts, the creditors had a right to sell the slave and settle their claims out of his price. However, if their claims would not be satisfied even after selling the slave, and the slave would die in that state of indebtedness, the creditors could not approach his master for the rest of their claims.

Here, the master was actually the owner of the whole business, the slave being merely an intermediary tool to carry out the business transactions. The slave owned nothing from the business. Still, the liability of the master was limited to the capital he invested including the value of the slave. After the death of the slave, the creditors could not have a claim over the personal assets of the master.

This is the nearest example found in the Islamic Fiqh, which is very much similar to the limited liability of the share holders of a company, which can be justified on the same analogy.

On the basis of these five precedents, it seems that the concepts of a juridical person and that of limited liability do not contravene any injunction of Islam. But at the same time, it should be emphasized, that the concept of 'limited liability' should not be allowed to work for cheating people and escaping the natural liabilities consequent to a profitable trade. So, the concept could be restricted, to the public companies only who issue their shares to the general public and the number of whose shareholders is so large that each one of them cannot be held responsible for the day-to-day affairs of the business and for the debts exceeding the assets.

As for the private companies or the partnerships, the concept of limited liability should not be applied to them, because, practically, each one of their shareholders and partners can easily acquire knowledge of the day-to-day affairs of the business and should be held responsible for all its liabilities.

There may be an exception for the sleeping partners or the shareholders of a private company who do not take part in the business practically and their liability may be limited as per agreement between the partners.

If the sleeping partners have a limited liability under this agreement, it means, in terms of Islamic jurisprudence, that they have not allowed the working partners to incur debts exceeding the value of the assets of the business. In this case, if the debts of the business increase from the specified limit, it will be the sole responsibility of the working partners who have exceeded the limit.

The upshot of the foregoing discussion is that the concept of limited liability can be justified, from the Shariah viewpoint, in the public joint-stock companies and those corporate bodies only who issues their shares to general public. The concept may also be applied to the sleeping partners of a firm and to the shareholders of a private company who take no active part in the business management. But the liability of the active partners in a partnership and active shareholders of a private company should always be unlimited.

At the end, we should again recall what has been pointed out at the outset. The issue of limited liability, being a modern issue, which requires a collective effort to find out its solution in the light of Shariah, the above discussion should not be deemed to be a final verdict on the subject. This is only the outcome of an initial thinking, which always remains subject to further study and research.

3

Islamic Economic System

ISLAM'S CARE FOR MAN'S LIVELIHOOD

Today, economic problems come at the head of man's present plights. They may be regarded as the root of life problems that leave a pervasive impact on man's material interests and social conditions. The result is that there is a direct effect not only on the life of the individual but also on the community and on the level of their material progress and civil development.

Economic conditions of the ummah (Muslim community), like elsewhere, have a backlash on security and stability, and consequently, advances in health, scientific gains and the process of achieving social justice. In Islam, life's stability is viewed as a base in up a committed Muslim community. Similarly, catering man's basic necessities is a factor conducive to solidifying piety and winning divine rewards in the Hereafter.

Present life and the Hereafter, economic welfare and moral and spiritual ascendancy are tightly connected together through a sound insight in having all-embracing way of life, which only Islam can offer.

Allah, the Exalted, says:

"And seek by means of what Allah has given you the future abode, and do not neglect your portion of this world..."

Holy Qur'an (28:77)

A Prophetic tradition from the Holy Messenger (S.A.W.) pointedly records:

"He is not from us who gives up his worldly life in favour of his Hereafter, nor is he who gives up his Hereafter in favour of his worldly life."

The Prophet (S.A.W.) is further quoted to saying:

"How excellent is wealthiness in strengthening man's fear of Allah."

Imam al-Sadiq (A.S.), in interpreting the following verse,

(...Our Lord! grant us good in this world and in the Hereafter, and save us from the punishment of the fire) (Qur'an 2:201) has elabourated that the good referred is associated together in seeking the pleasure of Allah and Paradise in the Hereafter and the provision and good morals in worldly life.

Imam al-Sadiq (A.S.) is quoted himself to have said:

"There is no good in him who does not like to collect wealth lawfully, by which he satisfies his needs, pays off his debts and keeps up his relations with his relatives."

"How excellent is worldly life when it helps one to prepare oneself for the Hereafter".

"Wealthiness that prevents you from wronging others is better than poverty that leads you to do evils."

The Prophet (S.A.W.) has also said:

"O Lord! Make bread blessed for us. Do not separate us form it. If it were not for bread we would not have kept up prayers, fast not have discharged our divine duties."

"It is better for the faithful to wake in the morning or in the evening at the loss of a beloved one than to go in the morning or the evening plundering others' property. We take refuge in Allah from plundering others' possessions."

Through these Islamic texts about the importance of the economic side of man's life, the role of the growth of money and wealth in a Muslim's life, in relation to his quest on earth can be seen. They present a clear understanding of Islam's concern with economic life and the necessity of fair distribution of wealth, and the providing of a satisfactory standard of living to every individual so as to keep his faith sound and his life stable.

Based on this plain concept is Islam's stress on man's management of his financial life and its concern to set up a fair economic system based on the belief in man's lawful right to satisfy his natural needs. These include providing an adequacy of foodstuff, clothing, residence and the rest of material, ideological and psychological needs on whose availability, the justice of an economic system and the betterment of the community's welfare depend.

Qur'anic ayahs (verses) and Prophetic traditions are bountiful in dealing with the concerns of everyday economic life of individuals. So exactly and meticulously they attend to production, earnings, distribution of wealth, management of money and all aspects of the economy that they never fail to draw admiration of economists and political scientists the world over.

How all perfect is the Qur'anic concept of Islam's view of daily economic life in which it confirms man's right to seek comfort. It is vividly expressed in this Qur'anic address to Adam (A.S.):

"Surely it is (ordained for you that you shall not be hungry therein nor bare of clothing."

Holy Qur'an (20:118)

Man's economic needs should be met, whether he himself, achieves this goal or someone else, be it an individual, a group of people or the state. The following verse enriches this concept:

"...so let them worship the Lord of this House, Who feeds them against hungry and gives them security against fear."

Holy Qur'an (106:3-4)

It makes it clearer and more positive the connection of Allah's worthiness of being worshipped to favouring man by providing his basic necessities of life. Tackling starvation and furnishing the basic economic needs of man, in the shadow of peace and security and is explained by this verse. It is a sacred feature of man's relationship with Allah and a stimulus to worship and submit to His will.

It is quite evident, in Islam's view, that the issues raised and questions emerging from thanksgiving, or to which worship is related, must be the focus of man's concern. They must be provided, for they form the path leading to worship and the causes of thankfulness and gratitude.

In a nutshell, Islam's view of man's rights to earn a daily living can be outlined as:-

1. Money and property are Allah's. People are equal in gaining them and making use of them. Imam Ali (A.S.) is reported to have said:
   "Were it my money I would have distributed it among them equally. But it is Allah's."
2. Man has an inalienable right to earn his livelihood. Under no circumstances should he be deprived of it and at the time of infirmity or incapability, it must be provided for him.
3. Man is obliged to exert his utmost efforts in working and utilizing nature's resources to his interests. Allah, the Exalted, says:

"...therefore go about in the spacious sides thereof, and eat of His provision, and to Him is the return after death."

Holy Qur'an (67:15)

4. The system of economic life and the methods of earning money, distributing wealth and consumption should be in accordance with a specific moral and legal line. Man's freedom and his economic rights should be similarly subjected to this lawful commitment, which safeguards the rights of all and balances everyone's interests.

Misconceptions

Two main points related to the economic system and the distribution of wealth and productivity in Islam need further consideration as a prelude to delve into related issues. Primarily these are:

1. Islamic economic thought has become vague in the minds of many scholars and cultured people and has led them to deny the existence of such system in Islam. This has been caused on the basis that Muslim thinkers have not studied economic and financial percepts and concepts and presented them in a related way in which contemporary thought has tackled them and treated within modern idioms and methodology.

   It is due to this lack of development that Islamic economic thought has remained texts and concepts scattered in the Holy Qur'an, books of traditions, books of history and Islamic studies on *fiqh* (jurisprudence).

   Muslim researchers did not consider them except in the recent past and in a limited and narrow scope. The need has been to have them to be more meticulously examined, gathered, studied, analyzed, deduced and reshaped and where the outcome should be easily comprehensible and encapsulates all man's economic problems as well as covering all related aspects, such as the themes of wealth, its production and distribution within the Muslim community.

   In respect, the *fuqaha'* took great pains to study these items extensively on the basis of *fiqh*. They also examined *zakat* (poor-rate), *khums* (an Islamic tax), *kharaj* (land tax levied on non-Muslims), working systems for companies, trade, ijarah (hiring someone or something for specific purposes), *hawalah* (transfer of debt from one person to another), purchases, usury, farming, speculation, usurpation, property, conduct of business...etc. By so doing, they provided basic ideological material conducive to form an economic view, and a clear-cut viewpoint on an Islamic economic system. Many contemporary Muslim intellectuals have made use of this basic ideological material and have studied economic systems, ownership, distribution, consumption in its light. They have also developed it in analyzing production relationships and offering an explanation to economic problems and so forth.

When Muslim intellectuals systematically delve into this field, in line with Islam's methodology of research and employing a comprehensive economic method, an economic overview can be presented, that make up entire systems providing solutions for man's problems, for which he has failed to find an answer. Instead man has been left groping in the long dark tunnels of the communist, socialist and capitalist theories, when satisfactory answers are at hand to alleviate doubts adduced by the enemies of Islam. Such have spared no effort to present, to the sons of Islam and others, that Islamic economic thought is a shallow mould, which is unable to accommodate today's problems. They charge Islam, due to their ignorance, obstinacy, and fear from its justice, as well as its threat to their boundless self-centeredness and greed, that it falls short of successfully treating the more complicated daily economic issues. Islamic economic system is not still, as they maliciously claim, composed of a set of varying charity-oriented questions and moral commandments, which cannot tackle deep-seated problems, nor can it resolve the ever-complicated crises of inhumanity because of the immense phenomena, related to financial considerations present in human society.

These efforts are clearly made in a bid to turn attention of Muslims and others from returning to an economic system that frees humanity from exploitation, injustice and avarice and leads it to an economic life of welfare, where man finds comfort, care and dignity.

2. The second misconception, which must be warned of, is the mixing up of Islam with other economic systems and without distinguishing between the two. Many researchers and academics are they Muslims or non-Muslims still mingle the Islamic economic system with the capitalist and social systems. Even, some of them go to the extent of mixing it up with the communist systems. This confusion can be ascribed to the comprehensible concepts found in Islam, including the principles of freedom,

sponsorship, or insurance or through the intervention of the Islamic state in directing the economy and keeping watch over the distribution and production, etc.

Those, who examine the conception of economic, political and individual freedom in Islam, look at Islam within a capitalist framework. Yet, those observe Islam's rejection of, for instance, the capitalist amassing of wealth or the state's role in economic life, think Islam is a socialist system.

Re-examining these ideological aspects and analyzing them scientifically, meticulously and unbiasedly, it will be noticed however, that there is a wide gap between Islam's view and cures and those of capitalism and socialism. The only conclusions that can be made about attempts to converge manmade systems with Islam is that they are clear distortions in line with other misconception that are invented to belittle the everlasting message of the Holy Prophet (S.A.W.).

To emphasize the difference, the following four points underline the key difference between Islam and these two ideological systems, in particular, and other social and political systems, in general:

a. Islam differs from socialism, capitalism and communism and other theories and perspectives in its ideological and doctrinal bases. Islam is a Divine Message with a special conception of the universe, life and man. It basically disagrees with socialist and capitalist views, which have their roots in their materialistic vision that has no religious base, nor any belief in Allah.

   Socialism, capitalism and communism and the like are merely concepts devoid of spiritual and moral values. The distance between them and Islam is unmistakably great. Islam has an all-embracing ideological and legislative make-up. In it, no barriers are to be found between morals, laws, worships, concepts and existence.

b. Islam differs from all man-made systems in that it has a lawful executive framework, which exactly expresses political, economic, and social concepts.

Regarding the social system, laws, which are the second stage of its ideological ladder, are based on founding principles of their own. They manage related affairs quite differently from man-written laws and legislation, in all domains whether they be economical, political, sociological, or appertaining to individual behaviour...etc.

Such matters as ownership, investment, economic, consumption are tackled in a unique way by Islam.

c. In its aims and objectives, Islam is distinguished from other systems, like it differs from them on the basis of contents and the legal organization of life. It treats related subjects in separate ways with specific points. The ultimate goal of Islam is to worship and seek the pleasure of Allah, the Exalted.

   In implementing the divine law and adhering to the divine order, a Muslim demonstrates he is a worshipper. His objective is to seek the reward and pleasure of Allah, the Exalted.

   Contrarily, the human objective in capitalist and socialist societies is purely a materialistic one, expressed in terms of materialistic gain regardless of the cost and fall out on society.

d. Even though there is a sort of analogy between Islam and other systems in certain respects, Islam has its own way and method of implementing its economic concepts and objectives.

For example, Islam believes in social justice and so it adopts just principles in distribution and production growth.

Socialism and capitalism attempt to call for similar concepts, which can be seen as generally logical and which man, by no means, can shun. But in trying to develop the conceptions and implement them, we will find the difference between Islam and secular systems in both method and way. In capitalism, freedom knows no boundaries. In theory, individuals can do what they desire to. In doing so, it believes that the non-existence of limits or restrictions results in economic freedom, in competition and the increase of production. But to achieve a suitable and satisfactory economic level is for all people, makeshift and inexorable laws have to be enforced, based upon such theories as the laws of wages, supply and demand...etc. while, on the other hand, socialism subscribes to the methods of confiscating the sources of wealth and means of production. The state, thanks to this system, becomes a massive capitalist party monopolizing all means of economic resources and turns individuals into production units, who take nothing from the fruit of their toil except that which the state allows them to have.

Unlike these two systems Islam adopts its own methods. It never opens the gates for individual selfishness to flourish like in capitalism, nor does it confiscate the means of production and acquiring wealth, turning people into machines on behalf of the state, like socialism. Islam believes in individual ownership, community ownership and state ownership, as it is expounded in the books of *fiqh*, traditions and in the Holy Qur'an. Lest selfishness and urges of greed prevail, and to prevent exploitation and economic injustice from sweeping over the community, Islam has laid down lawful and moral restrictions related to ownership, investment and consumption in defense of manipulation and deprivation.

The aim, which has in view, as duly explained, is to liberate man from both the greedy capitalist grip solidified by the democratic system and state capitalism thrust upon productive individuals in the socialist system by means of coercion and force, which are the monopoly of the government. In conformity with a delicately set economic plan, Islam grants freedom and responsibility to the Muslim individual and community within bounds, so each balance the other.

NATURE OF ECONOMIC PROBLEM

The central question which presents itself in the world of economics and wealth and which needs a comprehensive and exact answer is: What is the economic problem and what is its cause?

The answer to this question depends upon what is the approach and the nature of the system chosen. The identity of the economic system, which manages the distribution of wealth among human beings, conversely is outlined in accordance with the general comprehension of the problem and its nature. The solution to any economic problem thus lies within the system, in its formula. It gives the answer to the question, what the economic problem is and how it can be dealt with.

To analyze the problem overall from a philosophical point of view needs a comprehensive grasp of the nature of both man and wealth, the value of each and their significance in life as a prerequisite. It further relies on a deep, exact and efficient comprehension of the problem on one hand, and on the other, an objective analysis of the implemented system, which is immune to any prejudice that may caused by the personal bias of the concerned economist and those who invented its perspectives.

These factors, put together, help to give the shape of the answer and to plan an economic system with its stated hallmarks.

Now, let us see what answer Islam gives to our question: What is the economic problem and what is its mainspring?

1. Allah, the Exalted, says:

   "Corruption has appeared in the land and the sea on account of what the hands of people have wrought, that he may make them taste a part of that which they have done, so that they may return."

   Holy Qur'an (30:41)

2. And Allah has also said:

   "And you love wealth with exceeding love."

   Holy Qur'an (89:20)

3. "Decked out fair to mankind is the love of desires - Women, children, hoarded treasures of gold and silver, marked horses, cattle and tilth. That is the enjoyment of the life of this world; but Allah - with Him is the fairest return. Say: 'Shall I tell you of better than that?' For those

that are godfearing, with their Lord are Gardens underneath which rivers flow, therein dwelling forever, purified spouse, and Allah's good pleasure. And Allah sees His servants."

Holy Qur'an (3:14-15)

4. "...most surely man is ungrateful to his Lord. And most surely he is a witness of that. And most surely he is tenacious in the love of wealth..."

   Holy Qur'an (100:6-8)

5. "And those who made their abode in the city and in the faith before them love those who have fled to them, and do not find in their hearts a need of what they are given, and prefer (them) before themselves though poverty may afflict them, and whoever is preserved from the niggardliness of his soul, these it is that are the successful ones."

   Holy Qur'an (59:9)

6. "Therefore be careful of (your duty to) Allah as much as you can, hear and obey and spend, it is better for your souls; and whoever is saved from the greediness of his soul, these it is that are the successful."

   Holy Qur'an (64:16)

7. The Messenger of Allah (S.A.W.) is reported to have said:

"Refrain from doing injustice, for it is the darkness of the Judgement's Day. Avoid misery. It was misery that cut down those who were before you. It made them shed their blood and do haram (what is forbidden and harmful)".

8. And, the Holy Prophet (S.A.W.) is also quoted to have said:

"Two fierce wolves entering a pen of sheep are not as much harmful as avarice and love of a social rank to the faith of a Muslim."

Examining these quotations and compile their content, the following conclusions can be reached:

a. In the first quotation, the Qur'an blames man for causing his own problem. Corruption, be it political, economic or moral, is only man's making. Man encapsulates a host of stimuli and desires and he himself is spurred on to extremes in peculiar proclivities, to cause corruption, injustice and tyranny under which humanity suffers greatly.

"Corruption has appeared in the land and the sea on account of what the hands of people have wrought, that he may make them taste a part of that which they have done, so that they may return."

Holy Qur'an (30:41)

b. Quotations 2,3,4 and 8 emphasize that man's selfishness, avarice, his excessive love for property and wealth and his tendency to amass them, is the main cause of all his daily problems, in general, and his economic problems, in particular.

c. Quotations 5,6 and 7, from the Qur'an and holy Prophetic traditions, how that avarice itself which is a vice used with great eagerness and desire to obtain and keep wealth away from the bands of others, is the latent, effective factor behind man's greed and his predilection to monopoly wealth and deprive others from it.

In summary, we can assert an important fact in the world of economics, as clearly stated by Islam and known as the causeehind the problem of wealth distribution, is man's self-centeredness and his greed. For the worlds of the holy Qur'anic verses and Prophetic traditions lay great stress on avarice and greed as the root causes of the economic problems in the fields of distribution and consumption.

This view rules out the effect of external conditions, including means of production, whether in abundance or scarce, and distribution, for man, himself, controls distribution, His will controls it. His awareness identifies his view of justice, the value of money and wealth and the meaning of life. It is this very awareness that principally outlines the way he adopts in dealing with himself and others.

Everywhere and every time subjective factors are the root causes of the problems and the sources of economic injustice, regardless of the variation in conditions, means and quantity of production, which tend themselves to be by-products resulting from the original misdiagnosis.

The only way to save man from economic injustice and confusion is his daily life, re-shaping his existence and re-formulating his conceptions, his view of life, money, wealth, profit and moral pleasure, in a sound and objective way and in harmony with the Qur'an and in agreement with its deep, analytical views.

Allah, the Exalted, says:

"...surely Allah does not change the condition of a people until they change their own condition..."

Holy Qur'an (13:11)

Unless an independent, economic system is adhered to this change cannot be fully successful; a system, which takes upon itself the task of re-distributing human wealth and managing economic life in agreement with the principles of Islamic justice and equality and not on high-fluting theories that lose the essence of what the basic problem is:

Allah, the Exalted, says:

"And that if they should keep to the (right) way, I would certainly give them to drink of abundant water."

Holy Qur'an (72:16)

"And if the people of the towns had believed and guarded (against evil), I would certainly have opened up for them blessings from the heaven and the earth..."

Holy Qur'an (7:96)

There is no way to better man's life other than effecting a complete, psychological and ideological transformation. Yet to achieve this, a just system and law must be brought about, both socially and legally, to serve as a prelude in the building of a human community, where man can bask in righteousness and happiness and taste the flavor of freedom and dignity.

The Qur'an, in many of its ayahs and conceptions, emphasizes this method of transformation:

"Until they change your own condition and that if they should keep to the (right) way believed and guarded (against evil)."

By scrutinizing these words, we can arrive at the conclusion that the Qur'an made psychological change, and treading on the right path (*shari'ah* and the Divine system), having faith in them and insisting on adhering to their profound principles. Islam is prerequisite to human change for the better and the sources of good and man's economic welfare.

This is the true dimensions of the problem and of its overcoming. But what of the external factor that perpetuate and self-propel the ill-effects?

EXTERNAL FACTORS

Identifying human faults as an internal cause of the economic problem, Islam turns its attention to specify the external factors, which constitute the chief reasons behind exacerbating the problem. Islam attributes the economic problems to two factors:

1. The Human Factor- The subjective one and root cause as already has been explained.
2. External Factors- These objective factors can be deduced, by concerned researchers of Islamic economics, from the sources of legislation, morals, and concepts that deal with the social and economic aspects of man's life. By referring to the Qur'an, Prophetic Sunnah, books of *fiqh*, studies on morals, we can compile many texts, principles and thoughts which deal with each of these causes. To present a clearer picture of the Islamic view of the economic problem, it is necessary to consider all three causes separately.Briefly they can be summed as:

i. Inadequate Production

The main cause of poverty as well as being a principle factor behind the economic problem, under whose burden man is still suffering, is the decline in production in the view of Islam. That is why Islam has focused attention on it and blamed two main factors for it:

a. Unemployment and Disusing of Human Resources

Islam looks upon work as a holy and esteemed asset. It puts it on the same footing with jihad and worship. The Prophet (S.A.W.) is reported to have said:

"Worship is of seven parts the best of which is seeking halal (lawful) provision."

Islamic traditions and texts dealing with the importance of work are bountiful. They have one aspect in common urging man to work, mobilizing human beings to raise their production capabilities and fighting sloth and unemployment as the prime reasons of poverty and materialistic and social decline.

Of the traditions reported in regard to this point is one quoted from Imam Ali (A.S.):

"When things coupled, sloth and helplessness got together and engendered poverty."

Imam al-Ridha (A.S.) quotes his father Imam Musa al-Kadhim (A.S.), on the same subject that he said to one of his sons on his death-bed:

"Beware of laziness and boredom, because for they prevent you from your share of this world and in the Hereafter."

b. Ignorance and Lack of Experience about Methods of Productions

It includes the under-utilization of natural resources and man's creative powers. These factors play a critical and undeniable role in the decline of production and spread of need and destitution. Islam, for such consideration, urges Muslims to seek knowledge, make use of natural resources and gain in knowledge about work and management. The Prophet (S.A.W.) is quoted to have said:

"Allah surely loves the trustworthy professional."

Islam works towards mobilizing man bodily, psychologically and intellectually, employing his technical and scientific abilities for the sake of production, adequate supplies of needed commodities, and creating wealth. The Prophet (S.A.W.) reproached whoever has no interest in increasing his wealth through halal (lawful) work and expanding his ability to spend and meet his needs and the needs of his dependants.

In the words of the Holy Prophet (s.a.w.):

"There is no good in whoever does not like earning his living from halal work to satisfy his needs, pays his debts and strengthen his ties of kinship".

This Prophetic tradition emphasizes the necessity of man striving to earn his own way; that his earnings should outweigh his expenses. The Prophet (S.A.W.) laid stress on this point in, "relation to the good of his family and the community as a whole".

Islam's plan is simple and precise, directing man's energies into productive employment as a moral responsibility and a legal duty that fits into building a healthy Muslim society, where there is no unmet wanting.

ii. Ill-Distribution

Bad distribution is the second gravest external cause of the economic problem, which also results in the spread of poverty and need, and unbalanced economic life. As clearly seen from secular systems, different social classes have arisen. One of them lives in the lap of luxury, enjoying every kind of material pleasure, a massing wealth, monopolizing means and sources of riches. While the other is hardly able to have daily bread and scrape together a subsistence living.

This gross inequality in economic life, which represents a dangerous and harmful schism in society, has its main causes principally in bad distribution and the implementation of bland, man-made economic systems which have their own momentum is aggravating the catastrophe. Feudalism, capitalism, and communism and the like have merely exacerbated the crisis all the more.

Ill-distribution has a long historic experience, regardless of whatever secular economic system has been tried. Its consequence of an unjust spread of wealth is a prime basis of today's social tragedy of mankind.

Such is well established, by Muslim and non-Muslim experts alike, as exampled by one report in an Italian publication, and translated and published in the Kuwaiti daily, *Al-Qabas* back on August 15-8-1976 in its issue 1525:-

"Experts in the fields of development, food and population unanimously agree that the available natural resources in the world are so abundant that they can meet all the needs of the nations if goodwill was shown and if these resources were equally distributed among all nations. The root cause is the unjust distribution of the resources...and the failure of many nations to win their real independence, decide the fate of their wealth and distribute it justly and fairly."

"Russian scientist Ivan Shatilov has also said that cultivated areas now could satisfy the hunger of tens of billions of people if their crops were distributed equally and fairly among the nations of the world. He further points out: 'On the other hand, we must not lose sight of the fact that the advanced industrialized world has not, sofar, made use of the marine sources of food. The oceans constitute 71 percent of the total surface of the earth, whereas they produce no more that 1 percent of man's foodstuff."

Man will never be able to taste the flavor of happiness and dignity, as historical records testify, unless he sheds the shackles of short-sighted man-made systems, and blot out forever their traces in the human community, souls and life. Such systems proved themselves a failure. They only record their flagrant, tragic defeat, which victimize humanity and brings forth unspeakable cries of starvation, wars and deprivations. Man was metamorphosed into a machine working incessantly in favour of the ruling classes, whether being individuals as is the case in the capitalist and feudalis systems, or authorities, and parties as it is in the socialist and communist systems.

Only when man recovers his consciousness from the anaesthesia of propaganda manipulated by those who covet these principles from their won vested interest and breaks the fetters of servitude which subdues him by force and coercion, man will see the fountain of light and find the path to an honorable, free life, where he finds his righteousness and dignity. Only when man strives to seek and intensifies his efforts to win good and happiness will he find the key presented by Islam.

This concise discourse, is not intended to delve into great detail the major principles and important lines drawn by Islam in its unmatched economic system. It is but an outline of its just view.

iii. Ill-Consumption

The major third factor conducive to the economic problem and perpetuating the spread of poverty and destruction of human resources is ill-consumption, which the misuse of wealth and the non-usage of assets that could preserve and satisfy human demands in a calculated and balanced way.

Like all other fields, Islam has a unique diagnosis for consumption in its particularly caring way of embracing a complete formula for life. Its guidelines show the following steps:-

a. Limiting Consumption

Consumption is the most critical stage in dealing with the wealth and making use of it and Islam did not neglect this vital area but set a system with clear moral aspects that controls the process, utilizing the graces and favours bestowed on man by Allah so that man would not act excessively or unreasonably in regard to consuming life's resources, Islam projects a well-laid system, calculated and in accordance with its message and its distinctive way of handling matters at man's disposal.

b. Prohibition of Extravagance and Wastefulness:

Extravagance and wastefulness are nothing but harmful misusages of wealth. Islam exhorted man to confine himself to the necessities of life and to keep his lusts, avarice and the untoward behaviour in check.

Allah, the Exalted, says:

"O children of Adam! Attend to your embellishments at every time of prayer, and eat and drink and be not extravagant; surely He does not love the extravagant."

Holy Qur'an (7:31)

"And they who when they spend, are neither extravagant nor parimonious, and (keep) between these the just mean."

Holy Qur'an (25:67)

"And give to the near of kin his due and (to) the needy and the wayfarer, and do not squander wastefully. Surely the squanderers are the brothers of the Satan and Satan is ever ungrateful to his Lord."

Holy Qur'an (17:26-27)

"And do not make your hand to be shackled to your neck nor stretch it forth to the utmost (limit) of its stretching forth, lest you should (afterwards) sit down blamed, stripped off."

Holy Qur'an (17:29)

These exhortation and restrictions were purely to keep a balanced economy, perfectly organized. If wealth is employed in the interest of man, used as it was ordained and planned by Allah, all human needs are met.

Islam, in its legislation and perceptions, erect a structure of logical bases compatible with human make-up and instinctive needs.

Because man cannot always handle wealth, Allah's given services and favours are bestowed upon him in a strategically productive way, Islam puts before him the way according to which he can utilize and consume wealth efficiently and justly. If, however, these are ignored and neglected, the specific objective outlined by Allah will be lost to man with disastrous consequences as can be seen by the widespread plight of people all over the world.

All activities, including commodities and services, are put into two categories that best suit their nature, halal (lawful) and the *haram* (unlawful). Wine, gambling, revelry, debauchery, wasteful entertainment...etc, are strictly prohibited because they only dissipate man's wealth.

Instead of being wasted in vain, such huge sums of money should be spent in the services of human society to satisfy fundamental human needs and preserve wealth from being squandered and lost. It is an ailment that plagued all societies who lack the sound planning Islam presents to man.

Thousands of millions of dollars are wasted daily on wine, gambling, extravagant entertainment, debauchery, as well as on accumulating weapons of mass destruction and annihilation for wars and terrorizing other nations, whilst millions of people are straddled with hunger, deprivation and misery.

Islam makes such perverse and corrupt consumption *haram* because its aims are to employ wealth in fields that secure welfare for humanity. With its exact and perfectly planned economic system, Islam has placed in the hands of mankind the economic gifts of securing the cure of all financial woes and salvaging an equitable world from the abyss of poverty, deprivation and injustice in which millions still painfully suffer from and seemingly will continue to do so with ill-founded man-made equivalents.

GENERAL BASES OF DISTRIBUTION IN ISLAM

1. The distribution system of Islam is grounded in a general ideological base that "Allah is the only real owner".

As for man, he is not more than a deputizing vicegerent. He can only manage what he owns within certain limits, specified by Allah.

Allah, the Most High, says:

"And certainly you have come to Us alone as We created you at first, and you have left behind your backs the things which We gave you, and We do not see with you your intercessors about whom you asserted that they were (Allah's) associates in respect to you; certainly the ties between you are now cut off and what you asserted is gone from you."

Holy Qur'an (6:95)

"Believe in Allah and His Apostle, and spend out of what He has made to you to be successors of; for those of you who believe and spend shall have a great reward".

Holy Qur'an (57:7)

2. Man has natural, instinctive needs which must be met, and under no-circumstances can he be deprived of this right.

The aim of Islamic economic legislation is to provide needed commodities for man. Thus, in unmistakably made clear in this Prophetic tradition.

"Allah, the Exalted and mighty, looked at the wealth of the well-off. And He looked at the destitute. He ordained a portion from the wealth of the rich to be delivered to the poor to satisfy them. If it had not satisfied them He would certainly have increased their share."

The ability to earn wealth is put at man's disposal to better his life. It is not a goal in itself. Rather it is a means to manage man's economic and daily life. Wealth, therefore, has a social role. It serves man and makes him attain more noble and a more comfortable life. In its distribution, it must be spread into every cell of the human society's body so that it can cater for all needs.

"Whatever Allah has restored to His Apostle from the people of the towns, it is for Allah and for the Apostle, and for the near of kin and the orphans and the needy and the wayfarer, so that it may not be a thing taken by turns among the rich of you, and whatever the Apostle gives you, accept it, and from whatever he forbids you, keep back, and be careful of (your duty to) Allah; surely Allah is severe in retributing (evil)".

Holy Qur'an (59:7)

3. In Islam, ownership in various forms is lawful.

It includes individual, communal and state ownerships and which is an axiomatic fact in *fiqh* and Islamic legislation.

4. The method of gaining money, property and economic resources are restricted.

Certain law as Islam puts restraints on any tendency of greediness or other unscrupulous motives including exploitation. Islam adopts two important methods to tackle this critical point to frustrate the urges of greediness and exploitation. They are:

a. Rearing and cultivating Muslim individuals and society, both morally and spiritually

In a way that promotes virtuous aspirations to steer clear of greediness and selfishness and present the reality of wealth being only transitory aspects of a temporary life on earth. It is a life that belittles so much attention being paid to competition and making material gains merely for their own-sake, as man's existence has much greater goals to be achieved for his salvation.

Islam turns its attention to the process of upbringing and focuses its attention on developing the spirit of thrift, innovation and productive goals in line with its cultural values and guidance. Man is advised to overlook the fierce rat race, which in merely for grabbing more wealth and warns him not to drown himself extravagantly and excessively in lusts and corporal pleasures.

Islam calls upon man, to vie with his brothers, to create goodness and to give up a part of his property if able in favour of others in need. Man is spurred on by Islamic teachings to shun methods and amass wealth and property, which pollute the spirit, kill the conscience and dispose man to the wrath of Allah. In return, man's reward is ensured in the Hereafter. Undesirable and unproductive ways of accumulating wealth such as usury, hoarding, cheating and other unprincipled methods are forbidden by Islam.

There are bountiful texts and concepts in the Holy Our'an and the Prophetic Sunnah that instead nurture a noble human spirit and promote the qualities of altruism and benevolence deep in man.

Allah, the Almighty, says in the Our'an:

"And those who made their abode in the city and in the faith before them love those who have fled to them, and do not find in their hearts a need of what they are given, and prefer (them) before themselves though poverty may afflict them, and whoever is preserved from the niggardliness of his soul, these it is that are the successful ones."

Holy Qur'an (59:9)

"Say: In the grace of Allah and in His mercy, in that they should rejoice; it is better than that which they gather."

Holy Qur'an (10:58)

b. Laws are the second method employed by Islam to limit ways of accumulating riches and prohibit amassing through unlawful means

That does the utmost harm to the community and feeds off the blood of the impoverished social class.

It is the state that takes the responsibility of achieving economic justice as it is responsible far justice in every social realm. That is why laws strictly forbid usury, hoarding, cheating and manipulating prices ...etc. The state's responsibility is to protect and enforce laws and also to prevent such unlawful practices.

The letter written by Imam Ali (A.S.) to Malik al-Ashtar, his governor in Egypt, clearly testifies to this required intervention, when saying:

"Keep an eye on the activities of traders and industrialists, whether they are nearby or live in far-flung areas in your country. "Let it be known to you, however, that they are usually stingy misers, intensely self-centered and selfish, suffering from the obsession of grasping and accumulating wealth. They often hoard their goods to make more profit out of them by creating scarcity and black markets. Such practice is extremely injurious to the public on one hand, and defames the ruler on the other.

"So put an end to hoarding up wares because the Holy Prophet (S.A.W.) has prohibited it. Remember that trade should go on between purchasers and suppliers according to correct measures and weights, and on such responsible terms that neither the consumers nor the suppliers should have to face losses. But if traders and industrialists carry on hoarding and black marketeering, even though you have explicitly warned them earlier, then you must punish them according to the intensity of their crime."

5. Economic balances by means of Islamic taxes

Islam has laid down certain taxes like *zakat* (poor-rate) and *khums* (one-fifth of a Muslim's income paid to the treasury every year). They are taken from the well-off according to certain provisions, and delivered up to the destitute to satisfy their needs, solve the problem of poverty, and in doing so achieve economic justice. The ultimate goal of Islam here is to meet the economic needs of all Muslim individuals, so that no one is left deprived in the whole Muslim World.

Imam Ja'far bin Muhammad al-Sadiq (A.S.) is reported to have said:

"Surely, Allah the Almighty and Exalted ordained a portion from the wealth of the rich to be handed out to the poor which satisfies them. Otherwise, He would certainly have increased their share. If they, however, remain unsatisfied, that is because some people deny them their undisputed right."

In a dialogue between the Prophet (S.A.W.) and a man who came asking him about faith, the Prophet (S.A.W.) described *zakat* as a redress for the poor and a means to ensure a balance between the needy and the rich.

The man narrated that he had asked the Messenger of Allah (S.A.W.) what he called for and describes the following dialogue. "I call the servants of Allah to serve Allah," the Prophet (S.A.W.) replied.

"What do you say?" I enquired.

"Bear witness," the Prophet (S.A.W.) said, "that there is no god but Allah and that I, Muhammad, am the Messenger of Allah. You must believe in what He revealed to me, deny the deity of al- at and al-Uzzah, keep up prayer and pay zakat."

"And what is *zakat*?" I asked him.

"The well-off among us," he told me, "hand back the money set aside to the poor among us."

Looking at the statement of the Messenger of Allah (S.A.W.)in his using of the verb, "hand back" the Prophet (S.A.W.)reveals the objective basis on which the process of economic distribution in Islam depends and the secret of the balance of its concept of eeonomic justice in human society. The Prophet (S.A.W.)thus points out the effective role of Islamic taxes in addressing defeats in economic life. In the light of the Prophet's statement, the reason behind this is that the surplus wealth that ought to be distributed fairly and evenly among individuals goes directly, due to mismanagement, to the pockets of the well-off and tips the scale at the expense of the poor. Hence, the redress is made by handing back the money to their original and lawful owners, namely the poor.

The Prophet's statement sheds a glaring light on Islam's view of one of the main pillars on which distribution is based. It is the belief that these taxes are a lawful guarantee to protect the right that slips out of the hands of the poor, due to the self human attempts to bend the law or on the account of human failure in raising itself to the level where it can implement this natural law in economic life. These taxes underpin the ground on which the pillars of just distribution stand, in order to preserve the economy's stability, secure welfare to everyone and ensure balance is addressed on both sides of the economic scale.

6. Reciprocal social responsibility

Reciprocal social responsibility among Muslims is a further important safeguard towards a just distribution of wealth and combatting destitution and poverty in the Muslim community.

From an Islamic education, Islamic sentiments are developed for a Muslim to feel responsible for his brother. On no account should he bark for life pleasures and luxuries whereas his brothers suffer from the severe pains bitter hunger, and unsatisfied needs.

Islamic law lays down the principle of reciprocal social responsibility on spiritual and moral grounds to implement such concerned behaviour. By so doing, Islam builds up a strong, tenacious society, in which the individual shoulders his duties by identifying with his suffering brothers.

Numerous traditions and narrations emphasize this principle and urge Muslims to share the burden uniformly.

The Noble Messenger (S.A.W.) is quoted to have said:

"Never does he believe in me who goes to bed full while his neighbour is hungry. Never shall Allah on the Day of

Judgement look with favour at the people of a place who pass their night satisfied but among them is a hungry one."

He also said:

"Surely he is not a Muslim who does not take interest in the affairs of Muslims. And surely he is not a Muslim who hears a Muslim calling for help and does not respond to his call."

He further said:

"All of you are leaders and all of you are responsible for your subjects."

On this point Imam Ja'far al-Sadiq (A.S.) is quoted to have said:

"The right of the Muslim on the Muslim is that he should never eat his fill while his brother suffers, never should he quench his thirst while his brother suffers thirst, never should he clothe himself while his brother suffers inadequate clothing."

Another tradition reads:

"Any believer who denies another faithful something he can certainly offer him or can do for him, on his own or with others' help, Allah shall certainly resurrect him on the Day of Judgement black-faced, with withered eyes and hands tied up to his neck. Someone shall cry out, 'This is the traitor who betrayed Allah and his Messenger.' Then he shall be ordered to be thrown into hell-fire."

Deep in themselves, Muslims feel great human sentiments. With such cooperative, kindly manners, Muslims treat one another. They only act incompatible ways with Islam's excellent teachings, which leave their mark far more than any material and corporal power could do. Muslims move to act, urged by the reward stored for them and by their implanted benevolence more than by the whip of the dictatorial authority.

7. Economic Security

In Islam, state is liable for the demands and needs of every single subject be he Muslim or non-Muslim, should he be unable to provide for himself, through his own personal resources or his sponsor.

This point is best explained again in the letter Imam Ali (A.S.) wrote to his governor in Egypt, Malik al-Ashtar:

"Then I want to caution you about the poor. Fear Allah about their condition and your attitude towards them. They have no support, no resources and no opportunities. They are poor, they are destitute and many of them are crippled and unfit for work. Some of them come out begging and some (who maintain self-respect) do not beg, but their condition screams about their distress, poverty, destitution and wants. So, protect them and their rights. Allah has laid the responsibility of this on your shoulders. You must fix a share for them from the government treasury. Beside this reservation in cash, you must also reserve a share in kind of crops...etc. from government grain stores in cities, in which such grain are collected and cultivated on state-owned lands. Because, in this collection the share of those living far away from any particular city is equal to the share of those living nearby".

Islamic law, made by this quotation, allots sums of money from the treasury to support the infirm and needy, who can no longer work or that their incomes fall short of covering their expenses. It states clearly the principle the state's responsibility for economic security that applies to every citizen, irrespective of his/her religion.

It is narrated that one day Imam Ali (A.S.) saw a Christian *dimmi* (non-Muslim citizen living in an Islamic state) begging. Amir al-Mu'minin (A.S.) asked:

"Who is this?"

"Oh Amir al-Mu'minin!," said people, who were present.

"He is a Christian."

"You employed him," Amir al-Mu'minin (A.S.) retorted, "until he become old and infirm then you denied him help. Spend on him from the treasury."

8. Lawful sources of wealth

Sources of ownership, or the means by which man can gain wealth, property and amenities of life, are looked upon by Islam as important matters, which define the identity of the economic system, its method of distributing wealth among members of society, fighting poverty and need, and rooting out greed, exploitation and unlawful ways of gaining wealth. Islam sets two key ways of gaining wealth which are work and need. These are lawfully accepted ways of ownership.

a. Employment and natural resources

One may work in agriculture, mining, industry or any field of production or one may give one' s services in the fields of medicine, engineering, transportation, education, trade...etc. In Islam, employment in any field of lawful activity is the chief way of acquiring wealth and money. Islam lays out great emphasis on the personal role in securing wealth and obtaining money, as we have previously detailed.

b. Need

In the same way Islam made work a legal way of getting money and wealth, it made need a source of ownership for wealth to fight destitution and poverty. But ownership here is different from the former one.

For ownership, in the first case, is the fruit of the direct interaction between man, nature or raw materials, or services rendered to satisfy some needs. Man here becomes entitled to ownership in return for the fruits of his labour.

As for ownership by need, it is the process of conveying property or wealth from one owner to another one on account of the need for it by the new owner. In order of precedence, the latter kind of ownership comes second to the first one. Ownership by need is placed in the category of owning something by inheritance and maintenance as in the case given by the husband to his wife.

The needy, who cannot work, due to bodily infirmity or can finds no work, has a share in the money set aside from the taxes of *zakat* and *khums*, or from the money allotted by the state to meet the needs of the impoverished.

The ultimate result of this economic system being put into practice is that every single member of the Islamic community becomes economically secure. He neither fears poverty nor does he worry about his daily life. On the contrary he feels secure, and has confidence in the community and state he lives under its shade.

FEATURES OF THE ISLAMIC ECONOMIC SYSTEM

One of the forms of capitalism, which has been flourishing in non-Islamic societies, is the interest based investment. There are normally two participants in such transactions. One is the Investor who provides capital on loan and the other Manager who runs the business. The investor has no concern whether the business runs into profit or loss; he automatically gets an Interest (Riba) in both outcomes at a fixed rate on his capital. Islam prohibits this kind of trading and the Holy Prophet enforced the ruling, not in the form of some moral teaching, but as the law of land. It is very important to know the definition and forbiddance of Riba and the injunctions relating to its unlawfulness from different angles. On the one hand, there are severe warnings of the Qur'an and Sunnah and on the other, it has been taken today as an integral part of the world economy. The desired liberation from it seems to be infested with difficulties. The problem is very detail oriented and has to be taken up in all possible aspects.

First of all we have to deliberate into the correct interpretation of the Quranic verses on Riba and what has been said in authentic ahadith and then determine what Riba is in the terminology of the Quran and Sunnah, what transaction it covers, what is the underlying wisdom behind its prohibition and what sort of harm it brings to society. We will start from looking at the economic philosophy of Islam vis-à-vis interest.

THE ECONOMIC PHILOSOPHY OF ISLAM VIS-A-VIS INTEREST

The economic philosophy of Islam has no concept of Riba because according to Islam, Riba is that curse in society, which accumulates money around handful of people, and it results inevitably in creating monopolies, opening doors for selfishness, greed, injustice and oppression. Deceit and fraud prospers in the world of trade and business. Islam, on the other hand, primarily encourages highest moral ethics such as universal brotherhood, collective welfare and prosperity, social fairness and justice. Due to this reason, Islam renders Riba as absolutely haram and strictly prohibits all types of interest based transactions. The prohibition of Riba in the light of economic philosophy of Islam can be explained with the cost of distribution of wealth in a society.

DISTRIBUTION OF WEALTH

The distribution of wealth is one of the most important and most controversial subjects concerning the economic life of man, which has given birth to global revolutions in today's world, and has affected every sphere of human activity from international politics down to the private life of the individuals. For many centuries now, the question has been the center not only of fervent debates, oral and written both, but also of armed conflicts. The fact, however, is that whatever has been said on the subject without seeking guidance from Divine Revelation and relying merely on human reason, has had the sole and inevitable result of making the confusion worse confounded.

Islamic perspective of distribution of wealth

Before explaining the point, it seems to be imperative to clarify certain basic principles which one can derive from the Quran, and which distinguish the Islamic point of view in economics from non-Islamic systems of economy. Islam in this matter, such as we have been able to deduce from the Holy Qur'an, the Sunnah and the writings of the "Thinkers" on distribution of wealth in the Islamic context.

i. The importance of the economic goals

No doubt, Islam is opposed to monasticism, and views the economic activities of man quite lawful, meritorious, and some times even obligatory and necessary. It approves of the economic progress of man, and considers lawful or righteous livelihood an obligation of the secondary order. Notwithstanding all this, it is no less a truth that it does not consider "economic activity" to be the basic problem of man, nor does it view economic progress as the be-all and end-all of human life.

Many misunderstandings about Islamic economics arise just from confusion between the two facts of considering economics as the ultimate goal of life and considering it as a necessity in order to have a prosperous life through lawful means. Even common sense can suffice to show that the fact of an activity being lawful or meritorious or necessary separate from it being the ultimate goal of human life and the center of thought and action. It is, therefore, very essential to make the distinction as clear as possible at the very outset. In fact, the profound, basic and far-reaching difference between Islamic economics and materialistic economics is just this:

a. According to materialistic economics, "Livelihood is the fundamental problem of man and economic developments are the ultimate end of human life."

b. According to Islamic economics, "Livelihood may be necessary and indispensable, but cannot be the true purpose of human life."

So, while we find in the Holy Quran the disapproval of monasticism and the order to: "Seek the benevolence of Allah." At the same time we find in the Quran to restrain from the temptations or delusion for worldly life. And all these things in their totality have been designated as "Ad-Dunya" ("the mean") - a term which, in its literal sense, does not have a pleasant connotation.

Apparently one might feel that the two commands are contradictory, but the fact is that according to the Quranic view, all the means of livelihood are no more than just stages on man's journey, and his final destination lies beyond them. That destination is the sublimity of character and conduct, and, consequently, the felicity of the other world. The real problem of man and the fundamental purpose of his life is the attainment of these-two goals. But one cannot attain them without traversing the path of this world. So, all those things too which are necessary for his worldly life, become essential for man. It comes to mean that so long as the means of livelihood are being used only as a path leading towards the final destination, they are the benevolence of Allah, but as soon as man gets lost in the mazes of this pathway and allows himself to forget his real destination, the very same means of livelihood turn into an "temptation, or delusion" into a "trial": "And know that your possessions and your children are but a trial".

The Holy Quran has enunciated this basic truth very precisely in a brief verse: "Seek the other world by means of what Allah has bestowed upon you".

This principle has been stated in several other verses too. This attitude of the Holy Quran towards "the economic activity" of man and its two aspects would be very helpful in solving problems of man of Islamic economics.

ii. The real nature of wealth and property

The other fundamental principle, which can help to solve the problem of the distribution of wealth, is the concept of "wealth" in Islam. According to the illustration of the Holy Quran "wealth" in all its possible forms is a thing created by Allah, and is, in principle His "property". Allah delegates the right of property over a thing, which accrues to man, to Him. The Holy Quran explicitly says: "Give to them from the property of Allah which He has bestowed upon you."

According to Quran the reason for this philosophy is that all a man can do is invest his labour into the process of production. But Allah alone, and no one else, can cause this endeavor to be fruitful and actually productive. Man can do no more than sow the seed in the soil, but to bring out a seedling from the seed and make the seedling grow into a tree is the work of some one other than man. The Holy Quran says: "Have you considered what you till? Is it you yourselves who make it grow, or is it We who make it grow?"

And in another verse:

"Have they not seen that, among the things made by our own hands? We have created cattle for them, and thus they acquired the right of property over them?"

All these verses throw ample light on the fundamental point that "wealth", no matter what its form, is in principle "the property of Allah", and it is He who has bestowed upon man the right to exploit it. So Allah has the right to demand that man should subordinate his exploitation of this wealth to the commandments of Allah.

Thus, man has the "right of property" over the things he exploits, but this right is not absolute or arbitrary or boundless, it carries along with it certain limitations and restrictions, which have been imposed by the real owner of the 'wealth'. We must spend it where He has commanded it to be spent, and refrain from spending where He has forbidden. This point has been clarified more explicitly in the following verse:

"Seek the other world by means of what Allah has bestowed upon you, and do not be negligent about your share in this world. And, do good as Allah have done good to you and, do not seek to spread disorder on the earth."

This verse fully explains the Islamic point of view on the question of property. It places the following guidelines before us:

1. Whatever wealth man does possess has been received from Allah.
2. Man has to use it in such a way that his ultimate purpose should be the other world.
3. Since wealth has been received from Allah, its exploitation by man must necessarily be subject to the commandment of Allah.
4. Now, the Divine Commandment has taken into two forms:
    a. Allah may command man to convey a specified production of "Wealth" to another man. This Commandment must be obeyed, because Allah has done well to you, so He may command you to do good to others - "do good as Allah has done good to you".
    b. He may forbid you to use this "wealth" in a specified way. He has every right to do so because He cannot allow you to use "wealth" in a way which is likely to produce collective ills or to spread disorder on the earth.

This is what distinguishes the Islamic point of view on the question of property from the Capitalist and Socialist points of view both. Since the mental background of Capitalism is, theoretically or practically, materialistic, it gives man the unconditional and absolute right of property over his wealth, and allows him to employ it, as he likes. But the Holy Quran has adopted an attitude of disapprobation towards this theory of property, in quoting the words of the nation of Hazrat Shu'aib. They used to say: "Does your way of prayer command you that we should forsake what our fore?"

4

Commercial Interest and Usury

THE BACKGROUND OF BOTH TYPES

In the 17th century, two new technical terms of interest emerged after the establishment of banking system. These are namely:

1. Tijarti Sood (Commercial Interest): Interest paid on loan taken for productive & profitable purposes.
2. Sarfi Sood (Usury): Interest paid on loan taken for personal need and expenses.

The present day banking system, which has given interest the moral and legal license, is the backbone of the prevalent capitalism. When Muslim countries became subjugated to west in their economic field, some westernized Muslims in the 19th century, on one side, saw the increasing progress of the west in trade and industry and on the other side saw the shattering economic condition of fellow Muslims states. They also became conscious of the fact that banking is inevitable in the field of trade and industry not only on national level but also internationally. This prompted them to say that only usury is harâm (illegal) but not commercial interest because rendering commercial interest harâm would pose irresolvable problems to their way up to industrialization and economic progress. They only included usury in the term "Riba" as categorically prohibited in Qura'n and Sunnah and freed commercial interest from it, calling it totally different from the western concept of interest. Therefore, it was concluded that the prohibition of Riba was restricted to usury while commercial interest was perfectly Islamic.

There are two schools of thought on this issue. A detailed analysis of their arguments is discussed as under:

1. First School

This school presents two arguments to support their point that only usury (not commercial interest) is prohibited in Islam:

Argument 1: Riba as practiced during the days of the Prophet was only Usury.

Counter argument: This claim is groundless, since Islam when prohibiting something does not only prohibit one form of it that is prevalent but all forms that might erupt in future. The changed state does not change the ruling; e.g., Qura'n has prohibited the following:

a. Liquor (Khamar): During the time of Prophet its form and the way of production was totally different from that of the present day liquor but the ruling remains unchanged even though the form has changed.
b. Pork (Khinzeer): Irrespective how clean the present day breeding of pigs in high class farms may be, pork will stay prohibited and cannot be rendered halal (legal).
c. Corruption/Immorality (Al Fahsha): Although a lot of sophisticated ways have been developed of this evil from the time of Qura'nic revelations prohibiting it, the ruling stands forever. The same applies to interest and gambling. By claiming that it was in a different form during Prophet's time does not change its ruling. It remains unchanged just as in case of Khamar, Khinzeer and Al Fahsha.

Argument 2: Commercial Interest did not exist in the days of Prophet.

Counter argument: This claim is also wrong. If one glances through the Islamic and pre Islamic history of Arabia, it will be evident that the interest type at that time was not restricted to usury but loans were granted for commercial and profitable purposes. To quote some examples:

a. "The tribe of Umro bin Aamir used to take interest from the tribe of Mughairah and at the advent of Islam, Mughairah owed heavy interest to Umro bin Aamir." In this narration, the transaction of interest between two tribes of Arabia has been pointed out who actually operated as trading companies; both tribes were very wealthy. Could it be that two wealthy tribes transacted interest just for personal need and expenses? The interest was simply commercial.

b. History of the city of Ta'if tells us that it was only second to Makkah in trade (their main exports being liquor, raisins, currants, wheat, wood etc) and industry (major being leather and dyeing). The tribe of 'Saqeef" (Jewish tribe) advanced cash on interest, not only to the natives of Ta'if, but the business community of Makkah as well, eg., the tribe of Mughairah who were their permanent customer. This advancement, which was not only restricted to cash but also to commodities between wealthy tribes of Taif and Makkah who were usually traders and businessmen, was only for their commercial purposes and not for their consumption and personal needs. One of the ways of receiving interest was to double the principle amount plus interest in case of non payment of loan and this practice was applied to both cash as well as commodities. They had become accustomed to it. At the time of signing the peace treaty with the people of Ta'if, the Prophet imposed conditions: i) Total elimination of interest based transactions. ii) Giving up of interest owed to and from them.

c. The practice of making 2 trade trips, one to Yemen in winters and the other to Syria in summer was started by the tribe of Quraish of Makkah. These trips proved to be very profitable especially since being custodians of Kaa'ba, Quraish were looked at with respect, granted special concessions and protected in transit which was a necessity at that time. This way business and trade became their only means of livelihood. Investment became the order of the day in which women also took part and its circulation flourished and multiplied. With this background in mind, one can easily visualize that the city of Makkah more or less became the clearing house or the banking city and accustomed to their related amenities. It was only natural that interest was one of them. Since they advanced cash for commercial purposes and charged compound interest incase of default by the traders, and this earning of interest was their trade, they argued when Qura'n rendered interest haram (illegal) that the transaction of interest based loans is a type of trade in which the return on capital can be earned as in the case of rent received from assets. They could not differentiate between excess in shape of profit during a trade and excess in the shape of interest at the time of repayment of loan.

d. Therefore in pre Islamic days, we see that Syedna Abbas bin Abdul Muttalib and Syedna Khalid bin Waleed formed a company with joint capital whose prime business was cash advancement on interest. Similarly Syedna Usman was one of the wealthy businessmen who lent money on interest. There were many other traders dealing full time in interest extending a network of interest based transactions.

e. The way Syedna Zubair bin Awwam, who was famous for his trustworthiness, operated was quite similar to that of modern banking system. People used to deposit with him their capital as Amanah (trust or security). However, Syedna Zubair used to make it clear to the depositors that he would accept the deposits as a 'loan' and not as 'security' (Amanah). Because he knew that he will not be fully liable according to Shariah in case these Amanahs got destroyed but in case of having them as a loan, he will be fully liable to pay them back. He was afraid that in case of losing any deposited amount, his image as the trustworthy caretaker would be damaged. He therefore used the term 'loan' for such deposits to ensure guaranteed payment so that he enjoys everyone's confidence in him. Another reason for using the word 'loan' was to legalize trading and earning profits on such deposits. Because if he got those deposits as Amanah, he could not utilize it for his business, as it is not permissible in Shariah to use Amanah. This clearly shows that borrowing in those days was not only for consumption purposes but for commercial purposes as well. Syedna Zubair left a will with his son Syedna Abdullah bin Zubair before he died to sell his property to repay the loan, if required. The total amount calculated after his death for repayment by his son was 22 lacs. It is obvious that a rich Sahaba such as Syedna Zubair did not owe this loan of 22 lacs out of any need; rather it was an investment of securities that was circulating in trade.

Another Clear Argument: Syedna Abu Hurairah narrated that the Prophet said, "He who does not abandon Mokhabara, will be caught in a war against Allah & His Prophet." In this narration Prophet has rendered Mokhabara illegal just like riba and has declared a war against those who indulge in it just like riba.

Mokhabara is actually a division of the crop by agreement between the landlord and cultivator in which the landlord gives his land to cultivator for cultivation purposes in order to get his pre-agreed amounts of the crop irrespective whether the production is low or high. E.g., 'A' lends his land to 'B' for cultivation on the condition that B will get a predetermined portion on each crop, say, 5 mounds. Such a transaction is called Mokhabara. Prophet had called Mokhabara a form of riba. Now one should think over whether he referred to usury as the form of riba or he referred to commercial interest. It is similar to commercial interest as both Mokhabara and commercial interest are used for productive businesses. On the other hand, in the case of usury, the borrower uses the loan for personal use and not for productive purposes.

To sum up, Prophet included Mokhabara in riba that has no similarity with usury, rather with commercial interest. The fact that during Prophet's time, the dealing in commercial interest was common is proven and also that this form is prohibited.

2. Second School

This group presents two arguments justifying their points of view that are mentioned below:

Argument 1: The factor leading to prohibition of Riba (Interest) is that if a borrower faces a loss, he still has to pay an excess amount over the principal, which is basically an exploitation of his need, whereas the lender on the other hand gets an increase on his surplus capital without any effort which is unjust. But this factor is not found in commercial interest since both the borrower as well as the lender gets profit; the borrower on the amount he has circulated in business and the lender in shape of interest over his principle amount. Therefore, no one faces unfairness or injustice in this transaction.

Counter argument: This argument is quite appealing and attractive at the face value, as it is based on the assumption that no one suffers in case of commercial interest. But after analysis, it is proven that Quran has not only prohibited that one party faces a loss and the other gets profit but has also prohibited one party getting confirmed profit and the other party unconfirmed profit from the same investment as we have studied above in the case of Mokhabara.

Argument 2: This argument is based on the Qura'nic verse "O believers do not devour one another's possession wrongfully; rather than that, let there be trading by mutual consent" (Al Nisa verse 29). In the above verse, Qura'n has prohibited "Wrongful devouring" which will only arise if the consent of one of the parties is absent and naturally the party who is devouring consents, the other party never consents; he only gives in since he has no other option. So we come to the conclusion that if the consent and satisfaction of both parties is present in a deal, it cannot be called "Wrongful devouring". According to this logic, commercial interest is permissible since the mutual consent is present of both parties whereas riba is prohibited only when one party is getting the excess out of his selfishness and the other party is encountering the loss, as he has no other alternative.

Counter argument: This argument is of superficial nature. Mutual consent is not the criteria to render anything prohibited or not in Islam. Would the act of adultery be allowed if the condition of mutual consent is fulfilled? Similarly, there are many transactions in business, which are rendered illegal even with mutual consent. For reference see "Abwab ul Buyu al Batila" where Muhaqila and Talqi al Jalab being forms of Bai where the mutual consent and satisfaction is present and is prohibited by Prophet . Similarly, mutual consent is present in commercial interest and gambling too but in spite of that, it has been prohibited. Therefore no such criteria exist in the legality of any transaction that both parties approve; rather the approval should be on the transaction, which has not been prohibited by Shariah. To quote the words of Qura'n "Except the legitimate business......."

SIMPLE AND COMPOUND INTEREST

Riba An Nasiyah can be classified into two types-

1. Definition of Simple Interest (Sood-e-Mufrid): Interest calculated only on the initial investment.
2. Definition of Compound Interest (Sood-e-Murakkab): Reinvestment of each interest payment on money invested, to earn more interest. During the pre-Islamic era, when a borrower used to fail to pay back the principal and interest charged on him, then the lender used to extend the loan on the condition that the interest will also become part of the loan (essentially Compound Interest). The following verses of Quran were revealed in order to stop the people from such practices:

"O believers, take not doubled and redoubled interest, and fear God so that you may prosper." (Surah Al 'Imran, verses 130-1)

To eradicate this abominable practice of the period of ignorance, this verse was revealed. By mentioning the practice of doubling and redoubling, it was condemned and declared unlawful in view of its adverse impact on the community and the selfishness that it bred. It does not mean that if there is no doubling and redoubling (i.e., if there is simple interest, in today's jargon), then it is lawful. No. In Surah Al Baqarah (The Cow) and Surah An Nisa (The Women), the prohibition of interest in its entirety and in absolute terms is clearly mentioned, whether or not there is doubling and redoubling.

Since the aforementioned verse prohibits the compound interest only, some people misinterpret it even today that compound interest alone is forbidden in Islam, not the simple interest. They fail to see that there is absolute prohibition of simple interest in a number of other Quranic verses. The reason that the above verse specifically uses the words "doubled and redoubled interest" is to highlight the shameful aspect of compound interest and not to limit the scope of riba only to compound interest. This is similar to Allah's command "Do not bargain on my orders for paltry gains in this world." The reason for mentioning paltry gains is that even if all conceivable material goods and luxuries of this world are obtained in exchange for ignoring Allah's commands, even then this is a paltry gain. It does not obviously mean that it is prohibited to obtain paltry gains but permissible to obtain (by one's standard or judgment) a hefty price. Similarly, in the Ayat under consideration, the mention of doubling and redoubling is to condemn the shameful practice rather than limit its permissibility.

VERSES ON ABSOLUTE PROHIBITION OF SIMPLE AND COMPOUND INTEREST

"O believers, fear God and give up the interest that remains outstanding (i.e. whether it is simple interest or multiplied interest) if you are believers." (Surah Al-Baqarah, verse 278)

"If you do not do so, then be sure of being at war with God and His Messenger. But, if you repent, you can have your principal (only - not any kind of interest or premium). Neither should you commit injustice nor should you be subjected to it.

(Surah al Baqarah, verse 279)

The above two verses demand to abandon the amount of riba and directs that only the principal amount should be paid back, nothing in excess. The second verse explains that any excess on principal, no matter how insignificant, is cruel.

The following hadith also proves that both simple and compound interest are forbidden:

"Listen! All Riba liable to you in the pre-Islamic days have been completely eliminated. You have to pay back the principal amount only. Neither hurt someone nor gets hurt by someone. And the first riba to be completely eliminated is Abbas bin Mutalib's.

The above evidence proves that the claim that 'only compound interest is prohibited and any riba less than that are allowed in Islam,' is wrong. Any amount in excess of the principal fixed in the contract of a loan is called Riba An Nasiyah. If simple interest is accepted, it can also be used to give out additional loans, which will again pay out simple interest. In effect, the interest will keep on becoming part of the principal, which is essentially compound interest."

ISLAMIC CONTRACT

In Islamic jurisprudence what is the ruling of putting a condition on a contract or agreement? There are four basic rules for judging the validity of conditions in a contract:

1. A condition which is not against the contract is a valid condition.
2. A condition which seems to be against the contract, but it is in the market practice, that type of condition is not void, if its voidness is not proven with the clear injunctions of the Holy Quran and Sunnah. For example 'A' buys an air conditioner on a condition that the seller will provide him five-year guarantee and one year free service. This type of condition does not invalidate the contract.

3. A condition that is against the contract and not in the practice of market but it is in favor of one of the contractors or subject matter, this type of condition is void. For example if 'A' says he sells a car with a condition that he will use it on a fixed date every month, this contract will be void.
4. A condition which is against the contract, not in the market practices and not in favor of any contractor, is not a void condition.

Now, a question arises what is the ruling of void condition, whether it invalidates the contract or not?

The answer is that there is a detail about the impacts of void condition. Sometimes a void condition invalidates the contract and sometimes it does not invalidate the contract, however, the condition itself is annulled.

To elaborate this, Islamic jurists and scholars have written that the compensation (Uqood Muawadha) like sale, purchase, lease agreements become void by putting void condition. However, non-compensatory (voluntarily) agreements (Uqood Ghair Muawadha) like contract of loan (Qard-e-Hasanah) do not become void because of void condition. The void condition, however, becomes itself ineffective. For example if 'A' gives to 'B' a loan with a condition of premium at the time of repayment, this condition of interest is void. However, this condition does not invalidate the contract, therefore all transaction done by this borrowed money, will be valid. But the condition of interest itself is revoked; therefore 'B' is not liable for the payment of interest.

RIGHTS, RESPONSIBILITY AND OBLIGATION IN A CONTRACT

In Islamic Fiqh, some contracts are such that rights and obligations are also attached to the agent doing the contract on behalf of the Contracting Party, e.g., Sales Contract, Ijara, Istisna, Salam etc.where as in others, a Principle has all the responsibilities, rights and obligations, such as, Nikah.

A. Sale

1. Valid Sale (Bai Sahih)

A sale becomes valid if the following elements are present as well as the conditions are complied with:

a. Contract (Aqd)
b. Subject Matter (Mabe'e)
c. Price (Thaman)
d. Possession or delivery (Qabza)

2. Void/Non Existing Sale (Bai Baatil)

Sale will be void if any one of the conditions of offer and acceptance (1.1), conditions of Buyer & Seller (1.2) and sold good conditions (2.1 - 2.5) are not complied with. In a void sale, the buyer does not have title to subject matter and seller does not have title to price. Both subject matter and price cannot be used lawfully. The produce of both shall be unlawful.

3. Existing sale but void due to defect (Bai Fasid)

Sale will exist but will be void due to defect if the conditions of contract (1.3), sold good conditions (2.6 & 2.7) and conditions of price (3.1 & 3.2) are not complied with. However, if the defect is rectified the sale becomes valid. In a fasid sale, the buyer should not possess the subject matter. If possessed with the consent of the seller, title or ownership will pass to the buyer but usage of subject matter will be impermissible. He must return it to the seller.

4. Valid but disliked sale (Bai Makrooh)

A sale will be Makrooh when the transaction is complete and one gets possession of the goods but is disliked eg. sale after Juma Azaan, sale after hoarding or where a third party intervenes to buy something which was under negotiation of sale between other parties.

Types of Sales

Sale (Bai) is commonly defined in shari'ah as "the exchange of a thing of value by another thing of value with mutual consent". More specifically it means "the sale of a commodity in exchange of cash". Following are the common types of sales:

1. Bai Musawamah: It refers to normal sale in which cost price is not known.
2. Bai Murabaha: It refers to a sale in which cost and sale price is known to the buyer.
3. Bai Muqayada: It refers to barter sale excluding currency sale.
4. Bai Surf: It refers to the sale of gold, silver and currency.
5. Bai Salam: It is a kind of sale in which payment is spot while the delivery of the good is deferred.
6. Bai Istisna: It refers to such sale in which commodity is transacted before it comes into existence. It is basically an order to manufacture.
7. Bai Muajjal: It refers to such sale in which payment is delivery is spot while payment is deferred but cost is not known.

B. Ijarah Wa Iqtina

In Islamic Shariah, it is allowed that instead of sale, the lessor signs a separate promise to gift the leased asset to the lessee at the end of the lease period, subject to his payment of all amounts of rent. This arrangement is called 'Ijarah wa iqtina. It has been allowed by a large number of contemporary scholars and is widely acted upon by the Islamic banks and financial institutions. The validity of this arrangement is subject to two basic conditions:

a. The agreement of Ijarah itself should not be subjected to signing this promise of sale or gift but the promise should be recorded in a separate document.
b. The promise should be unilateral and binding on the promisor only. It should not be a bilateral promise binding on both parties because in this case it will be a full contract affected to a future date, which is not allowed in the case of sale or gift.

Sub-Lease

If the leased asset is used differently by different users, the lessee cannot sub-lease the leased asset except with the express permission of the lessor. If the lessor permits the lessee for subleasing, he may sub-lease it. If the rent claimed from the sub-lessee is less to or less than the rent payable to the owner or original lessor, all the recognized schools of Islamic jurisprudence are unanimous on the permissibility of the sub lease. However, the opinions are different in case the rent charged from the sub-lessee is higher than the rent payable to the owner. Imam Shafi and some other scholars allow it and hold that the sub lessor may enjoy the surplus received from the sub-lessee. This is the preferred view in the Hanbali School as well. On the other hand, Imam Abu Hanifah is of the view that the surplus received from the sub-lessee in this case is not permissible for the sub-lessor to keep and he will have to give that surplus in charity. However, if the sub-lessor has developed the leased property by adding something to it or has rented it in a currency different from the currency in which he himself pays rent to the owner/the original lessor, he can claim a higher rent from his sub-lessee and can enjoy the surplus.

Although the view of Imam Abu Hanifah is more precautious which should be acted upon to the best possible extent, in cases of need the view of Shafai and Hanbali schools may be followed because there is no express prohibition in the Holy Quran or in the Sunnah against the surplus claimed from the lessee. Ibn Qudamah has argued for the permissibility of surplus on forceful grounds.

Assigning of the Lease

The lessor can sell the leased property to a third party whereby the relation of lessor and lessee shall be established between the new owner and the lessee. However, the assigning of the lease itself (without assigning the ownership in the leased asset) for a monetary consideration is not permissible.

The difference between the two situations is that in the latter case the ownership of the asset is not transferred to the assignee, but he becomes entitled to receive the rent of the asset only. This kind of assignment is allowed in Shariah only where no monetary consideration is charged from the assignee for this assignment. For example, a lessor can assign his right to claim rent from the lessee to his son, or to his friend in the form of a gift. Similarly, he can assign this right to any one of his creditors to set off his debt out of the rentals received by him. But if the lessor wants to sell this right for a fixed price, it is not permissible, because in this case the money (the amount of rentals) is sold for money, which is a transaction subject to the principle of equality. Otherwise it will be tantamount to a riba transaction, hence prohibited.

C. Istisna

Istisna' is a sale transaction where a commodity is transacted before it comes into existence. It is an order to a manufacturer to manufacture a specific commodity for the purchaser. The manufacturer uses his material to manufacture the required goods. In Istisna', price must be fixed with consent of all parties involved. All other necessary specifications of the commodity must also be fully settled.

Cancellation of Contract

After giving prior notice, either party can cancel the contract before the manufacturing party has begun its work. Once the work starts, the contract cannot be cancelled unilaterally.

Difference between Istisna and Salam Istisna

The subject on which transaction of Istisna' is based, is always a thing which needs to be manufactured. The subject can be anything that need manufacturing or not.

The price in Istisna' does not necessarily need to be paid in full in advance. It is not even necessary to pay the full price at delivery. It can be deferred to any time according to the agreement of the parties. The payment may also be made in installments. The price has to be paid in full in advance. The time of delivery does not have to be fixed in Istisna'. The time of delivery is an essential part of the sale. The contract can be cancelled before the manufacturer starts the work. The contract cannot be cancelled unilaterally.

Difference between Istisna' and Ijarah

The manufacturer either uses his own material and if not available with him, he obtains it to make the ordered goods. The material is provided by the customer and the manufacturer uses only his labour and skill meaning that his services will be hired for a specified fee paid to him. The purchaser has a right to reject the goods after inspection as Shariah permits somebody who purchases a thing not seen by him, to cancel the sale after seeing it. The right of rejection only exists if the goods do not conform to the specifications agreed upon between the parties at the time of contract. Right of rejection of goods after inspection does not exist.

Time of delivery

As pointed out earlier, it is not necessary in Istisna' that the time of delivery is fixed. However, the purchaser may fix a maximum time for delivery which means that if the manufacturer delays the delivery after the appointed time, he will not be bound to accept the goods and to pay the price.

In order to ensure that the goods will be delivered within the specified period, some modern agreements of this nature contain a penal clause to the effect that in case the manufacturer delays the delivery after the appointed time, he shall be liable to a penalty which shall be calculated on daily basis. Can such a penal clause be inserted in a contract of Istisna' according to Shariah? Although the classical jurists seem to be silent about this question while they discuss the contract of Istisna', yet they have allowed a similar condition in the case of Ijarah . They say that if a person hires the services of a person to tailor his clothes, the fee may be variable according to the time of delivery. The hirer may say that he will pay Rs. 100/- in case the tailor prepares the clothes within one day and Rs. 80/- in case he prepares them after two days.

On the same analogy, the price in Istisna' may be tied up with the time of delivery, and it will be permissible if it is agreed between the parties that in the case of delay in delivery, the price shall be reduced by a specified amount per day.

Istisna' as a mode of financing

Istisna' may be used to provide financing for house financing. If the client owns a land and seeks financing for the construction of a house, the financier may undertake to construct the house on the basis of an Istisna'. If the client does not own the land and wants to purchase that too, the financier can provide him with a constructed house on a specified piece of land. The financier does not have to construct the house himself. He can either enter into a parallel Istisna' with a third party or hire the services of a contractor (other than the client). He must calculate his cost and fix the price of Istisna' with his client that allows him to make a reasonable profit over his cost. The payment of installments by the client may start right from the day when the contract of Istisna' is signed by the parties. In order to secure the payment of installments, the title deeds of the house or land, or any other property of the client may be kept by the financier as a security until the last installment is paid by the client. The financier will be responsible to strictly conform to the specifications in the agreement for the construction of the house. The cost of correcting any discrepancy would have to be borne by him.

Istisna' may also be used for similar projects like installation of an air conditioner plant in the client's factory, building a bridge or a highway.

The modern BOT (buy, operate and transfer) agreements may be formalized through an Istisna' agreement as well. So, if the government wants to build a highway, it may enter into an Istisna' contract with the builder. The price of Istisna' may be the right of the builder to operate the highway and collect tolls for a specific period.

Uses of Istisna'

House financing, Financing of plant / factory / building, Booking of apartments, BOT arrangements, and Construction of buildings and plants.

D. Salam

This mode of financing can be used by the modern banks and financial institutions especially to finance the agricultural sector. In Salam, the seller undertakes to supply specific goods to the buyer at a future date in exchange of an advanced price fully paid at spot. The price is in cash but the supply of purchased goods is deferred.

Purpose of use

To meet the need of small farmers who need money to grow their crops and to feed their family up to the time of harvest. When Allah declared Riba haram, the farmers could not take usurious loans. Therefore Holy Prophet allowed them to sell their agricultural products in advance.

Meeting the need of traders for import and export business: Under Salam, it is allowed for them that they sell the goods in advance so that after receiving their cash price, they can easily undertake the aforesaid business. Salam is beneficial to the seller because he received the price in advance and it was beneficial to the buyer also because normally the price in Salam is lower than the price in spot sales.

Conditions of Salam

The permissibility of Salam is an exception to the general rule that prohibits forward sale and therefore it is subject to strict conditions, which are as follows:

1. It is necessary for the validity of Salam that the buyer pays the price in full to the seller at the time of effecting of the sale. In the absence of full payment, it will be tantamount to sale of a debt against a debt, which is expressly prohibited by the Holy Prophet. Moreover the

basic wisdom for allowing Salam is to fulfill the "instant need" of the seller. If it is not paid in full, the basic purpose will not be achieved.

2. Only those goods can be sold through a Salam contract in which the quantity and quality can be exactly specified. E.g., precious stones cannot be sold on the basis of Salam because each stone differ in quality, size, weight and their exact specification is not possible.
3. Salam cannot be affected on a particular commodity or on a product of a particular field or farm. E.g., supply of wheat of a particular field or the fruit of a particular tree, since there is a possibility that the crop is destroyed before delivery and given such possibility, the delivery remains uncertain.
4. All details in respect to quality of goods sold must be expressly specified leaving no ambiguity, which may lead to a dispute.
5. It is necessary that the quantity of the commodity is agreed upon in absolute terms. It should be measured or weighed in its usual measure only, meaning what is normally weighed cannot be quantified and vice versa.
6. The exact date and place of delivery must be specified in the contract.
7. Salam cannot be affected in respect of things, which must be delivered at spot.
8. The commodity for Salam contract should remain in the market right from the day of contract up to the date of delivery or at least till the date of delivery.
9. The time of delivery should be at least fifteen days or one month from the date of agreement. Price in Salam is generally lower than the price in spot sale. The period should be long enough to affect prices. But Hanafi Fiqh did not specify any minimum period for the validity of Salam. It is all right to have an earlier date of delivery if the seller consents to it.
10. Since price in Salam is generally lower than the price in spot sale; the difference in the two prices may be a valid profit for the Bank.

11. A security in the form of a guarantee, mortgage or hypothecation may be required for a Salam in order to ensure that the seller delivers.
12. The seller at the time of delivery delivers commodities and not money to the buyer who would have to establish a special cell for dealing in commodities.

Benefits

There are two ways of benefiting from the contract of Salam:

1. After purchasing a commodity by way of Salam, the financial institution can sell it through a parallel contract of Salam for the same date of delivery. The period of Salam in the second parallel contract is shorter and the price is higher than the first contract. The difference between the two prices shall be the profit earned by the institution. The shorter the period of Salam the higher is the price and greater the profit. In this way, institutions can manage their short term financing portfolios.
2. The institution can obtain a promise to purchase from a third party. This promise should be unilateral from the expected buyer. The buyer does not have to pay the price in advance. When the institution receives the commodity, it can sell it at a pre-determined price to a third party according to the terms of the promise.

Parallel Salam

In arrangement of Salam, there must be two different and independent contracts; one where the bank is a buyer and the other in which it is a seller. The two contracts cannot be tied up and performance of one should not be contingent on the other. For example, if 'A' has purchased from 'B' 1000 bags of wheat by way of Salam to be delivered on 31 December, 'A' can contract a parallel Salam with 'C' to deliver to him 1000 bags of wheat on 31 December. But while contracting Parallel Salam with 'C', the delivery of wheat to 'C' cannot be conditioned with taking delivery from 'B'. Therefore, even if 'B' did not deliver wheat on 31 December, 'A' is duty bound to deliver 1000 bags of wheat to 'C'. He can seek whatever recourse he has against 'B', but he cannot rid himself from his liability to deliver wheat to 'C'. Similarly, if 'B' has delivered defective goods, which do not conform to the agreed specifications, 'A' is still obligated to deliver the goods to 'C' according to the specifications agreed with him.

A Salam arrangement cannot be used as a buy back facility where the seller in the first contract is also the purchaser in the second. Even if the purchaser in the second contract is a separate legal entity, but owned by the seller in the first contract; it would not tantamount to a valid parallel Salam agreement. For example, 'A' has purchased 1000 bags of wheat by way of Salam from 'B' - a joint stock company. 'B' has a subsidiary 'C', which is a separate legal entity but is fully owned by 'B'. 'A' cannot contract the parallel Salam with 'C'. However, if 'C' is not wholly owned by 'B', 'A' can contract parallel Salam with it, even if some share-holders are common between 'B' and 'C'.

ISTIJRAR

Istijrar means purchasing goods time to time in different quantities. In Islamic jurisprudence Istijrar is an agreement where a buyer purchases something from time to time; each time there is no offer or acceptance or bargain. There is one master agreement where all terms and conditions are finalized. There are two types of Istijrar:

1. Whereby the price is determined after all transactions of purchase are complete.
2. Whereby the price is determined in advance but the purchase is executed from time to time. The first kind is relevant with the Islamic mode of financing. This kind is permissible with certain conditions.
   a. In the case where the seller discloses the price of goods at the time of each transaction; the sale becomes valid only when the buyer possess the goods. The amount is paid after all transactions have been completed.
   b. If the seller does not disclose each and every time to the buyer the price of the subject matter, but the contractors know that it is being sold on market value

and the market value is specified and determined in such a manner that it does not vary and it does not lead to differences of the contractors.

c. If at the time of possession, the price of subject matter was unknown or contractors agree that whatever the price shall be, the sale will be executed. However, if there is significant difference in the market price and the agreed price, it may cause conflict. In such a case, at the time of possession, the sale will not be valid. However, at the time of settlement of the payment, the sale will be valid.

The validity will relate to the time of possession. Therefore the ownership of the buyer in the subject matter will be proved from the time of possession. After the payment of price the buyer's usage of the subject matter will be valid from the time of the possession.

As far as the use of Istijrar in Islamic banks is concerned, at present they are involved in four kinds of activities, namely Murabahah, Ijarah, Mudarabah and Musharakah. Out of these four, the concept of Istijrar can be applied to only the first three cases, due to the reason that Istijrar cannot be applied to borrowers of the bank. However, the same concept can however be applied to suppliers of the borrower.

However, Istijrar can work with suppliers of the borrower. In this case, the bank enters into a Murabahah with the suppliers on the basis of Istijrar. The bank enters into an Agreement to Purchase with the suppliers (which are mainly trading companies) that it will purchase assets from them at a market price or at a predetermined discount from the market price. Whenever the bank has a new customer, it can purchase the assets from the suppliers on the basis of Istijrar and sell it onwards to the customer on the basis of Murabahah.

It might very well be probable that the bank might enter into a pseudo-Istijrar agreement with the suppliers rather than a true one. This is the case when the bank enters into an agreement with the customer that it is going to sell certain assets in a certain quantity to them within a specified time period. The customer may then purchase the assets from the banks in tranches rather than at once and complete the whole purchase within the specified time period in order to complete the agreement.

The above type of Istijrar is referred to as Istijrar with Pre-agreed Sale due to the reason that the customer purchases a given amount of assets from the bank over a period of time but the price of the assets purchased is always known before the sale. Given the above, there is no difference of opinion between Shariah scholars as far as accepting this type of transaction as Bai-Ta'ati is concerned. However, the use of Ta'ati in case of a Murabahah transaction is not acceptable, as it leads indirectly to Riba in case the bank does not take possession of the assets before they are sold to the customer. Hence if Ta'ati is to be used in this case, then the only way to do it is that the bank should purchase the assets some time before selling it to the customer. This would ensure possession that is not just constructive but the bank would have title to the assets before they are sold to the customer. Given that the above conditions are complied with to their full extent, Istijrar can be used in case of a Murabahah.

A. Murabaha

All other services that can be sold in the form of package (i.e. services like education, medical etc. as a package).Securitization of Murabahah agreement (certificate) is allowed at per value only. Otherwise, certain rules of Islamic Finance must be met.

USES OF MURABAHAH

- Murabahah can be used in following conditions:
- Short / Medium / Long Term Finance for:
- Raw material
- Inventory
- Equipment
- Asset financing
- Import financing

- Export financing (Pre-shipment)
- Consumer goods financing
- House financing
- Vehicle financing
- Land financing
- Shop financing
- PC financing
- Tour package financing
- Education package financing

B. Mudarabah

This is a kind of partnership where one partner gives money to another for investing in a commercial enterprise. The investment comes from the first partner who is called "Rab-ul-Maal" while the management and work is an exclusive responsibility of the other, who is called "Mudarib" and the profits generated are shared in a predetermined ratio.

Types of Mudarabah

There are two types of Mudarabah, namely:

1. Al Mudarabah Al Muqayyadah: Rab-ul-Maal may specify a particular business or a particular place for the mudarib, in which case he shall invest the money in that particular business or place. This is called Al Mudarabah Al Muqayyadah (restricted Mudarabah).
2. Al Mudarabah Al Mutlaqah: However if Rab-ul-maal gives full freedom to Mudarib to undertake whatever business he deems fit, this is called Al Mudarabah Al Mutlaqah (unrestricted Mudarabah). However Mudarib cannot, without the consent of Rab-ul-Maal, lend money to anyone. Mudarib is authorized to do anything, which is normally done in the course of business. However if they want to have an extraordinary work, which is beyond the normal routine of the traders, he cannot do so without express permission from Rab-ul-Maal. He is also not authorized to keep another Mudarib or a partner mix his own investment in that particular Modarabah without the

consent of Rab-ul Maal. Conditions of offer & acceptance are applicable to both. A Rab-ul-Maal can contract Mudarabah with more than one person through a single transaction. It means that he can offer his money to 'A' and 'B' both so that each one of them can act for him as Mudarib and the capital of the Mudarabah shall be utilized by both of them jointly, and the share of the Mudarib .

Difference between Musharakah and Mudarabah

1. All partners invest. Only Rab-ul-Maal invests.
2. All partners participate in the management of the business and can work for it. Rab-ul-maal has no right to participate in the management which is carried out by the Mudarib only.
3. All partners share the loss to the extent of the ratio of their investment. Only Rab-ul-maal suffers loss because the Mudarib does not invest anything. However, this is subject to the condition that the Mudarib has worked with due diligence.
4. The liability of the partners is normally unlimited. If the liabilities of business exceed its assets and the business goes in liquidation, all the exceeding liabilities shall be borne pro rata by all partners. But if the partners agree that no partner shall incur any debt during the course of business, then the exceeding liabilities shall be borne by that partner alone who has incurred a debt on the business in violation of the aforesaid condition. The liability of Rab-ul-maal is limited to his investment unless he has permitted the Mudarib to incur debts on his behalf. As soon as the partners mix up their capital in a joint pool, all the assets become jointly owned by all of them according to the proportion of their respective investment. All partners benefit from the appreciation in the value of the assets even if profit has not accrued through sales. The goods purchased by the Mudarib are solely owned by Rab-ul-maal and the Mudarib can earn his share in the profit only in case he sells the goods profitably.

Investment

In Mudarabah, Rab-ul-maal provides the investment and Mudarib the management therefore the Rab-ul-maal should hand over the agreed investment to Mudarib and leaves everything to Mudarib with no interference from his side but he has the authority to oversee the Mudarib 's activities and Work with Mudarib if the Mudarib consents. In what form should the capital be? Should it be liquid or non-liquid assets like equipment, land etc. can these form a capital?

The basic principle is that the capital in Mudarabah is valid just the way as it is in Shirkah which according to Hanafi fiqh should be in liquid form but according to other scholars equipment, land etc can also be included as capital. However all agree on the assets other than cash can be used as an intermediate step, meaning- however this is subject to the determination of exact amount of the assets before it is used for Mudarabah. If the assets are not correctly evaluated, the Mudarabah is not valid.

Mudarabah Expenses

The Mudarib shares profit of the Mudarabah as per agreed rate with the investor but his expenses like meals, clothing, conveyance and medical are not borne by Mudarabah. However, if he is traveling on business and is overstaying the night, then the above expenses shall be covered from capital. If Mudarib goes for a journey which constitutes Safar-e-Sharai (more than 48 miles) but does not overstay the night, his expenses will not be borne by Mudarabah.

All expenses which are incidental to the Mudarabah's function like wages of employees/workers or Commission in buying/selling or stitching, dyeing expenses etc have to be paid by the Mudarabah. However all expenses will be included in the cost of commodities which Mudarib is selling. E.g., if he is selling ready made garments then the stitching, dyeing, washing expenses etc. can be included by the Mudarib in the total cost of the garments.

If the Mudarib manages the Mudarabah within his city, he will not be allowed any expenses, only his profit share. Similarly, if he keeps an employee, this employee will not be allowed any expenses, just his salary.

If the Mudarabah agreement becomes Fasid due to any reason, the Mudarib 's status will be like an employee, meaning - whether he is traveling or doing any business in his city, he will not be entitled to any expenses such as meals, conveyance, clothing, medicine etc. He will not be sharing any profit and will just get Ujrat-e-Misl (ordinary pay) for his job.

Distribution of Profit and Loss

It is necessary for validity of Mudarabah that the parties agree, right at the beginning, on a definite proportion of the actual profit to which each one of them is entitled. The Shariah has prescribed no particular proportion; rather it has been left to their mutual consent. They can share the profit in equal proportions and they can also allocate different proportions for Rab-ul-Maal and Mudarib. However in extreme case where the parties have not predetermined the ratio of profit, the profit will be calculated at 50:50.

The Mudarib and Rab-ul-Maal cannot allocate a lump sum amount of profit for any party nor can they determine the share of any party at a specific rate tied up with the capital. For example, if the capital is Rs.100,000/-, they cannot agree on a condition that Rs.10,000 out of the profit shall be the share of the Mudarib nor can they say that 20% of the capital shall be given to Rab-ul-Maal. However they can agree that 40% of the actual profit shall go to the Mudarib and 60% to the Rab-ul-Maal or vice versa.

It is also allowed that different proportions are agreed in different situations. For example, the Rab-ul-Maal can say to Mudarib "If you trade in wheat, you will get 50% of the profit and if you trade in flour, you will have 33% of the profit". Similarly, he can say "If you do the business in your town, you will be entitled to 30% of the profit and if you do it in another town, your share will be 50% of the profit".

Apart from the agreed proportion of the profit, as determined in the above manner, the Mudarib cannot claim any periodical salary or a fee or remuneration for the work done by him for the Mudarabah.

All schools of Islamic Fiqh are unanimous on this point. However, Imam Ahmad has allowed for the Mudarib to draw his daily expenses of food only from the Mudarabah Account. The Hanafi jurists restrict this right of the Mudarib only to a situation when he is on a business trip outside his own city. In this case he can claim his personal expenses, accommodation, food, etc. but he is not entitled to get anything as daily allowances when he is in his own city.

If the business has incurred loss in some transactions and has gained profit in some others, the profit shall be used to offset the loss at the first instance, and then the remainder, if any, shall be distributed between the parties according to the agreed ratio. The Mudarabah becomes void (Fasid) if the profit is fixed in any way. In this case, the entire amount (Profit + Capital) will be the Rab-ul-Maal's. The Mudarib will just be an employee earning Ujrat-e-Misl. The remaining amount will be called (Profit). This profit will be shared in the agreed (pre-agreed) ratio.

Roles of the Mudarib

Ameen (Trustee): To look after the investment responsibly, except in case of natural calamities.

Wakeel (Agent): To purchase from the funds provided by Rab-ul-Maal.

Shareek (Partner): Sharing in any profit.

Zamin (Liable): To provide for the loss suffered by the Mudarabah due to any act on his part.

Ajeer (Employee): When the Mudarabah gets Fasid due to any reason; the Mudarib is entitled to only the salary, Ujrat-e-Misl.

In case there is a loss, the Mudarib will not even get the Ujrat-e-Misl.

Termination of Mudarabah

The Mudarabah will stand terminated when the period specified in the contract expires. It can also be terminated any time by either of the two parties by giving notice. In case Rab-ul-Maal has terminated services of Mudarib, he will continue to act as Mudarib until he is informed of the same and all his acts will form part of Mudarabah.

If all assets of the Mudarabah are in cash form at the time of termination, and some profit has been earned on the principal amount, it shall be distributed between the parties according to the agreed ratio. However, if the assets of Mudarabah are not in cash form, it will be sold and liquidated so that the actual profit may be determined. All loans and payables of Mudarabah will be recovered. The provisional profit earned by Mudarib and Rab-ul-Maal will also be taken into account and when total capital is drawn, the principal amount invested by Rab-ul-Maal will be given to him, balance will be called profit which will be distributed between Mudarib and Rab-ul-Maal at the agreed ratio. If no balance is left, Mudarib will not get anything. If the principal amount is not recovered fully, then the profit shared by Mudarib and Rab-ul-Maal during the term of Mudarabah will be withdrawn to pay the principal amount to Rab-ul-Maal. The balance will be profit, which will be distributed between Mudarib and Rab-ul-Maal. In this case too if no balance is left, Mudarib will not get anything.

USES OF MUSHARAKAH / MUDARABAH

These modes can be used in the following areas (or can replace them according to Shariah rules).

- Asset Side Financing
- Short/medium/long - term financing
- Project financing
- Small & medium enterprises setup financing
- Large enterprise financing
- Import financing

- Import bills drawn under import letters of credit
- Inland bills drawn under inland letters of credit
- Bridge financing
- LC without margin (for Mudarba)
- LC with margin (for Musharakah)
- Export financing (Pre-shipment financing)
- Working capital financing
- Running accounts financing / short term advances
- Liability Side Financing
- For current /saving/mahana amdani/investment accounts (deposit giving Profit based on Musharkah / Mudarabah with predetermined ratio)
- Inter- Bank lending / borrowing
- Term Finance Certificates & Certificate of Investment
- T-Bill and Federal Investment Bonds / Debenture.
- Securitization for large projects (based on Musharkah)
- Certificate of Investment based on Murabahah (Eg: Al Meezan Riba Free)
- Islamic Musharakah bonds (based on projects requiring large amounts – profit based on the return from the project).

C. Musharakah

The literal meaning of Musharakah is sharing. The root of the word "Musharakah" in Arabic is Shirkah, which means being a partner. It is used in the same context as the term "shirk" meaning partner to Allah. Under Islamic jurisprudence, Musharakah means a joint enterprise formed for conducting some business in which all partners share the profit according to a specific ratio while the loss is shared according to the ratio of the contribution. It is an ideal alternative for the interest based financing with far reaching effects on both production and distribution. The connotation of this term is little limited than the term "Shirkah" more commonly used in the Islamic jurisprudence. For the purpose of clarity in the basic concepts, it will be pertinent at the outset to explain the meaning of each term, as distinguished from the other. "Shirkah" means "Sharing" and in the terminology of Islamic Fiqh, it has been divided into two kinds:

1. Shirkat-ul-milk (Partnership by joint ownership): It means joint ownership of two or more persons in a particular property. This kind of "Shirkah" may come into existence in two different ways:
   i. Optional (Ikhtiari): At the option of the parties e.g., if two or more persons purchase equipment, it will be owned jointly by both of them and the relationship between them with regard to that property is called "Shirkat-ul-Milk Ikhtiari" Here this relationship has come into existence at their own option, as they themselves elected to purchase the equipment jointly.
   ii. Compulsory (Ghair Ikhtiari): This comes into operation automatically without any effort/action taken by the parties. For example, after the death of a person, all his heirs inherit his property, which comes into their joint ownership as a natural consequence of the death of that person. There are two more types of Joint ownerships (Shirkat-ul-Milk) - Shirkat-ul-Ain and Shirkat-ul-Dain.

A property in shirkat-ul-milk is jointly owned but not divided yet, is called Musha. In Shirkat-ul-milk undivided shares or other assets can be used in the following manner:

a. Mushtarik Intifa: Mutually or jointly using an asset by taking turns under circumstances where the partners or joint owners are on good terms.
b. Muhaya: Under this arrangement the owners will set turns in days for example one may use the product for 15 days and then the other may use it for the rest of the month.

Taqseem: Referring to division of the jointly owned asset. This may be applied for property where the asset that is owned can be divided permanently for example jointly taking a 1,000 sq. yards plot and making a house on 500 yards by each of the 2 owners.

Under a situation where the partners are not satisfied with Muhaya arrangement, the property or asset jointly held can be sold off and proceeds divided between the partners.

2. Partnership by contract (Shirkat-ul-Aqd): This is the second type of Shirkah, which means, "a partnership effected by a mutual contract". For the purpose of brevity it may also be translated as "joint commercial enterprise." Shirkat-ul-Aqd is further divided into three kinds:

Shirkat-ul-Amwal (Partnership in capital) where all the partners invest some capital into a commercial enterprise.

Shirkat-ul-Aamal (Partnership in services) where all the partners jointly undertake to render some services for their customers, and the fee charged from them is distributed among them according to an agreed ratio. For example, if two people agree to undertake tailoring services for their customers on the condition that the wages so earned will go to a joint pool which shall be distributed between them irrespective of the size of work each partner has actually done, this partnership will be a shirkat-ul-aamal which is also called Shirkat-ut-taqabbul or Shirkat-us-sanai or Shirkat-ul-abdan.

Shirkat-ul-wujooh (Partnership in goodwill)

The word has its root in the Arabic word Wajahat meaning goodwill. Here the partners have no investment at all. They purchase commodities on deferred price, by getting capital on loan because of their goodwill and sell them at spot. The profit so earned is distributed between them at an agreed ratio.Each of the above three types of Shirkat-ul-Aqd are further divided into two types:

a. Shirkat-Al-Mufawada: (Capital & labour at par): All partners share capital, management, profit, and risk in absolute equals. It is a necessary condition for all four categories to be shared amongst the partners; if any one category is not is not shared, then the partnership becomes Shirkat-ul-Ainan. Every partner who shares equally is a Trustee, Guarantor and Agent on behalf of the other partners.
b. Shirkat-ul-Ainan: A more common type of Shirkat-ul-Aqd where equality in capital, management or liability might be equal in one case but not in all respect meaning either profit is equal but not labour or vice versa.

All these modes of "Sharing" or partnership are termed as "Shirkah" in the terminology of Islamic Fiqh, while the term "Musharakah" is not found in the books of Fiqh. This term (i.e. Musharakah) has been introduced recently by those who have written on the subject of Islamic modes of financing and it is normally restricted to a particular type of "Shirkah", that is, the Shirkat-ul-Amwal, where two or more persons invest some of their capital in a joint commercial venture. However, sometimes it includes Shirkat-ul-Aamal also where partnership takes place in the business of services.

It is evident from this discussion that the term "Shirkah" has a much wider sense than the term "Musharakah" as is being used today. The latter is limited to "Shirkat-ul-Amwal" only i.e. all the partners invest some capital into a commercial enterprise, while the former includes all types of joint ownership and those of partnership.

Rules and Conditions of Shirkat-ul-Aqd

Common conditions are three which are as follows:

1. The existence of Muta'aqideen (Partners): Capability of Partners: Must be sane & mature and be able of entering into a contract. The contract must take place with free consent of the parties without any fraud or misrepresentation.
2. The presence of the commodity: This means the price and commodity itself.
3. Special Conditions
    a. The commodity should be capable of an Agency: The object in the contract must qualify as a commodity having value and not as a free good which is accessible to all. For example, grass or wood cannot be made the subject matter. As each partner is responsible for managing the project, he will directly influence the overall profitability of the business. As a result, each member in Shirkat-ul-Aqd should duly qualify as legally being eligible of becoming an agent and of carrying on business, e.g., 'A' has written a book and

owns it, 'B' cannot sell it unless 'A' appoints 'B' as his agent.

b. The rate of profit sharing should be determined: The share of each partner in the profit earned should be identified at the time of the contract. If however, the ratio is not determined before hand the contract becomes void (Fasid). Therefore identifying the profit share is necessary.

c. Profit and Loss Sharing: All partners will share in profit as well as loss. By placing the burden of loss solely on one or a few partners makes the partnership invalid. A condition for Shirkat-ul-Aqd is that the partners will jointly share the profit. However, defining an absolute value is not permissible, therefore only a percentage of the total return is allowed.

The Basic Rules of Musharakah

Musharakah or Shirkat-ul-amwal is a relationship established by the parties through a mutual contract. Therefore, it goes without saying that all the necessary ingredients of a valid contract must be present here also. For example, the parties should be capable of entering into a contract; the contract must take place with free consent of the parties without any duress, fraud or misrepresentation, etc.

But there are certain ingredients, which are peculiar to the contract of Musharakah. They are summarized here as below:

i. Basic Rules of Capital

The capital in a Musharakah agreement should be:

a. Quantified (Ma'loom): Meaning how much etc.

b. Specified (Muta'aiyan): Meaning specified currency etc.

c. Not necessarily be merged: The mixing of capital is not required.

d. Not necessarily be in liquid form: Capital share may be contributed either in cash/liquid or in the form of commodities. In case of a commodity, the market value of the commodity shall determine the share of the partner in the capital.

ii. Management of Musharakah

The normal principle of Musharakah is that every partner has a right to take part in its management and to work for it. However, the partners may agree upon a condition that the management shall be carried out by one of them, and no other partner shall work for the Musharakah. But in this case the sleeping partner shall be entitled to the profit only to the extent of his investment, and the ratio of profit allocated to him should not exceed the ratio of his investment, as discussed earlier.

However, if all the partners agree to work for the joint venture, each one of them shall be treated as the agent of the other in all matters of business. Any work done by one of them in the normal course of business shall be deemed as authorized by all partners.

iii. Basic Rules of Distribution of Profit

1. The ratio of profit for each partner must be determined in proportion to the actual profit accrued to the business and not in proportion to the capital invested by him. E.g. if it is agreed between them that 'A' will get 1% of his investment, the contract is not valid.
2. It is not allowed to fix a lump sum amount for anyone of the partners or any rate of profit tied up with his investment. Therefore if 'A' & 'B' enter into a partnership and it is agreed between them that 'A' shall be given Rs.10,000/- per month as his share in the profit and the rest will go to 'B', the partnership is invalid.
3. If both partners agree that each will get percentage of profit based on his capital percentage, whether both work or not, it is allowed.
4. It is also allowed that if an investor is working, his profit share (%) could be more than his capital base (%) irrespective whether the other partner is working or not. E.g. if 'A' & 'B' have invested Rs.1000/- each in a business and it is agreed that only 'A' will work

and will get 2/3rd of the profit while 'B' will get 1/3rd. Similarly if the condition of work is also imposed on 'B' in the agreement, then also the proportion of profit for 'A' can be more than his investment.

5. If a partner has put an express condition in the agreement that he will not work for the Musharakah and will remain a sleeping partner throughout the term of Musharakah, then his share of profit cannot be more than the ratio of his investment. However, Hanbali school of thought considers fixing the sleeping partners share more than his investment to be permissible.
6. It is allowed that if a partner is not working, his profit share can be established as less than his capital share.
7. If both are working partners, the share of profit can differ from the ratio of investment. E.g., Zaid & Bakar both have invested Rs.1000/- each. However Zaid gets 1/3rd of the total profit and Bakar 2/3rd, this is allowed. This opinion of Imam Abu Hanifa is based on the fact that capital is not the only factor for profit but also labour and work are. Therefore although the investment of two partners is the same but in some cases quantity and quality of work might differ.
8. If only a few partners are active and others are only sleeping partners, then the share in the profit of the active partner could be fixed at higher than his ratio of investment eg. 'A' & 'B' put in Rs.100 each and it is agreed that only 'A' will work, then 'A' can take more than 50% of the profit as his share. The excess he receives over his investment will be compensation for his services.

iv. Basic rules of distribution of Loss

All scholars are unanimous on the principle of loss sharing in Shariah based on the saying of Syedna Ali ibn Talib that is as follows:

"Loss is distributed exactly according to the ratio of investment and the profit is divided according to the agreement of the partners."

Therefore, the loss is always subject to the ratio of investment eg. if 'A' has invested 40% of the capital and 'B' 60%, they must suffer the loss in the same ratio, not more, not less. Any condition contrary to this principle shall render the contract invalid.

Powers & Rights of Partners in Musharakah

After entering into a Musharakah contract, partners have the following rights:

i. The right to sell the mutually owned property, since all partners are representing each other in Shirkah and all have the right to buy & sell for business purposes.
ii. The right to buy raw material or other stock, on cash or credit, using funds belonging to Shirkah for putting into business.
iii. The right to hire people for carrying out business if needed.
iv. The right to deposit money & goods of the business belonging to Shirkah as depositor trust, where and when necessary.
v. The right to use Shirkah's fund or goods in Mudarabah.
vi. The right of giving Shirkah's funds as hiba (gift) or loan: If one partner for purpose of investing in the business has taken a Qard-e-Hasana, then paying it becomes liable on both.

Termination of Musharakah

Musharakah will stand terminated in the following cases:

i. If the purpose of forming the Shirkah has been achieved: For example, if two partners had formed a Shirkah for a certain project, say, e.g., for buying a specific quantity of cloth in order to sell it and the cloth is purchased and sold with mutual investment, the rules are simple and clear in this case. The distribution of profit will be as per the agreed rate whereas in case of loss, each partner will bear the loss according to his ratio of investment.

ii. Every partner has the right to terminate the Musharakah at any time after giving his partner a notice that will cause the Musharakah to end. For dissolving this partnership, if the assets are liquidated, they will be distributed pro-rata between the partners. However, if this is not the case, the partners may agree either: a): to liquidate the assets, or b): to distribute the assets as they are.

iii. In case of a dispute between partners whether to seek liquidation of assets or distribute non-liquid assets, the distribution of non-liquid assets will be preferred. Because after the termination of Musharakah, all the assets are in the joint ownership of the partners and a co-owner has a right to seek partition or separation and no one can compel him on liquidation. But if the assets are in a form that cannot be distributed such as machinery, then they shall be sold and the sale-proceeds shall be distributed.

iv. In case of a death of any one of the partners or any partner becoming insane or incapable of effecting commercial transaction, the Musharakah stands terminated.

v. In case of damage to the share capital of one partner before mixing the same in the total investment and before affecting the purchase, the partnership will stand terminated and the loss will only be borne by that particular partner. However, if the share capital of all partners has been mixed and could not be identified singly, then the loss will be shared by all and the partnership will not be terminated.

Termination of Musharakah without Closing the Business

If one of the partners wants termination of the Musharakah, while the other partner or partners like to continue with the business, this purpose can be achieved by mutual agreement. The partners who want to run the business may purchase the share of the partner who wants to terminate his partnership, because the termination of Musharakah with one partner does not imply its termination between the other partners.

However, in this case, the price of the share of the leaving partner must be determined by mutual consent. If there is a dispute about the valuation of the share and the partners do not arrive at an agreed price, the leaving partner may compel other partners on the liquidation or on the distribution of the assets themselves.

The question arises whether the partners can agree, while entering into the contract of the Musharakah, on a condition that the liquidation or separation of the business shall not be effected unless all the partners or the majority of them wants to do so. And that a single partner who wants to come out of the partnership shall have to sell his share to the other partners and shall not force them on liquidation or separation.

This condition may be justified, especially in the modern situations, on the ground that the nature of business, in most cases today, requires continuity for its success, and the liquidation or separation at the instance of a single partner only may cause irreparable damage to the other partners.

If a particular business has been started with huge amounts of money which has been invested in a long-term project, and one of the partners seeks liquidation in the infancy of the project, it may be fatal to the interests of the partners, as well as to the economic growth of the society, to give him such an arbitrary power of liquidation or separation. Therefore, such a condition seems to be justified, and it can be supported by the general principle laid down by the Holy Prophet in his famous hadith:

"All conditions agreed upon by the Muslims are upheld, except a condition which allows what is prohibited or prohibits what is lawful".

Dispute Resolution

There shall be a provision for adjudication by a Review Committee to resolve any difference that may arise between the bank and its clients (partners) with respect to any of the provisions contained in the Musharakah Agreement.

Security in Musharakah

In case of Musharakah agreement between the Bank and the client, the bank shall in its own right and discretion, obtain adequate security from the party to ensure safety of the capital invested/ financed as also for the profit that may be earned as per profit projection given by the party. The securities obtained by the bank shall, also as usual, be kept fully insured at the party's cost and expenses till Islamic mode of insurance i.e. Takaful becomes operational. The purpose of this security is to utilize this only in case of damage or loss of the principal amount due to the negligence of the client.

Interest based Financing Musharakah

A fixed rate of return on a loan advanced by the financier is predetermined irrespective of the profit earned or loss suffered by the debtor. Musharakah does not envisage a fixed rate of return. The return is based on the actual profit earned by the joint venture.

The financier cannot suffer loss. The financier can suffer loss, if the joint venture fails to produce fruits. Results in injustice either to the creditor or to the debtor: If the debtor suffers a loss, it is unjust on the part of the creditor to claim a fixed rate of profit. Also if the debtor earns a very high rate of profit, it is injustice to the creditor to give him only small proportion of the profit leaving the rest for the debtor. The returns of the creditor are tied up with the actual profits accrued through the enterprise.The greater the profits of enterprise the higher the rate of return to the creditor. If the enterprise earns enormous profits, all of it cannot be secured by the debtor exclusively but will be shared by common people e.g. depositors in the bank.

Issues relating to Musharakah

Musharakah is a mode of financing in Islam. Following are some issues relating to the tenure of Musharakah, redemption in Musharakah and the mixing of capital in conducting musharakah. These were discussed earlier. These are explained in detail here.

Liquidity of Capital

A question commonly asked in the operation of Musharakah is whether the capital invested needs to be in liquid form or not. The answer as to whether the contract in Musharakah can be based on commodities only or on money varies among the different schools of thought in Islam. For example if Zaid and Bakar agree to invest Rs.1000 each in a garment business and both keep their investments with themselves. Then if Zaid buys cloth with his investment will it be considered belonging to both Zaid and Bakar or only to Zaid? Furthermore if the cloth is sold, can Zaid alone claim the profit or loss on the sale? In order to answer this question the prime consideration should be whether the partnership becomes effective without mixing the two investments profit or loss. This issue can be resolved in the light of the following schools of thought of different fiqhs:

Imam Malik is of the view that liquidity is not a condition for the validity of Musharakah. Therefore even if a partner contributes in kind to the partnership his share can be determined on the basis of the evaluation according to the prevalent market price at the date of the contract. However Imam Hanifa and Imam Ahmad do not allow capital of investment to be in kind. The reason for this restriction is as follows:

a. Commodities contributed by one partner will always be distinguishable from the commodities given by the other partners therefore they cannot be treated as homogenous capital.
b. If in case of redistribution of share capital to the partners tracing back each partners share becomes difficult. If the share capital was in the form of commodities then redistribution cannot take place because they may have been sold at that time.

Imam Shafi has an opinion dividing commodities into:

Dhawat-ul-Amthal: Commodities which if destroyed can be compensated by similar commodities in quality and quantity, such as, rice, wheat, etc.

Dhawat-ul-Qeemah: Commodities that cannot be compensated by similar commodities like animals.

Imam Shafi is of the view that commodities of the first kind may be contributed to Musharakah in the capital while the second type of commodities cannot be a part of the capital. In case of Dhawat-ul-Amthal redistribution of capital may take place by giving to each partner the similar commodities he had invested and earlier the commodities need to be mixed so well together that the commodity of one partner cannot be distinguished from commodities contributed by the other. Therefore, it should be remembered that the illiquid goods can be made capital of investment and the market value of the commodities shall determine the share of the partner in the capital.

Mixing of the Capital

In case the liquid capital is used the mixing of capital is an issue. According to Imam Shafi partners' capital should be mixed so well that it cannot be discriminated and this mixing should be done before any business is conducted. Therefore, partnership will not be completely enforceable if any kind of discrimination is present in the partners' capital. His argument is based on the reasoning that unless both investments will be mixed the investment will remain under the ownership of the original investor and any profit or loss on trade of that investment will be entitled to the original investor only. Hence such a partnership is not possible where the investment is not mixed.

According to Imam Abu Hanifa, Imam Malik and Imam Ahmed bin Hunbul the partnership is complete only with an agreement and the mixing of capital is not important. They are of the opinion that when two partners agree to form a partnership without so far mixing their capital of investment, then if one partner bought some goods for the partnership with his share of investment of Rs. 100,000, these goods will be accepted as being owned by both partners and hence any profit or loss on sale of these goods should be shared according to the partnership agreement.

However, if the share of investment of one person is lost before mixing the capital or buying anything for the partnership business, then the loss will be borne solely by the person who's owned the capital and will not be shared by other partners. However if the capital of both had been mixed and then a part of whole had been lost or stolen the loss would have been borne by both.

Since in Hanafi, Maliki and Hanbali schools of thought mixing of the capital is not important therefore a very important present day issue is addressed with reference to this principle. If some companies or trading houses enter into partnership for setting up an industry to conduct business they need to open LC for importing the machinery. This LC reaches the importer through his bank. Now when the machinery reaches the port and the importing companies need to pay for taking possession the latter need to show those receipts in order to take possession of the goods.

Under Shafi school of thought, the imported goods cannot become the capital of investment but will remain in the ownership of the person opening the LC because at the time of opening the LC the capital has not been mixed and without mixing the capital Musharakah cannot come into existence. Under this situation if the goods are lost during shipment the burden of loss will fall upon the opener of the LC, even though the goods were being imported for the entire industry. This is because even though a group of companies had asked for the machinery or imported goods the importers had not mixed their capital at the time of investment.

Contrary to this since the other three schools of thought believe that partnership comes into existence at the time of agreement rather than after the capital has been mixed therefore the burden of loss will be borne by all. This has two advantages:

In case of loss the burden of loss will not fall upon one rather will be shared by all firms of the partner. If the capital is provided at the time of the agreement it stays blocked for the period during which the machinery is being imported.

While if the capital was not kept idle, till the actual operation could be conducted with the machinery the same capital could have been used for something else as well. This shows that the decision of the three combined schools of thought is better equipped to handle the current import export situation.

Tenure of Musharakah

For conducting a Musharakah agreement, questions arise pertaining to fixing the period of the agreement. For fixing the tenure of the Musharakah following conditions should be remembered:

The partnership is fixed for such a long time that at the end of the tenure no other business can be conducted. Can be for a very short time period during which partnership is necessary and neither partner can dissolve the partnership.

Under the Hanafi school of thought a person can fix the tenure of the partnership because it is an agreement and an agreement should have a fixed period of time. In the Hanbal school of thought the tenure can be fixed for the partnership as it's an agency agreement and an agency agreement in this school can be fixed. The Maliki School however says that Shirkah cannot be subjected to a fixed tenure. Shafi School like the Maliki considers fixing the tenure to be not permissible. Their argument is that fixing the period will prohibit conducting the business at the end of that period which in turn means that the fixing will prevent them from conducting the business.

Diminishing Musharakah

Another form of Musharakah, developed in the near past, is 'Diminishing Musharakah'. According to this concept, a financier and his client participate either in the joint ownership of a property or an equipment, or in a joint commercial enterprise. The share of the financier is further divided into a number of units and it is understood that the client will purchase the units of the share of the financier one by one periodically, thus increasing his own share until all the units of the financier are purchased by him so as to make him the sole owner of the property, or the commercial enterprise, as the case may be.

The Diminishing Murabahah based on the above concept has taken different shapes in different transactions. Some examples are given below:

It has been used mostly in house financing. The client wants to purchase a house for which he does not have adequate funds. He approaches the financier who agrees to participate with him in purchasing the required house. 20% of the price is paid by the client and 80% of the price by the financier. Thus, the financier owns 80% of the house while the client owns 20%. After purchasing the property jointly, the client uses the house for his residential requirement and pays rent to the financier for using his share in the property. At the same time, the share of financier is further divided in eight equal units, each unit representing 10% ownership of the house. The client promises to the financier that he will purchase one unit after three months. Accordingly, after the first term of three months he purchases one unit of the share of the financier by paying 1/10th of the price of the house. It reduces the share of the financier from 80% to 70%. Hence, the rent payable to the financier is also reduced to that extent. At the end of the second term, he purchases another unit increasing his share in the property to 40% and reducing the share of the financier to 60% and consequently reducing the rent to that proportion. This process goes on in the same fashion until after the end of two years, the client purchases the whole share of the financier reducing the share of the financier to 'zero' and increasing his own share to 100%.

This arrangement allows the financier to claim rent according to his proportion of ownership in the property and at the same time allows him periodical return of a part of his principal through purchases of the units of his share. 'A' wants to purchase a taxi to use it for offering transport services to passengers and to earn income through fares recovered from them, but he is short of funds. 'B' agrees to participate in the purchase of the taxi. Therefore, both of them purchase a taxi jointly. 80% of the price is paid by 'B' and 20% is paid by 'A'. After the taxi is purchased, it is employed to provide transport to the passengers whereby the net income of Rs. 1000/- is earned on daily basis. Since 'B' has 80% share in the taxi, it is agreed that 80% of the fare will be given to him and the rest of 20% will be retained by 'A' who has a 20% share in the taxi. It means that Rs. 800/- is earned by 'B' and Rs. 200/- by 'A' on daily basis. At the same time the share of 'B' is further divided into eight units. After three months 'A' purchases one unit from the share of 'B'. Consequently the share of 'B' is reduced to 70% and share of 'A' is increased to 30% meaning thereby that as from that date 'A' will be entitled to Rs. 300/- from the daily income of the taxi and 'B' will earn Rs 700/-. This process will go on until after the expiry of two years, the whole taxi will be owned by 'A' and 'B' will take back his original investment along with income distributed to him as aforesaid.

'A' wishes to start the business of ready-made garments but lacks the required funds for that business. 'B' agrees to participate with him for a specified period, say two years. 40% of the investment is contributed by 'A' and 60% by 'B'. Both start the business on the basis of Musharakah. The proportion of profit allocated for each one of them is expressly agreed upon. But at the same time 'B's share in the business is divided to six equal units and 'A' keeps purchasing these units on gradual basis until after the end of two years 'B' comes out of the business, leaving its exclusive ownership to 'A'. Apart from periodical profits earned by 'B', he gains the price of the units of his share which, in practical terms, tend to repay to him the original amount invested by him. Analyzed from the Shariah point of view this arrangement is composed of different transactions, which come to play their role at different stages. Therefore, each one of the foregoing three forms of diminishing Musharakah is discussed below in the light of the Islamic principles:

House Financing on the basis of Diminishing Musharakah

The proposed arrangement is composed of the following transactions:

i. Creating a joint ownership of the property (Shirkat-ul-Milk);
ii. Giving the share of the financier to the client on rent;

iii. Having promise from the client to purchase the units of share of the financier;
iv. Actual purchasing of the units at different stages; and
v. Adjusting the rental according to remaining share of the financier in the property.

Steps in detail of the Arrangement

i. The first step in the above arrangement is to create a joint ownership in the property. It has already been explained in the beginning of this chapter that 'Shirkat-ul-Milk' (joint ownership) can come into existence in different ways including joint purchase by the parties. All schools of Islamic jurisprudence have expressly allowed this. Therefore no objection can be raised against creating this joint ownership.
ii. The second part of the arrangement is that the financier leases his share in the house to his client and charges rent from him. This arrangement is also above board because there is no difference of opinion among the Muslim jurists in the permissibility of leasing one's undivided share in a property to his partner. If the undivided share is leased out to a third party its permissibility is a point of difference between the Muslim jurists. Imam Abu Hanifa and Imam Zufar are of the view that the undivided share cannot be leased out to a third party, while Imam Malik and Imam Shafi'i, Abu Yusuf and Muhammad Ibn Hasan hold that the undivided share can be leased out to any person. But so far as the property is leased to the partner himself, all of them are unanimous on the validity of 'Ijarah '.
iii. The third step in the aforesaid arrangement is that the client purchases different units of the undivided share of the financier. This transaction is also allowed. If the undivided share relates to both land and building, the sale of both is allowed according to all the Islamic schools. Similarly if the undivided share of the building is intended to be sold to the partner, it is also allowed unanimously by all the Muslim jurists. However, there is a difference of opinion if it is sold to the third party.

It is clear from the foregoing three points that each one of the transactions mentioned herein above is allowed, but the question is whether this transaction may be combined in a single arrangement. The answer is that if all these transactions have been combined by making each one of them a condition to the other, then this is not allowed in Shariah, because it is a well settled rule in the Islamic legal system that one transaction cannot be made a pre-condition for another.

However, the proposed scheme suggests that instead of making two transactions conditional to each other, there should be one sided promise from the client, firstly, to take share of the financier on lease and pay the agreed rent, and secondly, to purchase different units of the share of the financier of the house at different stages. This leads us to the fourth step, which is the enforceability of such a promise.

iv. It is generally believed that a promise to do something creates only a moral obligation on the promisor, which cannot be enforced through courts of law. However, there are a number of Muslim jurists who declare that promises are enforceable, and the court of law can compel the promisor to fulfill his promise, especially, in the context of commercial activities. Some Maliki and Hanafi jurists can be cited, in particular, who have declared that the promises can be enforced through courts of law in cases of need. The Hanafi jurists have adopted this view with regard to a particular sale called 'bai-bilwafa'. This bai-bilwafa is a special arrangement of sale of a house whereby the buyer promises to the seller that whenever the latter gives him back the price of the house, he will resell the house to him. This arrangement was in vogue in countries of central Asia, and the Hanafi jurists have declared that if the resale of the house to the original seller is made a condition for the initial sale, it is not allowed. However, if the first sale is affected without any condition, but after affecting the sale the buyer promises to resell the house whenever the seller offers to him the same price, this promise is acceptable and it creates not only a moral obligation, but also an enforceable right of the original seller. The Muslim jurists allowing this arrangement have based their view on the principle that "the promise can be made enforceable at the time of need".

Even if the promise has been made before effecting of the first sale, after which the sale has been put to effect without a condition, it is also allowed by certain Hanafi jurists.

One may raise an objection that if the promise of resale has been taken before entering into an actual sale, it practically amounts to putting a condition on the sale itself, because the promise is understood to have been entered into between the parties at the time of sale, and therefore, even if the sale is without an express condition, it should be taken as conditional because a promise in an express term has preceded it.

This objection can be answered by saying that there is a big difference between putting a condition in the sale and making a separate promise without making it a condition. If the condition is expressly mentioned at the time of sale, it means that the sale will be valid only if the condition is fulfilled, meaning thereby, that if the condition is not fulfilled in future then the present sale will become void. This makes the transaction of sale contingent on a future event, which may or may not occur. It leads to uncertainty (Gharar) in the transaction, which is totally prohibited in Shariah.

Conversely, if the sale is without any condition, but one of the two parties has promised to do something separately, then the sale cannot be held to be contingent or conditional with fulfilling of the promise. It will take effect irrespective of whether or not the promisor fulfills his promise. Even if the promisor backs out of his promise, the sale will remain effective. The most the promisee can do is to compel the promisor through court of law to fulfill his promise and if the promisor is unable to fulfill the promise, the promisee can claim actual damages he has suffered because of the default.

This makes it clear that a separate and independent promise to purchase does not render the original contract conditional or contingent. Therefore, it can be enforced. On the basis of this analysis, the diminishing Musharakah may be used for house financing on the following conditions:

a. The agreement of joint purchase, leasing and selling different units of the share of the financier should not be tied-up together in one single contract. However, the joint purchase and the contract of lease may be joined in one document whereby the financier agrees to lease his share, after joint purchase, to the client. This is allowed because, as explained in the relevant chapter, Ijarah can be affected for a future date. At the same time the client may sign one-sided promise to purchase different units of the share of the financier periodically and the financier may undertake that when the client will purchase a unit of his share, the rent of the remaining units will be reduced accordingly.
b. At the time of the purchase of each unit, sale must be affected by the exchange of offer and acceptance at that particular date.
c. It will be preferable that the purchase of different units by the client is affected on the basis of the market value of the house as prevalent on the date of purchase of that unit, but it is also permissible that a particular price is agreed in the promise of purchase signed by the client.

Diminishing Musharakah for Carrying Business of Services

The second example given above for diminishing Musharakah is the joint purchase of a taxi run for earning income by using it as a hired vehicle. This arrangement consists of the following ingredients:

Creating joint ownership in a taxi in the form of Shirkat ul-Milk: As already stated, this is allowed in Shariah. Musharakah in the income generated through the services of the taxi. It is also allowed as mentioned earlier in this chapter. Purchase of different units of the share of the financier by the client. This is again subject to the conditions already detailed in the case of House financing. However, there is a slight difference between House financing and the arrangement suggested in this second example. The taxi, when used as a hired vehicle, normally depreciates in value over time, therefore, depreciation in the value of the taxi must be kept in mind while determining the price of different units of the share of the financier.

Diminishing Musharakah in Trade

The third example of diminishing Musharakah as given above is that the financier contributes 60% of the capital for launching a business of ready-made garments, for example. This arrangement is composed of two ingredients only:

1. In the first place, the arrangement is simply a Musharakah whereby two partners invest different amounts of capital in a joint enterprise. This is obviously permissible subject to the conditions of Musharakah.
2. Purchase of different units of the share of the financier by the client. This may be in the form of a separate and independent promise by the client. The requirements of Shariah regarding this promise are the same as explained in the case of House financing with one very important difference. Here the price of units of the financier cannot be fixed in the promise to purchase, because if the price is fixed before hand at the time of entering into Musharakah, it will practically mean that the client has ensured the principal invested by the financier with or without profit, which is strictly prohibited in the case of Musharakah.

Therefore, there are two options for the financier about fixing the price of his units to be purchased by the client. One option is that he agrees to sell the units on the basis of valuation of the business at the time of the purchase of each unit. If the value of the business has increased, the price will be higher and if it has decreased the price will be less. Such valuation may be carried out in accordance with the recognized principles through the experts, whose identity may be agreed upon between the parties when the promise is signed. The second option is that the financier allows the client to sell these units to any body else at whatever price he can, but at the same time he offers a specific price to the client, meaning thereby that if he finds a purchaser of that unit at a higher price, he may sell it to him, but if he wants to sell it to the financier, the latter will be agreeable to purchase it at the price fixed by him before hand.

Although both these options are available according to the principles of Shariah, the second option does not seem to be feasible for the financier, because it would lead to injecting new partners in the Musharakah which will disturb the whole arrangement and defeat the purpose of Diminishing Musharakah in which the financier wants to get his money back within a specified period. Therefore, in order to implement the objective of Diminishing Musharakah, only the first option is practical.

Uses

All purchase of fixed assets house financing plant & factory financing car / transport financing project financing of fixed assets.

FIVE KHIYARS

The term khiyar refers to the option or right of the buyer and seller to rescind a contract of sale. There are five khiyars in a sale contract which are as follows:

i. Khiyar-e-Shart (Optional condition): At the time of sale Buyer or Seller can put a condition that he has an option to rescind the sale within the specific 4 days. This option is called Khiyar-e-Shart.

   Specification of the days is necessary for this Khiyar. Within this period, he has the right to rescind/dissolve the sale without any reason. If the buyer puts the condition, it is called Khiyar-e-Mushtari (option of buyer) and when put by the seller it is called Khiyar-e-Bai (option of seller). This Khiyar is not transferred to heirs.

ii. Khiyar-e-Roiyyat (Option of inspecting goods): Where the goods can be returned after inspection. This applies automatically to all contracts. E.g. 'A' buys machinery from 'B' without seeing. However, 'A' has the option to return the machinery after inspection.

iii. Khiyar-e-Aib (Option of defect): Where the goods can be returned if found defective. It is the responsibility of the seller to supply goods free of error/defect or point out the defect to the buyer. No way is he allowed to cover the defect of the goods which constitutes as fraud. In one of the hadiths, Prophet has stated "He is not amongst us who indulges in fraud." Therefore the buyer has the right to return the good in case of a defect which is considered a defect in the market and which depreciates the value of the goods. E.g., 'A' buys batteries from 'B'. However, 'A' has the option to return them to 'B' if the batteries are found to be defective or not in working condition.

iv. Khiyar-e-Wasf (Option of quality): Where the goods are sold by specifying a certain quality by the Seller but which is absent in the goods. E.g. 'A' buys a car from 'B' who has specified automatic transmission of the car. However when 'A' uses the car, he finds the transmission to be manual. Therefore he can return the car to 'B' in the absence of a specific quality.

v. Khiyar-e-Ghaban (Option of price): Where the seller sells the goods at a price which is far expensive than the market price, a Buyer has the right to return it to the seller. E.g., a Parker pen is sold to 'A' by 'B' at a price of Rs.500/-. However after the sale, 'A' discovers its market price to be Rs.250/-, he has the option to return the pen to 'B'.

Iqala (Recession of Contract)

Where parties freely consent to rescind the contract i.e. each party will give back the consideration received by it. Neither the buyer nor the seller has the sole right to rescind the contract after execution of a contract. Often the buyer wants to rescind the contract after buying goods. In this case, it is necessary that he gets the seller's consent. Therefore this mutual agreement between buyer and seller to rescind the contract is called Iqala.

In one of the hadiths, Prophet has stated "He who does the Iqala (rescinding of the contract) with a Muslim who is not happy with his transaction, Allah will forgive his sins on the Day of Judgment."

However, it may be noted that the price of the goods being returned under Iqala will remain unchanged. Effect on third parties Iqala is treated as a new sale as if a new contract is entered into between the parties rescinding the original contract.

BAI' MUAJJAL

Bai' Muajjal is the Arabic acronym for "sale on deferred payment basis". The deferred payment becomes a loan payable by the buyer in a lump sum or installment (as agreed between the two parties). In Bai' Muajjal all those items can be sold on deferred payment basis which come under the definition of capital where quality does not make a difference but the intrinsic value does. Those assets do not come under definition of capital where quality can be compensated for by the price and Shariah scholars have an 'ijmah' (consensus) that demanding a high price in deferred payment in such a case is permissible.

Conditions for Bai' Muajjal

1. The price to be paid must be agreed and fixed at the time of the deal. It may include any amount of profit without qualms about riba.
2. Complete/total possession of the object in question must be given to the buyer, while the deferred price is to be treated as debt against him.
3. Once the price is fixed, it cannot be decreased in case of earlier payment nor can it be increased in case of default.
4. In order to secure the payment of price, the seller may ask the buyer to furnish a security either in the form of mortgage or in the form of an item.
5. If the commodity is sold on installments, the seller may put a condition on the buyer that if he fails to pay any installment on its due date, the remaining installments will become due immediately.

5

Islamic Financing

FINANCING

There are four main areas where the Islamic banks find it difficult to finance under the PLS scheme: a) participating in long-term low-yield projects, b) financing the small businessman, c) granting non-participating loans to running businesses, and d) financing government borrowing.

a. Long-term Projects

Table 5.1 shows the term structure of investment by 20 Islamic Banks in 1988. It is clear that less than 10 percent of the total assets go into medium- and long-term investment. Admittedly, the banks are unable or unwilling to participate in long-term projects. This is a very unsatisfactory situation.

Table 5.1

Term Structure of Investment by 20 Islamic Banks, 1988

Type of Investment	Amount*	% of Total
Short-term	4,909.8	68.4
Social lending	64.2	0.9
Real-estate investment	1,498.2	20.9
Medium- and long-term investment	707.7	9.8

The main reason of course is the need to participate in the enterprise on a PLS basis which involves time consuming complicated assessment procedures and negotiations, requiring expertise and experience. The banks do not seem to have developed the latter and they seem to be averse to the former. There are no commonly accepted criteria for project evaluation based on PLS partnerships. Each single case has to be treated separately with utmost care and each has to be assessed and negotiated on its own merits. Other obvious reasons are: a) such investments tie up capital for very long periods, unlike in conventional banking where the capital is recovered in regular instalments almost right from the beginning, and the uncertainty and risk are that much higher, b) the longer the maturity of the project the longer it takes to realise the returns and the banks, therefore, cannot pay a return to their depositors as quick as the conventional banks can. Thus it is no wonder that the banks are averse to such investments.

b. Small businesses

Small scale businesses form a major part of a country's productive sector. Besides, they form a greater number of the bank's clientele. Yet it seems difficult to provide them with the necessary financing under the PLS scheme, even though there is excess liquidity in the banks. The observations of Iqbal and Mirakhor are revealing:

> Given the comprehensive criteria to be followed in granting loans and monitoring their use by banks, small-scale enterprises have, in general encountered greater difficulties in obtaining financing than their large-scale counterparts in the Islamic Republic of Iran. This has been particularly relevant for the construction and service sectors, which have large share in the gross domestic product (GDP). The service sector is made up of many small producers for whom the banking sector has not been able to provide sufficient financing. Many of these small producers who were traditionally able to obtain interest-based credit facilities on the basis of collateral are now finding it difficult to raise funds for their operations.

c. Running businesses

Running businesses frequently need short-term capital as well as working capital and ready cash for miscellaneous on-the-spot purchases and sundry expenses. This is the daily reality in the business world. Very little thought seems to have been given to this important aspect of the business world's requirement. The PLS scheme is not geared to cater to this need. Even if there is complete trust and exchange of information between the bank and the business it is nearly impossible or prohibitively costly to estimate the contribution of such short-term financing on the return of a given business. Neither is the much used mark-up system suitable in this case. It looks unlikely to be able to arrive at general rules to cover all the different situations.

Added to this is the delay involved in authorising emergency loans. One staff member of the Bank of Industry and Mines of Iran has commented:

Often the clients need to have quick access to fresh funds for the immediate needs to prevent possible delays in the project's implementation schedule. According to the set regulations, it is not possible to bridge-finance such requirements and any grant of financial assistance must be made on the basis of the project's appraisal to determine type and terms and conditions of the scheme of financing.

The enormity of the damage or hindrance caused by the inability to provide financing to this sector will become clear if we realise that running businesses and enterprises are the mainstay of the country's very economic survival.

d. Government borrowing

In all countries the Government accounts for a major component of the demand for credit - both short-term and long-term. Unlike business loans these borrowings are not always for investment purposes, nor for investment in productive enterprises. Even when invested in productive enterprises they are generally of a longer-term type and of low yield. This latter only multiplies the difficulties in estimating a rate of return on these loans if they are granted under the PLS scheme. In Iran,...... it has been decreed that financial transactions between and among the elements of the public sector, including Bank Markazi [the central bank] and commercial banks that are wholly nationalised, can take place on the basis of a fixed rate of return; such a fixed rate is not viewed as interest. Therefore the Government can borrow from the nationalised banking system without violating the Law.

While the last claim may be subject to question, there is another serious consequence; continued-borrowing on a fixed rate basis by the Government would inevitably index bank charges to this rate than to the actual profits of borrowing entities.

LEGISLATION

Existing banking laws do not permit banks to engage directly in business enterprises using depositors' funds. But this is the basic asset acquiring method of Islamic banks. Therefore new legislation and/or government authorisation are necessary to establish such banks. In Iran a comprehensive legislation was passed to establish Islamic banks. In Pakistan the Central Bank was authorised to take the necessary steps. In other countries either the banks found ways of using existing regulations or were given special accommodation. In all cases government intervention or active support was necessary to establish Islamic banks working under the PLS scheme.

In spite of this, there is still need for further auxiliary legislation in order to fully realise the goals of Islamic banking. For example, in Pakistan, the new law has been introduced without fundamental changes in the existing laws governing contracts, mortgages, and pledges. Similarly no law has been introduced to define modes of participatory financing, that is, Musharaka*h* and PTCs. It is presumed that whenever there is a conflict between the Islamic banking framework and the existing law, the latter will prevail. In essence, therefore, the relationship between the bank and the client, that of creditor and debtor is left unchanged as specified by the existing law. The existing banking law was developed to protect mainly the credit transactions; its application to other modes of financing results in the treatment of those modes as credit transactions also. Banks doubt whether some contracts, though consistent with the Islamic banking framework, would be acceptable in the courts. Hence, incentives exist for default and abuse.

In Iran, although the law establishing interest-free banking is comprehensive, the lack of proper definitions of property rights may have constrained bank lending. Thus far there has been no precise legislative and legal expression of what is viewed as "lawful and conditional" private property rights. This may also have militated against investment lending in agricultural and industrial sectors and thus encouraged increased concentration of assets in short-term trade financing instruments.

Iran and Pakistan are countries committed to ridding their economies of riba and have made immense strides in towards achieving it. Yet there are many legal difficulties still to be solved as we have seen above. In other Muslim countries the authorities actively or passively participate in the establishment of Islamic banks on account of their religious persuasion. Such is not the case in non-Muslim countries. Here establishing Islamic banks involves conformation to the existing laws of the concerned country which generally are not conducive to PLS type of financing in the banking sector.

INVOLVEMENT IN SPECIALISED NON-BANK ACTIVITIES

Dr Hasanuz-Zaman, lists the traditional tasks of the bank and then questions its ability to take on the additional functions it is called upon to perform under the PLS scheme:

It is due to historical reasons that banks have evolved purely as a financial institution. They are suited to attract money, keep it in safe custody, lend it under safety, invest it profitably and enjoy the capacity to create the means of payment. A bank has to maintain a balance between income, liquidity and flexibility. While allocating its funds it has to be meticulously sensitive about the factors like capital position and rate of profitability of various types of loans, stability of deposit, economic conditions, influence of monetary and fiscal policy, ability and experience of bank's personnel and credit needs of the area. So far these banks thrive on a fixed rate of return a portion of which is passed on by them to the depositor. Thus the entire effort of a bank is directed towards money management and it is not geared to act as an entrepreneur, trader, industrialist, contractor or caterer.

The question arises: with all these limitations can a bank claim any competence in trading or entrepreneurship which is necessary for musharakah or mudarba contract, or can it act as an owner of a large variety of heavy machinery, transport vehicles or real estate to take the position of a lessor or, can it act as a stockist to buy and resell the entire stock of imports and exports that are needed by genuine traders?

Then he raises the even more serious question:

In case the bank is historically and practically not competent to do all these jobs its claim to share a portion of profits as a working partner, trader or lessor becomes questionable.

Traditional banks do perform a certain amount of project evaluation when granting large medium- and long-term loans. But doing such detailed evaluation as would be required to embark on a PLS scheme, such as determining the rates of return and their time schedule, is beyond the scope of conventional banks. So is the detailed accounting and monitoring necessary to determine the actual performance.

Under Islamic banking these exercises are not limited to relatively few large loans but need to be carried out on nearly all the advances made by the bank. Yet, widely acceptable and reliable techniques are yet to be devised. This is confounded by the fact that no consensus has yet been reached on the principles. Both the unprecedented nature of the task as well as the huge amount of work that need be done and the trained and experienced personnel needed to carry them out seems a daunting prospect.

RE-TRAINING OF STAFF

The bank staff will have to acquire many new skills and learn new procedures to operate the Islamic banking system.

This is a time consuming process which is aggravated by two other factors. One, the sheer number of persons that need to be re-trained and, two, the additional staff that need to be recruited and trained to carry out the increased work.

Principles are still to be laid down and techniques and procedures evolved to carry them out. It is only after the satisfactory achievement of these that proper training can begin. This delay and the resulting confusion appear to be among the main reasons for the banks to stick to modes of financing that are close to the familiar interest-based modes.

OTHER DISINCENTIVES

Among the other disincentives from the borrower's point of view are the need to disclose his accounts to the bank if he were to borrow on the PLS basis, and the fear that eventually the tax authorities will become wise to the extent of his business and the profits. Several writers have lashed out at the lack of business ethics among the business community, but that is a fact of life at least for the foreseeable future. There is a paucity of survey or case studies of clients to see their reaction to current modes of financing. As such we are not aware of further disincentives that might be there.

ACCOUNTS

When a business is financed under the PLS scheme it is necessary that the actual profit/loss made using that money be calculated. Though no satisfactory methods have yet been devised, the first requirement for any such activity is to have the necessary accounts. On the borrowers' side there are two difficulties: one, many small-time businessmen do not keep any accounts, leave alone proper accounts. The time and money costs will cut into his profits. Larger businesses do not like to disclose their real accounts to anybody. On the banks' side the effort and expense involved in checking the accounts of many small accounts is prohibitive and will again cut into their own share of the profits. Thus both sides would prefer to avoid having to calculate the actually realised profit/loss. To quote Iqbal and Mirakhor:

The commercial banks do face an element of moral hazard owing to the non-existence of systematic book-keeping in this sector. Additionally the reluctance of small producers to submit their operations to bank audits and the perceived enormous cost of auditing and monitoring relative to the small size of the potential credits makes banks unwilling to extend credit on the basis of new modes of financing to these small producers. These reduced lending to small producers may also explain the existence of excess liquidity in the banking system.

TAX

The bank is a big business and it has to declare its profit and loss and is legally required to present an audited account of its operations. Once the bank's accounts are known it doesn't take much for the tax collectors to figure out the share of the businesses financed by the bank under the PLS scheme. Thus it's no surprise that businesses are not too very happy about the situation. The fact that suggestions have been made to use the banks to collect taxes due has not helped the matter either.

EXCESS LIQUIDITY

Presence of excess liquidity is reported in nearly all Islamic banks. This is not due to reduced demand for credit but the due to the inability of the banks to find clients willing to be funded under the new modes of financing. Here we have a situation where there is money available on the one hand and there is need for it on the other but the new rules stand in the way of bringing them together! This is a very strange situation especially in the developing Muslim countries where money is at a premium even for ordinary economic activities, leave alone development efforts. Removal of riba was expected to ease such difficulties, not to aggravate the already existing ones!

UNEASY QUESTIONS OF MORALITY

The practices in use by the Islamic banks have evoked questions of morality. Do the practices adopted to avoid interest really do their job or is it simply a change of name? It suffices to quote a few authors.

The Economist writes:

..... Muslim theoreticians and bankers have between them devised ingenious ways of coping with the interest problem. One is murabaha. The Koran says that you cannot borrow $100m from the bank for a year, at 5% interest, to buy the new machinery your factory needs? Fine. You get the bank to buy the machinery for you - costing $100m - and then, you buy the stuff from the bank, paying it $105m a year from now. The difference is that the extra $5m is not interest on loan, which the Koran (perhaps) forbids, but your thanks to the bank for the risk it takes of losing money while it is the owner of the machinery: this is honest trading, okay with the Koran. Since with modern communications the bank's ownership may last about half a second, its risk is not great, but the transaction is pure. It is not surprising that some Muslims uneasily sniff logic-chopping here.

Dr Ghulam Qadir says of practices in Pakistan:

Two of the modes of financing prescribed by the State Bank, namely financing through the purchase of client's property with a buy-back agreement and sale of goods to clients on a mark-up, involved the least risk and were closest to the old interest-based operations. Hence the banks confined their operations mostly to these modes, particularly the former, after changing the simple buy-back agreement (prescribed by the State Bank) to buy-back agreement with a mark-up, as otherwise there was no incentive for them to extend any finances. The banks also reduced their mark-up-based financing, whether through the purchase of client's property or through the sale of goods to clients, to mere paper work, instead of actual buying of goods (property), taking their possession and then selling (back) to the client. As a result, there was no difference between the mark-up as practised by the banks and the conventional interest rate, and hence it was judged repugnant to Islam in the recent decision of the Federal Shari'ah court.

As banks are essentially financial institutions and not trading houses, requiring them to undertake trading in the form of buy-back arrangements and sale on mark-up amounts to imposing on them a function for which they are not well equipped. Therefore, banks in Pakistan made such modifications in the prescribed modes which defeated the very purpose of interest-free financing. Furthermore, as these two minimum-risk modes of financing were kept open to banks, they never tried to devise innovative and imaginative modes of financing within the framework of musharakah and mudarba.

Prof. Khurshid Ahmad says:

Murabaha (cost-plus financing) and bai' mu'ajjal (sale with deferred payment) are permitted in the Shari'ah under certain conditions. Technically, it is not a form of financial mediation but a kind of business participation. The Shari'ah assumes that the financier actually buys the goods and then sells them to the client. Unfortunately, the current practice of "buy-back on mark-up" is not in keeping with the conditions on which murabaha or bai' mu'ajjal are permitted. What is being done is a fictitious deal which ensures a predetermined profit to the bank without actually dealing in goods or sharing any real risk. This is against the letter and spirit of Shari'ah injunctions.

While I would not venture a fatwa, as I do not qualify for that function, yet as a student of economics and Shari'ah I regard this practice of "buy-back on mark-up" very similar to riba and would suggest its discontinuation. I understand that the Council of Islamic Ideology has also expressed a similar opinion.

Dr Hasanuz Zaman is more scathing in his condemnation:

It emerges that practically it is impossible for large banks or the banking system to practise the modes like mark-up, bai' Salam, buy-back, murabaha , etc. in a way that fulfils the Shari'ah conditions. But in order to make themselves eligible to a return on their operations, the banks are compelled to play tricks with the letters of the law. They actually do not buy, do not posses, do not actually sell and deliver the goods; but the transition is assumed to have taken place. By signing a number of documents of purchase, sale and transfer they might fulfil a legal requirement but it is by violating the spirit of prohibition.

It seems that in large number of cases the ghost of interest is haunting them to calculate a fixed rate percent per annum even in musharakah, mudarba, leasing, hire-purchase, rent sharing, murabaha , (bai' mu'ajjal, mark-up), PTC, TFC, etc. The spirit behind all these contracts seems to make a sure earning comparable with the prevalent rate of interest and, as far as possible, avoid losses which otherwise could occur.

To sum up, in Dr Hasanuz Zaman's words:

Many techniques that the interest-free banks are practising are not either in full conformity with the spirit of Shari'ah or practicable in the case of large banks or the entire banking system. Moreover, they have failed to do away with undesirable aspects of interest. Thus, they have retained what an Islamic bank should eliminate.

ISLAMIC BANKING IN NON-MUSLIM COUNTRIES

The modern commercial banking system in nearly all countries of the world is mainly evolved from and modelled on the practices in Europe, especially that in the United Kingdom. The philosophical roots of this system revolve round the basic principles of capital certainty for depositors and certainty as to the rate of return on deposits. In order to enforce these principles for the sake of the depositors and to ensure the smooth functioning of the banking system Central Banks have been vested with powers of supervision and control. All banks have to submit to the Central Bank rules. Islamic banks which wish to operate in non-Muslim countries have some difficulties in complying with these rules. We will examine below the salient features.

1. Certainty of capital and return

While the conventional banks guarantee the capital and rate of return, the Islamic banking system, working on the principle of profit and loss sharing, cannot, by definition, guarantee any fixed rate of return on deposits. Many Islamic banks do not guarantee the capital either, because if there is a loss it has to be deducted from the capital. Thus the basic difference lies in the very roots of the two systems. Consequently countries working under conventional laws are unable to grant permission to institutions which wish to operate under the PLS scheme to functions as commercial banks. Two official comments, one from the UK and the other from the USA suffice to illustrate this.

Sir Leigh Pemberton, the Governor of the Bank of England, told the Arab Bankers' Association in London:

- It is important not to risk misleading and confusing the general public by allowing two essentially different banking systems to operate in parallel;
- A central feature of the banking system of the United Kingdom as enshrined in the legal framework is capital certainty for depositors. It is the most important feature which distinguished the banking sector from the other segments of the financial system;
- Islamic banking is a perfectly acceptable mode of financing but it does not fall within the definition of what constitutes banking in the UK;
- The Bank of England is not legally able to authorise under the Banking Act, an institution which does not take deposits as defined under that Act; and
- The Islamic facilities might be provided within other areas of the financial system without using a banking name.

In the United States, Mr Charles Schotte, the US Treasury Department specialist in regulatory issues has remarked:

There has never been an application for an Islamic establishment to set up either as a bank or as anything else. So there is no precedent to guide us. Any institution that wishes to use the word 'bank' in its title has to guarantee at least a zero rate of interest - and even that might contravene Islamic laws.

2. Supervision and control

Besides these, there are other concerns as well. One is the Central Bank supervision and control. This mainly relates to liquidity requirements and adequacy of capital. These in turn depend on an assessment of the value of assets of the Islamic banks. A financial advisor has this to say:

The bank of England, under the 1979 Act, would have great difficulty in putting a value on the assets of an Islamic institution which wanted to operate as a bank in the UK. The traditional banking system has much of its assets in fixed interest instruments and it is comparatively easy to value that. For example, if they are British Government instruments they will have a quoted market value; and there are recognised methods for valuing traditional banking assets when they become non-productive. But it is very difficult indeed to value an Islamic asset such as a share in a joint venture; and the Bank of England would have to send a team of experienced accountants into every Islamic bank operating in the UK as a bank under the 1979 Act, to try to put a proper and cautious value on its assets.

Another financial analyst states:

Even if a method could be found for assessing the risks to calculate the capital necessary, little comfort could be taken from the profitability which is usually relied upon to cover day-to-day losses arising from the bank's business, because a substantial part of an Islamic bank's portfolio is venture capital without any guaranteed return.

It is evident then that even if there is a desire to accommodate the Islamic system, the new procedures that need be developed and the modifications that need be made to existing procedures are so large that the chances of such accommodation in a cautious sector such as banking is very remote indeed. Any relaxation of strict supervision is precluded because should an Islamic bank fail it would undermine the confidence in the whole financial system, with which it is inevitably identified. As Suratgar puts it:

There could be potential dangers for the international system, where the failure of such an institution could bring with it the failure of other associated institutions, or of all the Western banking institutions which come closely tied to with such an operation.

CENTRAL BANKS IN MUSLIM COUNTRIES

Another important consideration is the tax procedures in non-Muslim countries. While interest is a 'passive' income, profit is an earned income which is treated differently. In addition, in trade financing there are title transfers twice - once from seller to bank and then from bank to buyer - and therefore twice taxed on this account decreasing the profitability of the venture. The Director of the International Islamic Bank of Denmark says:

Tax laws are against the Islamic philosophy and pose the greatest difficulty. In most OECD countries Mudarabha is constrained by fiscal acts which define profits as an after tax item for the profit creator and a fully taxable item for the profit receiver.

DISCUSSION AND SUGGESTIONS

People have needs-food, clothes, houses, machinery, services; the list is endless. Entrepreneurs perceive these needs and develop ways and means of catering to them. They advertise their products and services, peoples expectations are raised and people become customers of the entrepreneur. If the customers' needs are fulfilled according to their expectations they continue to patronise the entrepreneur and his enterprise flourishes. Otherwise his enterprise fails and people take to other entrepreneurs.

Banks too are enterprises; they cater to peoples' needs connected with money - safe-keeping, acquiring capital, transferring funds etc. The fact that they existed for centuries and continue to exist and prosper is proof that their methods are good and they fulfil the customers' needs and expectations. Conventional commercial banking system as it operates today is accepted in all countries except the Islamic world where it is received with some reservation. The reservation is on account of the fact that the banking operations involve dealing in interest which is prohibited in Islam. Conventional banks have ignored this concern on the part of their Muslim clientele. Muslims patronised the conventional banks out of necessity and, when another entrepreneur - the Islamic banker - offered to address their concern many Muslims turned to him. The question is: has the new entrepreneur successfully met their concerns, needs and expectations? If not he may have to put up his shutters!

Broadly speaking, banks have three types of different customers: depositors, borrowers and seekers of banks' other services, such as, money transfer. Since services do not generally involve dealing in interest Muslims have no problem transacting such businesses with conventional banks; neither do Islamic banks experience any problems in providing these services. Among the depositors there are current account holders who too, similarly, have no problems. It is the savings account holders and the borrowers who have reservations in dealing with the conventional banks. In the following paragraphs we will see how well the Islamic banks have succeeded in addressing their customers' special concern.

SAVINGS ACCOUNTS AND CAPITAL GUARANTEE

As pointed out earlier, our concern here is the savings account holders. As the name itself indicates the primary aim of the saving account depositor is the safe-keeping of his savings. It is correctly perceived by the conventional banker and he guarantees the return of the deposit in toto. The banker also assumes that the depositor will prefer to keep his money with him in preference to another who might also provide the same guarantee if the depositor is provided an incentive. This incentive is called interest, and this interest is made proportional to the amount and length of time it is left with the bank in order to encourage more money brought into the bank and left there for longer periods of time. In addition, the interest rate is fixed in advance so that the depositor and the banker are fully aware of their respective rights and obligations from the beginning. And laws have been enacted to guarantee their enforcement. In Economic theory the interest is often taken to be the "compensation" the depositors demand and receive for parting with their savings. The fact that the depositors accept the paid interest and that, given other things being equal, they prefer the bank or the scheme which offers the highest interest proves the banker's assumption correct.

The scheme is simple, transparent and seems to have satisfied the requirements of all types of savers- from teenagers to old-age pensioners, from individuals to large institutions, pension funds and endowments, from small amounts to millions, and from a few weeks or months to years. It has survived over centuries and operates across national, cultural and religious borders.

The situation is very different in the Islamic banks. Here too the depositor's first aim is to keep his savings in safe custody. Islamic bankers divide the conventional savings account into two categories (alternatively, create a new kind of account): savings account and investment account. The investment accounts operate fully under the PLS scheme - capital is not guaranteed, neither is there any pre-fixed return. Under the savings account the nominal value of the deposit is guaranteed, but they receive no further guaranteed returns. Banks may consider funds under the savings accounts too as part of their resources and use it to create assets. This is theory. In practice, however, the banks prefer, encourage and emphasise the investment accounts. This is because since their assets operate under the PLS scheme they might incur losses on these assets which losses they cannot pass onto the savings accounts depositors on account of the capital guarantee on these accounts. In the process the first aim of the depositor is pushed aside and the basic rule of commercial banking -capital guarantee- is broken.

It is suggested that all Islamic banks guarantee the capital under their savings accounts. This will satisfy the primary need and expectation of an important section of the depositors and, in Muslim countries where both Islamic and conventional banks co-exist, will induce more depositors to bank with the Islamic banks. At the same time, it will remove the major objection to establishing Islamic banks in non-Muslim countries. .

LOANS WITH A SERVICE CHARGE

All the problems of the Islamic banks arise from their need to acquire their assets under the PLS scheme. A simple solution does, in fact, already exist in the current theories of Islamic banking. It need only be pointed out and acted upon. We will examine the provisions in the Iranian, Pakistani and the Siddiqi models.

All three models provide for loans with a service charge. Though the specific rules are not identical, the principle is the same. We suggest that the funds in the deposit accounts (current and savings) be used to grant loans (short- and long-term) with a service charge. By doing this the Islamic banks will be able to provide all the loan facilities that conventional banks provide while giving capital guarantee for depositors and earning an income for themselves. This would also remove the rest of the obstacles in opening and operating Islamic banks in non-Muslim countries.

The bonus for the borrowers is that the service charge levied by the Islamic banks will necessarily be less than the interest charged by conventional banks.

Let us now look at the existing relevant rules in the three models. The Iranian model provides for *Gharz-al hasaneh* whose definition, purpose and operation are given in Articles 15, 16 and 17 of Regulations relating to the granting of banking facilities:

Article 15

Gharz-al-hasaneh is a contract in which one (the lender) of the two parties relinquishes a specific portion of his possessions to the other party (the borrower) which the borrower is obliged to return to the lender in kind or, where not possible, its cash value.

Article 16

The banks ... shall set aside a part of their resources and provide Gharz-al-hasaneh for the following purposes:

a. To provide equipment, tools and other necessary resources so as to enable the creation of employment, in the form of co-operative bodies, for those who lack the necessary means;
b. To enable expansion in production, with particular emphasis on agricultural, livestock and industrial products; and
c. To meet essential needs.

Article 17

The expenses incurred in the provision of Gharz-al-hasaneh shall be, in each case, calculated on the basis of the directives issued by Bank Markazi Jomhouri Islami Iran and collected from the borrower.

In Pakistan, permissible modes of financing include:

Financing by lending:

a. Loans not carrying any interest on which the banks may recover a service charge not exceeding the proportionate cost of the operation, excluding the cost of funds and provisions for bad and doubtful debts. The maximum service charge permissible to each bank will be determined by the State Bank from time to time.
b. Qard-e-hasana loans given on compassionate grounds free of any interest or service charge and repayable if and when the borrower is able to pay.

Siddiqi has suggested that 50 percent of the funds in the 'loan' (i.e. current and savings) accounts be used to grant short-term loans. A fee is to be charged for providing these loans:

An appropriate way of levying such a fee would be to require prospective borrowers to pay a fixed amount on each application, regardless of the amount required, the term of the loan or whether the application is granted or rejected. Then the applicants to whom a loan is granted may be required to pay an additional prescribed fee for all the entries made in the banks registers. The criterion for fixing the fees must be the actual expenditure which the banks have incurred in scrutinising the applications and making decisions, and in maintaining accounts until loans are repaid. These fees should not be made a source of income for the banks, but regarded solely as a means of maintaining and managing the interest-free loans.

It is clear from the above that all three models agree on the need for having cash loans as one mode of financing, and that this service should be paid for by the borrower. Though the details may vary, all seem to suggest that the charge should be the absolute cost only. We suggest that a percentage of this absolute cost be added to the charge as a payment to the bank for providing this service. This should enable an Islamic bank to exist and function independently of its performance in it's PLS operations.

INVESTMENT UNDER PLS SCHEME

The idea of participatory financing introduced by the Islamic banking movement is a unique and positive contribution to modern banking. However, as we saw earlier, by making the PLS mode of financing the main (often almost the only) mode of financing the Islamic banks have run into several difficulties. If, as suggested in the previous section, the Islamic banks would provide all the conventional financing through lending from their deposit accounts (current and savings), it will leave their hands free to engage in this responsible form of financing innovatively, using the funds in their investment accounts. They could then engage in genuine Mudaraba financing. Being partners in an enterprise they will have access to its accounts, and the problems associated with the non-availability of accounts will not arise.

Commenting on Mudaraba financing, *The Economist* says:

.... some people in the West have begun to find the idea attractive. It gives the provider of money a strong incentive to be sure he is doing something sensible with it. What a pity the West's banks did not have that incentive in so many of their lending decisions in the 1970s and 1980s. It also emphasises the sharing of responsibility, by all the users of money. That helps to make the free-market system more open; you might say more democratic.

Islamic banking is a very young concept. Yet it has already been implemented as the only system in two Muslim countries; there are Islamic banks in many Muslim countries and a few in non-Muslim countries as well. Despite the successful acceptance there are problems. These problems are mainly in the area of financing.

With only minor changes in their practices, Islamic banks can get rid of all their cumbersome, burdensome and sometimes doubtful forms of financing and offer a clean and efficient interest-free banking. All the necessary ingredients are already there. The modified system will make use of only two forms of financing - loans with a service charge and Mudaraba participatory financing - both of which are fully accepted by all Muslim writers on the subject.

Such a system will offer an effective banking system where Islamic banking is obligatory and a powerful alternative to conventional banking where both co-exist. Additionally, such a system will have no problem in obtaining authorisation to operate in non-Muslim countries.

Participatory financing is a unique feature of Islamic banking, and can offer responsible financing to socially and economically relevant development projects. This is an additional service Islamic banks offer over and above the traditional services provided by conventional commercial banks.

ISLAMIC BANKING TODAY

Islamic banking as a concept has gained momentum world over and in India over the past few years. Several foreign banks operating in India, like Citibank, Standard Chartered Bank, HBSC are operating interest free windows in several West Asian countries, Europe and USA. There is also a growing awareness about the concept among Indian banks and it is

6

Concepts in Islamic Banking

Islamic banking is an ethical and equitable mode of financial services that derives its principles from the Shariah (Islamic law). The Shariah is based on the Quran and the Sunnah of the Prophet Muhammad (PBUH), and it governs all aspects of personal and collective life.

The most distinctive element of Islamic banking is the prohibition of interest, whether "nominal" or "excessive," simple or compound, fixed or floating. Other elements include the emphasis on equitable contracts, the linking of finance to productivity, the desirability of profit sharing, and the prohibition of gambling and certain types of uncertainty. These parameters define the nature and scope of Islamic banking, as interpreted by the Shariah scholars that work with Islamic financial institutions.

EQUITY INSTRUMENTS

Islamic law states an explicit preference for equity financing over debt financing. The classical forms of equity financing (musharaka and Mudaraba) require partnership and profit sharing, to which the contemporary devices of venture capital, investment management and project financing can be compared.

In financial markets, investing in stocks and equity funds is permitted but must conform to certain guidelines. Not unlike ethical or socially responsible investing, undesirable companies and industries are screened out on the basis of both qualitative criteria (nature of business) and quantitative criteria (level of involvement with interest). Islamic investment also discourages speculation and precludes short selling, conventional debt instruments and conventional derivatives. These views go back to the prohibition of interest, gambling and certain types of uncertainty in Islamic law.

DEBT INSTRUMENTS

Conventional debt financing is ruled out in Islamic banking because of the prohibition of interest. Asset-backed debt financing can be designed, however, on the basis of sale (murabaha) or leasing (ijara) contracts that provide fixed income alternatives to conventional debt financing. The capital provider must have ownership of the asset, however (even if briefly), and bear the risk that comes with that ownership. Recently, cash financing (tawarruq) has also been introduced by reversing the concept of murabaha.

THE BANKING INDUSTRY

The Islamic banking industry today stands at several hundred billion dollars (estimates vary), and consists of more than 300 financial institutions in and outside the Muslim world. It is the product of the collective effort of bankers, economists, and Islamic legal scholars over the past several decades to develop financial solutions that meet the religious requirements of Muslims.

It is a young industry and a growth industry, and continues to evolve and expand both financially and geographically. It is indigenous and community-focused: it caters to devout Muslims in indigenous Muslim societies as well as in Muslim minorities of non-Muslim countries. Furthermore, it is an inclusive paradigm: non-Muslim individuals and communities that seek ethical financial solutions have also been attracted to Islamic banking.

The first modern Islamic financial institutions emerged in the 1960s and 1970s. Since then, Islamic banking has spread to a large number of Muslim countries, including the GCC and the Arab world at large, South and Southeast Asia, and even Muslim communities in the West. Bahrain is considered a hub for Islamic banking, with significant activity also taking place in Kuala Lumpur and London. Islamic financial institutions have taken the form of commercial banks, investment banks, investment and finance companies, insurance companies, and financial service companies. They follow different banking models: private institutions in a conventional economy (as in the GCC and the West), attempts at national Islamic banking systems (as in Sudan, Iran and Pakistan), and dual banking models (as in Malaysia). They also take different forms: wholly Islamic institutions, Islamic subsidiaries of conventional banking groups, and Islamic banking windows within conventional banks.

This is an industry that is still evolving, developing and growing. It has gone from commercial banking to syndicated transactions and equities, and more recently, into debt issuance and structured products. Its sophistication and product offering have developed along with this change. At an earlier stage, industry growth was in part a reflection of economic growth in the Islamic world, fuelled primarily by oil wealth. This created a growing middle-wealth segment and hence made banking a necessary service to the larger segment of the population. In the past several years, increased awareness about Islamic banking has led to conversion from conventional banking and continued high growth (15-20% in key markets).

FINANCIAL INSTRUMENTS

HSBC Amanah applies a variety of Islamic financial instruments to develop its products. Often the same instrument is used in a variety of products, each product meeting the needs of a different type of customer. This section presents the three most common Islamic financial instruments and illustrates their uses in representative products offered by HSBC Amanah.

Each instrument is explained with a definition, an overview of the transaction process and its illustration in a representative HSBC Amanah product.

MUDARABA

A Mudaraba transaction is an investment partnership. In a mudarab arrangement, the contract is between an investor (and financier) and an entrepreneur or investment manager known as the mudarib. Risk and rewards are shared. In the case of a profit, both parties receive their agreed-upon share of the profit. In the case of a loss, the investor bears any loss of capital while the mudarib loses his time and effort.

TRANSACTION PROCESSES

Mudaraba Process

A generic Mudaraba process could take the following basic form:

Step 1: The investor and the mudarib agree on the nature of the venture and the terms of profit sharing.

Step 2: The investor provides capital to the mudarib.

Step 3: The mudarib undertakes the venture agreed upon between the parties.

Step 4: Profits from the investment are shared between the investor and the mudarib.

Ijara

An ijara is an Islamic lease. The bank purchases an asset and leases it to a client for fixed monthly payments. An ijarah may include an option for the lessee to buy the asset at the end of the lease, though such a provision is not required.

Generic Ijarah process

A generic ijarah process could take the following basic form:

Step 1: The bank and the client agree on the terms of the lease.

Step 2: The bank purchases the asset from the seller.

Step 3: The client leases the asset from the bank, paying a fixed monthly rental.

Step 4: The client purchases the asset from the bank at the end of the lease period Murabaha.

A murabahah transaction is a sale at a stated profit. In a murabahah transaction, the bank purchases something from a third party and it sells it to the client at a stated profit on a deferred payment basis. In this way, the client can buy something without taking an interest-based loan.

Generic murabahah process

A generic murabahah process could take the following basic form:

Step 1: The client expresses intent to engage in a murabahah transaction facilitated by the bank and, subject to bank approval, signs a "Promise to Buy".

Step 2: The bank purchases the item from the seller.

Step 3: The client purchases the item, in instalments, at the purchase price plus a stated profit.

THE TREND IN ISLAMIC BANKING

If implemented correctly, Islamic banking and finance should be able to co-operate and co-exist with any kind of capitalism, while still adhering to ethical guidelines set by Islamic Sacred Law.

Islamic banking, which implies the avoidance of interest, has become a substantial industry during the last four decades. One obvious question is whether its emergence further segregates Muslims from Western values and norms, creating a financial ghetto.

An alternative view is that as increasing numbers of people in the West are dissatisfied or skeptical about the banking services they receive, and see them as exploitative or even unethical, the emergence of Islamic banking with its own distinctive morality results in Islam projecting a much more positive face.

Many Western bankers view Islamic finance as a curiosity, and perhaps even a business opportunity, but seldom as a threat comparable to that from Muslim extremism. Indeed, Islamic banking and finance can be regarded as a gentler aspect of Islam, and one that lends itself to dialogue between Westerners and Muslims.

Islamic retail financial institutions, including the Islamic Bank of Britain, the European Islamic Investment Bank, and Lariba Bank in California, are now well-established in a number of Western countries. Furthermore, the leading international banks, including Citibank, HSBC Amanah, Deutsche Bank and UBS of Switzerland, all offer Islamic deposits and Shari'a-compliant financing facilities.

There has been much dialogue between the Western bankers working in these institutions and the Shari'a scholars who advise what is, and what is not, permissible. This dialogue extends to insurance, where Islamic takaful companies have become increasingly active, their distinguishing feature being that they do not hold conventional interest-yielding bonds, and that shareholder funds and premiums paid by policy holders cannot be co-mingled, which could result in the former exploiting the latter's misfortune.

As Shari'a is about universal, divinely inspired principles rather than national laws, leading international law firms have also become involved in Islamic banking and finance, as contracts need to be drafted under English or American law in a way that is consistent with Shari'a. Indeed, the main job of the Shari'a committee members who serve on the boards of Islamic banks and conventional banks offering Islamic products is to ensure that new contracts are compatible with Shari'a principles and, if they are not, to pursue a dialogue with the lawyers concerning amendments and redrafting.

The aspiration of many Islamists is to have divinely inspired Shari'a replacing man-made laws, perhaps even the establishment of a universal caliphate under which everyone,

Muslim and non-Muslim, should live. Not surprisingly, such an aspiration is unacceptable for most non-Muslims, and indeed for many Muslims, as it denies choice.

Islamic banking and finance can point to the way forward: it is about extending choice, not restricting options. As each institution has its own Shari'a board, Shari'a compliance is effectively privatized, rather than being a matter of national law. Indeed, each Shari'a board passes its own fatwas, or religious rulings, which further extends choice in the marketplace for religious ideas. Religion, of course, flourishes under competitive conditions and Islam is no exception, whereas when it is nationalized, its adherents soon become alienated.

The Islamic Republic of Iran can be regarded as an example of how not to encourage the development of Islamic banking and finance. There, all banking has been Shari'a - compliant since the Law on Interest Free Banking was passed in 1983. Bank clients have therefore no choice but to use the Shari'a system. The banks, however, are state-owned and have little autonomy, even in determining what deposit and financing products to offer. They also do not have Shari'a committees, the argument being that this is unnecessary as the law ensures Shari'a compliance in any case.

The result has been that banking development has been slow, there is little financial innovation, and most Iranians do not have bank accounts. In contrast, on the Arab side of the Gulf and in Malaysia, where Islamic and conventional banks compete, Islamic banks have attractive products on offer and a growing client base. Al Rajhi Bank of Saudi Arabia has become the world's largest Islamic retail bank, and its range of services and delivery channels compares favorably with the best that Western banks can offer.

Islamic banking is here to stay, it is an opportunity rather than a threat, and it has an exciting future. Gaps remain-there is no Islamic bank in Israel, for example, to serve its Muslim population. But if the Central Bank of Israel licensed such an entity it could create much goodwill. It might also encourage the Jewish population living there to question whether the operations of their own banks are compatible with religious teaching in Leviticus and Deuteronomy.

Ultimately Islamic banking and finance is about the emergence of a distinctively Islamic form of capitalism that may co-exist and interact with Western, Chinese, Russian or any other capitalism. Such a development should be welcomed and facilitated, and not hindered or suppressed.

Proponents of the ancient practice, which looks to sharia law for guidance and bans interest and trading in debt, have been promoting Islamic finance as a cure for the global financial meltdown.

This week, Kuwait's commerce minister, Ahmad Baqer, was quoted as saying that the global crisis will prompt more countries to use Islamic principles in running their economies. U.S. Deputy Treasury Secretary Robert M. Kimmet, visiting Jiddah, said, "Experts at his agency have been learning the features of Islamic banking."

As advocates maintain that though the trillion-dollar Islamic banking industry faces challenges with the slump in real estate and stock prices, the system has built-in protection from the kind of runaway collapse that has afflicted so many institutions. For one thing, the use of financial instruments such as derivatives, blamed for the downfall of banking, insurance and investment giants, is banned. So is excessive risk-taking.

The beauty of Islamic banking and the reason it can be used as a replacement for the current market is that you only promise what you own. Advocates maintain that Islamic banks are not protected if the economy goes down. "But you don't lose your shirt", said Majed al-Refaie, who heads Bahrain-based Unicorn Investment Bank.

The theological underpinning of Islamic banking is scripture that declares that collection of interest is a form of usury, which is banned in Islam. In the modern world, that translates into an attitude toward money that is different from that found in the West: Money cannot just sit and generate more money. To grow, it must be invested in productive enterprises.

"In Islamic finance you cannot make money out of thin air." said Amr al-Faisal, a board member of Dar al-Mal al-Islami, a holding company that owns several Islamic banks and financial institutions. "Our dealings have to be tied to actual economic activity, like an asset or a service. You cannot make money off of money. You have to have a building that was actually purchased, a service actually rendered, or a good that was actually sold."

In the Western world, bankers designing investment instruments have to satisfy government regulators. In Islamic banking, there is another group to please - religious regulators called a sharia board. Finance lawyers work closely with Islamic finance scholars, who study and review a product before issuing a fatwa, or ruling, on its compliance with sharia law.

Islamic bankers describe depositors as akin to partners - their money is invested, and they share in the profits or, theoretically, the losses that result. (In interviews, bankers couldn't recall a case in which depositors actually lost money; this shows that banks put such funds only in very low-risk investments, they said.)

Rather than lend money to a home buyer and collect interest on it, an Islamic bank buys the property and then leases it to the buyer for the duration of the loan. The client pays a set amount each month to the bank, and then at the end he obtains its full ownership. The payments are structured to include the cost of the house, plus a predetermined profit margin for the bank.

Sharia-compliant institutions also cannot invest in alcohol, pornography, weapons, gambling, tobacco or pork.

Computer engineer Tarek al-Bassam said the crisis made him glad that he had chosen an Islamic bank to take his money. His Islamic savings account has made about 4 per cent profit, he said. "Usually it's a very low risk or a very low gain. But I'm happy with it," Bassam said.

He has also borrowed from an Islamic bank, to buy a building. Even if he's late in his payments, he said, he will not have to pay cumulative interest or a larger sum than the one agreed upon. But he notes that under this system, it can be harder to get a loan than from a conventional bank. Islamic banks have stricter lending rules and require that their borrowers provide more collateral and have higher income.

Islamic banking has grown by about 15 per cent a year since its modern inception in the 1970s, fueled by the Middle East oil boom of that decade. "There was a lot of hostility when we first started out. We were regarded with suspicion, especially by the regulatory authorities. We were an odd fish. Authorities only acquiesced when they saw the huge demand," said Dar al-Mal al-Islami's Faisal, who has been in Islamic finance since the late 1970s.

Islamic finance now accounts for about 1 per cent of the global market, according to Majid Dawood, chief executive of Yasaar, a Dubai-based sharia financing consultancy. "We had expected to be at 12 per cent of the global market by 2025, but now with this financial crisis, we expect to get there much faster," he said in a telephonic interview from New York, where he was speaking at a conference on Islamic banking.

Growth in Islamic banking picked up even before the current financial crisis, mainly because of strong client demand for safe, religiously acceptable investments and a recent explosion in new and innovative financial instruments, said Jane Kinninmont, an analyst at the Economist Intelligence Unit, a research and advisory company.

Islamic banks now offer credit cards in which the full balance must be paid off at month's end. They have devised a kind of commercial paper known as sukuk, which generates a predetermined return that is called a profit, not interest. It is tied to a specific asset and conveys ownership of it. A sukuk might be issued by a government or a company that is building a hospital or a bridge, for example.

Work in Islamic banking by the King and Spalding law firm has grown roughly forty-fold in the past four years, according to Jawad Ali, a Dubai-based partner at the firm. The firm has thirty five lawyers "who do nothing but structure sharia-compliant investment and financing on a daily basis," he said.

Islamic finance first sparked interest in the United States in the late 1990s. The Dow Jones Islamic Index was established in 1999, and the Dow Jones Islamic Fund, which invests in sharia-compliant companies, the following year.

But interest cooled after some Islamic banks were accused of financing terrorism in a lawsuit filed by family members of Sept. 11, 2001, victims, and a lot of Persian Gulf money left the United States for Europe.

In 2004, the German state of Saxony-Anhalt issued a 100 million-euro sovereign Islamic bond. That same year, the first Islamic bank opened in Britain, which now has six Islamic financial institutions, including a retail bank.

Although the biggest Islamic banks are in the Persian Gulf - Dubai Islamic Bank, Kuwait Finance House and Saudi Arabia's al-Rajhi Bank - Malaysia and London are growing as major centers of Islamic banking as well.

Islamic institutions are not immune to ills plaguing other banks, such as corruption charges and bad investments. Differences of interpretation between sharia scholars about what is permissible and what isn't also create confusion. The sukuk market, which had doubled each year since 2004, growing to a total of about $90 billion in bonds issued, fell 50 per cent this year after a Bahrain-based group of Islamic scholars decreed that most of the bonds were not compatible with sharia law.

But as banks turn borrowers away in these times of economic turmoil, Islamic institutions continue to close deals in Europe, the Gulf and the United States, bankers said. "Banks feel safer and more comfortable with us because we put down more money, more equity. We are not allowed to borrow with very little down," said Tariq Malhance, a former chief financial officer for the city of Chicago who now heads Unicorn

Investment Bank's U.S. office. And those who have been in Islamic banking for a long time now feel vindicated.

"The current financial collapse is an opportunity. The ugly side of Wall Street is exposed; it's always been there but covered by a layer of glamour that is now stripped away," Faisal said. "We are more conservative and sober in our investments. That used to be considered a handicap. Now it's considered the height of wisdom."

CORPORATE GOVERNANCE IN ISLAMIC BANKING

Corporate governance in banking has been analysed almost exclusively in the context of conventional banking markets. For example, there has recently been some discussion of the role 'market discipline' exerted by bank shareholders and depositors in constraining the risk taking behaviour of bank management. At the same time, there is growing interest in, and analysis of, banks as stockholders in companies themselves playing a central role in corporate governance, especially in Germany and other countries with universal banking structures of the traditional type.

By contrast, little is written on governance structures in Islamic banking, despite the rapid growth of Islamic banks since the mid 1970s and their increasing presence on world financial markets. There are now over 180 financial institutions world-wide which adhere to Islamic banking and financing principles. These banks operate in 45 countries encompassing most of the Muslim world, along with Europe, North America and various offshore locations. Islamic financing increasingly is a market segment of interest of Western banks, and the latest addition to the list of Islamic banks in October 1996 in the Citi Islamic Investment Bank, Bahrain a wholly owned subsidiary of Citicorp.

Islamic banking represents a radical departure from conventional banking, and from the viewpoint of corporate governance, it embodies a number of interesting features since equity participation, risk and profit-and-loss sharing arrangements from the basis of Islamic financing. Because of the bank on interest (riba), an Islamic bank cannot charge any fixed return in advance, but rather participates in the yield resulting from the use of funds. The depositors also share in the profits according to predetermined ratio, and are rewarded with profit returns for assuming risk. Unlike a conventional bank which is basically a borrower and lender of funds, an Islamic bank is essentially a partner with its depositors, on the one side, and also a partner with entrepreneurs, on the other side, when employing depositors' funds in productive direct investment.

These financial arrangements imply quite different stockholder relationships, and by corollary governance structures, from the conventional model since depositors have a direct financial stake in the bank's investment and equity participations. In addition, the Islamic bank is subject to an additional layer of governance since the suitability of its investment and financing must be in strict conformity with Islamic law and the expectations of the Muslim community. For this purpose, Islamic banks employ an individual sharia Advisor and/or Board.

My examination of corporate governance in Islamic banking begins with the comparing governance structures in the Islamic bank and will continue with the principles of Islamic banking. This study compares the Islamic banking, financial model and its implications for governance structures. The study intends to give a small picture on the principles of Islamic banking.

THE ISLAMIC BANK

Governance structures are quite different from these under Islamic banking because the institution must obey a different set of rules - those of the *Holy Qur'an* - and meet the expectations of Muslim community by providing Islamically-acceptable financing modes. These profit-and-loss sharing methods, in turn, imply different relationships than under interest-based borrowing and lending.

There are two major differences from the conventional framework. First, and foremost, an Islamic organisation must serve God. It must develop a distinctive corporate culture, the main purpose of which is to create a collective morality and spirituality which, when combined with the production of goods and services, sustains the growth and advancement of the Islamic way of life. To quote janachi (1995):

'Islamic banks have a major responsibility to shoulder ....all the staff of such banks and customers dealing with them must be reformed Islamically and act within the framework of an Islamic formula, so that any person approaching an Islamic bank should be given the impression that he is entering a sacred place to perform a religious ritual, that is the use and employment of capital for what is acceptable and satisfactory to God' (p.42).

There are equivalent obligations upon employees:

'The staff in an Islamic bank should, throughout their lives, be conducting in the Islamic way, whether at work or at leisure' (p.28).

Further, obligations also extend to the Islamic community:

'Muslims who truly believe in their religion have a duty to prove, through their efforts in backing and supporting Islamic banks and financial institutions, that the Islamic economic system is an integral part of Islam and is indeed for all times ... through making legitimate and Halal *profits*' (p.29).

Second, interest-free banking is based on the Islamic legal concepts of *shirkah* (partnership) and Mudaraba (profit-sharing). An Islamic bank is conceived as financial intermediary mobilising savings from the public on a Mudaraba basis and advancing capital to entrepreneurs on the same basis. A two-tiered profit-and-loss sharing arrangement operates under the following rules:

a. The bank receives funds from the public on the basis of unrestricted Mudaraba. There are no restrictions imposed on the bank concerning the kind of activity, duration, and location of the enterprise, but the funds cannot be applied to activities which are forbidden by Islam.

b. The bank has the right to aggregate and pool the profit from different investments, and share the net profit (after deducting administrative costs, capital depreciation and Islamic tax) with depositors according to a specified formula. In the event of losses, the depositors lose a proportional share or the entire amount of their funds. The return to the financier has to be strictly maintained as a share of profits.

c. The bank applies the restricted from of Mudaraba when funds are provided to entrepreneurs. The bank has the right to determine the kind of activities, the duration, and location of the projects and monitor the investments. However, these restrictions may not be formulated in a way which harms the performance of the entrepreneur, and the bank cannot interfere with the management of the investment. Loan covenants and other such constraints usual in conventional commercial bank lending are allowed.

d. The bank cannot require any guarantee such as security and collateral from the entrepreneur in order to insure its capital against the possibility of an eventual loss.

e. The liability of the financier is limited to the capital provided. On the other hand, the liability of the entrepreneur is also restricted, but in this case solely to labour and effort employed. Nevertheless, if negligence or mismanagement can be proven, the entrepreneur may be liable for the financial loss and be obliged to remunerate financier accordingly.

f. The entrepreneur shares the profit with bank according to previously agreed division. Until the investment yields a profit, the bank is able to pay a salary to the entrepreneur based on the ruling market salary.

Many of the same restrictions apply to musharaka financing, except that in this instance the losses are borne proportionately to the capital amounts contributed. Thus under these two Islamic modes of financing, the project is managed by the client and not by the bank, even though the bank shares the risk. Certain major decisions such as changes in the existing lines of business and the disposition of profits may be subject to the bank's consent. The bank, as a partner, has the right to full access to the books and records, and can exercise monitoring and follow-up supervision. Nevertheless, the directors and management of the company retain independence in conducting the affairs of the company.

These conditions give the finance many of the characteristics of non-voting equity capital. From the viewpoint of the entrepreneur, there are no fixed annual payments needed to service the debt as under interest financing, while the financing does not increase the firm's risk in the way that other borrowings do through increased leverage. Conversely, from the bank's viewpoint, the returns come from profits - much like dividends - and the bank cannot take action to foreclose on the debt should profits no eventuate.

GOVERNANCE STRUCTURES

These structures are depicted in Figure 2 which sketches the conceptual framework of corporate governance for Islamic bank. Central to such a framework is the Sharia Supervisory Board (SSB) and the internal controls which support it. The SSB is vital for two reasons. First, those who deal with an Islamic bank require assurance that it is transacting with Islamic law. Should the SSB report that the management of the bank has violated the *sharia,* it would quickly lose the confidence of the majority of its investors and clients. Second, some Islamic scholars argue that strict adherence to Islamic religious principles will act as a counter to the incentive problems outlined above. The argument is that the Islamic moral code will prevent Muslims from behaving in ways which are ethically unsound, so minimising the transaction costs arising from incentive issues. In effect, Islamic religious ideology acts as its own incentive mechanism to reduce the inefficiency that arises from asymmetric information and moral hazard.

Such matters are obviously basic to the successful operation of Islamic modes of finance, and they are assessed in the next section when I examine Principles of Islamic Banking.

PRINCIPLES OF ISLAMIC BANKING

An Islamic bank is based on the Islamic *faith* and must stay within the limits of Islamic Law or the *sharia* in all of its actions and deeds. The original meaning of the Arabic word *sharia* was 'the way to the source of life' and it is now used to refer to legal system in keeping with the code of behaviour called for by the *Holly Qur'an* (Koran). Four rules govern investment behaviour which gives Islamic banking its distinctive religious identity:

a. Riba

Perhaps the most far reaching of these is the prohibition of interest (riba). The payment of riba and the taking as occurs in a conventional banking system is explicitly prohibited by the *Holy Qur'an*, and thus investors must be compensated by other means. Technically, riba refers to the addition in the amount of the principal of a loan according to the time for which it is loaned and the amount of the loan. While earlier there was a debate as to whether riba relates to interest or usury, there now appears to be consensus of opinion among Islamic scholars that the term extends to all forms of interest.

In banning riba, Islamic seeks to establish a society based upon fairness and justice *(Qur'an 2.239)*. A loan provides the lender with a fixed return irrespective of the outcome of the borrower's venture. It is much fairer to have a sharing of the profits and losses. Fairness in this context has two dimensions: the supplier of capital possesses a right to reward, but this reward should be commensurate with the risk and effort involved and thus be governed by the return on the individual project for which funds are supplied.

Hence, what is forbidden in Islamic is a predetermined return. The sharing of profit is legitimate and that practice has provided the foundation for Islamic banking.

b. Ghirar

Another feature condemned by Islamic is economic transactions involving elements of speculation, *ghirar*. Buying goods or shares at low and selling them for higher price in the future is considered to be illicit. Similarly an immediate sale in order to a void a loss in the future is condemned. The reason is that speculators generate their private gains at the expense of society at large.

c. Zakat

A mechanism for the redistribution of income and wealth is inherent is Islam, so that every Muslim is guaranteed a fair standard of living, *nisab*. An Islamic tax, *Zakat* (a term derived from the Arabic *zaka*, meaning "pure") is the most important instrument for the redistribution of wealth. This tax is a compulsory levy, one of the five basic tenets of Islam and the generally accepted amount of the *zakat* is one fortieth (2.5 per cent) of Muslim's annual income in cash or kind from all forms of assessed wealth exceeding *nisab*.

Every Islamic bank has to establish a *zakat* fund for collecting the tax and distributing it exclusively to the poor directly or through other religious institutions. This tax is imposed on the initial capital of the bank, on the reserves, and on the profits as described in the Handbook of Islamic Banking.

d. Haram

A strict code of 'ethical investment' operates. Hence it is forbidden for Islamic banks to finance activities or items forbidden in Islam, *haram*, such as trade of alcoholic beverage and pork meat.

Furthermore, as the fulfilment or materials needs assures a religious freedom for Muslims, Islamic banks are required to give priority to the production of essential goods which satisfy the needs of the majority of the Muslim community, while the production and marketing of luxury activities, *israf wa traf* is considered as unacceptable from a religious viewpoint.

In order to ensure that the practices and activities of Islamic banks do not contradict the Islamic ethical standards, Islamic banks are expected to establish a *Sharia Supervisory Board*, consisting of Muslim jurisprudence, which acts as adviser to the banks.

PROFIT-SHARING AGREEMENTS

Although the restriction against the use of interest might seem to be a binding constraint upon expansion, Islamic banks and financial institutions have in fact grown rapidly. It shows that the total assets of these reporting banks amounted to US $155 billion in 1994, with employment in excess of 220,000 (data supplied by the International Association of Islamic Banks).

If the paying and receiving of interest is prohibited, how do Islamic banks operater It is necessary to distinguish between the expressions 'rate of interest' and 'rate of return'. Whereas Islam clearly forbids the former, it not only permits, but rather encourages, trade. In the interest-free system sought by adherents to Muslim principles, people are able to earn a return on their money only by subjecting themselves to the risk involved in profit sharing. As the use of interest rates in financial transactions is prevented, Islamic banks are expected to undertake operations only on the basis of *Profit and Loss Sharing* (PLS) arrangements or other acceptable modes of financing. Mudaraba and musharaka are the two profit-sharing arrangements preferred under Islamic law.

Mudaraba

A Mudaraba can be defined as contract between at least two parties whereby one party, the financier *(sahib al-mal)*, entrusts funds to another party, the entrepreneur (mudarib), to undertake an activity or venture. This type of contract is in contrast with musharaka.

In arrangements based on *musharaks* there is also profit-sharing, but all parties have the right to participate in managerial decisions. In Mudaraba, the financier is not allowed a role in management of the enterprise. Consequently, Mudaraba represents a PLS contract where the return to lenders is a specified share in the profit/loss outcome of the project in which they have a stake, but no voice.

In interest lending, the loan is not contingent on the profit or loss outcome, and is usually secured, so that the debtor has to repay the borrowed capital plus the fixed interest amount regardless of the resulting yield of the capital.

Under Mudaraba, the yield is not guaranteed in profit-sharing and financial losses are borne completely by the lender. The entrepreneur as such losses only the time and effort invested in the enterprise. This distribution effectively treats human capital with equally financial capital.

Musharaka

Under musharaka, the entrepreneur adds some of his own to that supplied by the investors, so exposing him to the risk of capital loss. Profits and losses are shared according to pre-fixed proportions, but these proportions need not coincide with the ratio of financing input. The bank sometimes participates in the execution of the projects in which it has subscribed, perhaps by providing managerial expertise.

Mudaraba and musharaka constitute, at least in principle if not always in practice, the twin pillars of Islamic banking.

The two methods conform fully to Islamic principles, in that under both arrangements lenders share in the profits and losses of the enterprises for which funds are provided and *shirkah* (partnership) is involved. The musharaka principle in invoked in the equity structure of Islamic banks and is similar to the modern concepts of partnership and joint stock ownership.

TWO-TIERED MUDABARA

For banking operations, the Mudaraba concept has been extended to include three parties: the depositors as financiers, the bank as an intermediary, and the entrepreneur who requires funds. The bank acts as an entrepreneur when it receives funds from depositors and as financier when it provides the funds to entrepreneurs. In other words, the bank operates a two-tier Mudaraba system in which it acts both as the mudarib on the saving side of the equation and as the *rubbul-mal* (owner of capital) on the investment portfolio side. Insofar as the depositors are concerned, an Islamic bank acts as a mudarib which manages the funds of the depositors to generate profits subject to the rules of Mudaraba. The bank may in turn use the depositors' funds on a Mudaraba basis in addition to other lawful (but less preferable) modes of financing, including mark up or deferred sales, lease purchase and beneficence loans. The funding and investment avenues are now listed.

SOURCES OF FUNDS

Besides their own capital and equity, Islamic banks rely on two main sources of funds, a) transaction deposits, which are risk free but yield no return and, b) investment deposits, which carry the risks of capital loss for the promise of variable. In all, there are four main types of accounts:

i. Current accounts

Current accounts are based on the principle of *al-wadiah,* whereby the depositors are guaranteed repayment of their funds. At the same time, the depositor does not receive remuneration for depositing funds in a current account, because the guaranteed funds will not be used for PLS ventures. Rather, the funds accumulating in these accounts can only be used to balance the liquidity needs of the bank and for short-term transactions on the bank's responsibility.

ii. Savings accounts

Savings accounts also operate under the *al-wadiah* principle. Savings accounts differ from current deposits in that they earn the depositors income: depending upon financial results, the Islamic bank may decide to pay a premium, *hiba,* at its discretion, to the holders of savings accounts.

iii. Investment accounts

An investment account operates under the Mudaraba *al-mutlaqa* principle, in which the mudarib (active partner) must have absolute freedom in the management of the investment of the subscribed capital. The conditions of this account differ from those of the savings accounts by virtue of: a) a higher fixed minimum amount, b) a longer duration of deposits, and

c) most importantly, the depositor may lose some of or all his funds in the event of the bank making losses.

iv. Special investment accounts

Special investment accounts also operate under the Mudaraba principle, and usually are directed towards larger investors and institutions. The difference between these accounts and the investment account is that the special investment account is related to a specified project, and the investor has the choice to invest directly in a preferred project carried out by the bank.

USES OF FUNDS

The Mudaraba and musharaka modes, referred to earlier, are supposedly the main conduits for the outflow of funds from banks. In practice, however, other important methods applied by Islamic banks include:

i. Murabaha (mark-up): The most commonly used mode of financing seems to be the 'mark-up' device. In murabaha transactions, the bank finances the purchase of a good or assets by buying it on behalf of its client and adding a mark-up before reselling it to the client on a 'cost-plus' basis profit contract.
ii. Bai' muajjal (deferred payment): Islamic banks have also been resorting to purchase and resale of properties on a deferred payment basis. It is considered lawful in fiqh (jurisprudence) to charge a higher price for a good if payments are to be made at a later date. According to fiqh this does not amount to charging interest, since it is not a lending transaction but a trading one.
iii. Bai'salam (pre-paid purchase). This method is really the opposite of the murabaha. There the bank gives the commodity first, and receives the money later. Here the bank pays the money first and receives the commodity later, and is normally used to finance agricultural products.
iv. Istisana (manufacturing): This is a contract to acquire goods on behalf of a third party where the price is paid

to the manufacturer in advance and the goods produced and delivered at a later date.

v. Ijara *and* ijara *wa* iqtina (leasing): Under this mode, the banks buy the equipment or machinery and lease it out to their clients who may opt to buy the items eventually, in which case the monthly payments will consist of two components, i.e. rental for the use of the equipment and instalment towards the purchases price.

vi. Qard hasan (beneficence loans): This is the zero return type of loan that the *Holly Qura'n* urges Muslims to make available to those who need them. The borrower is obliged to repay only the principal amount of the loan, but is permitted to add a margin at his own discretion.

vii. Islamic securities: Islamic financial institutions often maintain an international Islamic equity portfolio where the underlying assets comprise ordinary shares in well run businesses, the productive activities of which exclude those on the prohibited list (alcohol, pork, armaments) and financial service based on interest income.

ACCEPTABILITY OF ISLAMIC BANKING

Islam prohibits the payment of interest on loans, so observant Muslims require specialized alternative arrangements from their banks. Many of the largest global financial companies, including Deutsche Bank and JPMorgan Chase, have established thriving subsidiaries that strive to meet these requirements. As a result, optimists speculate that the common pursuit of lucre-divinely sanctioned, filthy, or otherwise-will bring bickering civilizations together. They may be right.

The Islamic aversion to interest collection comes from the Qur'an. Not that the term "interest" is ever used: the Arabic injunction forbids something called *riba*. The Qur'an offers no exact definition of what riba meant in seventh-century Arabia, the time and place of the Prophet Mohammed-let alone what the term should mean today. In particular, the passages are ambiguous on the question of whether riba refers to *all* kinds of interest collection, or only usurious interest-that is, lending practices that are, according to some ill-defined standard, unfair and exploitative. What is clear in the divine financial critique is that, whatever riba may be, Jews are doing it. At one point God warns that they will face a "painful day of doom" if they keep it up.

This ambiguity was a practical problem for the early Muslim jurists, who formalized religious rules in a code called *sharia*. They were divided on the subject, but as time went on, the weight of consensus came to rest on the side of prohibiting all interest collection.

The financial instruments that 20th-century Islamic theorists championed were updated versions of medieval commercial instruments, still known in the Islamic financial sector by their Arabic names: in addition to bonds, known as *sukuk*, there are profit-and-loss sharing instruments known as *musharaka* or *Mudaraba*, Islamic leases known as *ijara* , and a commercial trade instrument called *murabaha* , the flexibility of which has made it extremely popular among Islamic financial firms.

Banking, as an institution, evolved at the same time as the unprecedented economic growth in Europe over the past 500 years. That growth was made possible in part by the codification, in the 12th century, of a distinction between usury and interest in the Christian tradition.

The Islamic world witnessed the development of corporate contract law and the European banking system from afar. A mixture of traditional arrangements and, later, imported Western practices prevailed in Muslim countries. But it wasn't until the 1960s that anyone tried to combine the two, governing a modern bank according to Islamic law.

You don't have to be Islamic to bank in accordance with sharia. All you need is a board of religious scholars to approve your operation.

Islamic financial institutions, the argument went, would boost the economic development of Muslim societies. The fraternal style of Islamic banking-with its emphasis on equity financing rather than lending-would enhance social responsibility. In practice, however, Islamic finance has had to bend to the same pressures as any other kind of finance. Social, religiously oriented investment in the development of the Islamic world is something people are more interested in publicly championing than personally doing. Khalid Ikram, who represented the World Bank in Egypt, says of Islamic banking, "it hasn't had a lot to do with development."

Pinning down the growth of Islamic banking is a challenge. Whether a banking system truly counts as *halal*-that is, compliant with the laws of sharia, or, in another religious context, kosher-is a religious question, hard for accountants to answer. Take Iran: should the country's whole banking system, which is nominally Islamic, be counted as part of the sector even though many experts raise questions about its legitimacy?

Rodney Wilson, professor of economics at Durham University in Britain and editor of the essay collection *The Politics of Islamic Finance*, estimates total assets within halal banking systems at just under $500 billion. That's roughly the size of Wells Fargo Bank, America's fourth-largest. Hussein A. Hassan of Deutsche Bank predicts that Islamic finance will be the world's fastest-growing banking sector for years, based on what he calls a modest estimate of 20 per cent annual increases in deposits.

So its big business, getting bigger, and those who hesitate to enter it now risk suffering an expertise deficit later. The number of professionals trained to structure sharia-compliant products, and of religious scholars qualified to certify them, is small enough to be already causing problems. Governments are getting in the game, too: Japan is planning to become the first non-Muslim country to issue sharia-compliant bonds; the UK, Gordon Brown announced last summer, is revising its laws to make London the "gateway" for Islamic finance in Europe; and Malaysia has proposed substantial tax incentives in its 2007 budget for its Islamic financial sector.

Deutsche Bank, Chase, and HSBC, the giant London-based financial institution with an extensive presence in Asia, have all entered the sector within the last ten years. Their moves coincide with rising oil prices, echoing a phenomenon three decades ago. When the 1970s oil boom gave Muslims and their governments wealth that seemed barely countable, Islamic financial institutions bloomed: the Islamic Development Bank (1975), the Kuwait Finance house (1977), the Faisal Islamic Bank of Egypt (1977), the Jordan Islamic Bank (1978), and others. In 1979, Bank Misr, a conventional financial house in Egypt, became the first mainstream bank to build a halal subsidiary, which in the late 1990s began to attract more capital than its chief domestic competitor, the Faisal Islamic Bank.

Oil prices and religious fervor are both on the rise again. This time, Western financial firms have noticed that you don't have to be Islamic to bank in accordance with sharia. All you need is a board of religious scholars to approve your operation. Muslim is as Muslim does.

The Islamic world witnessed the development of corporate contract law and the European banking system from afar.

Hussein Hassan of Deutsche Bank is an example of the sort of expert required. He structures specialized Islamic bonds, or sukuk. For a bond to qualify as sharia-compliant there must be an underlying asset backing it. One cannot simply issue bonds to raise money, the way it's been done elsewhere for centuries, in return for a promise of a fixed rate of return. To be Islamic in nature, the securities that look like bonds must represent fractions of an equity asset, rather than fractions of a loan.

According to sharia scholars signing off on the prospectuses, the practices of the multinationals are fully Islamic. That is good news for corporations that want to raise money from Muslims, and for the observant clients themselves. But the potential clientele is by no means captive. As Hassan put it to me, "money always looks for the best deal." if Islamic finance couldn't provide results close to those of secular institutions, it wouldn't exist.

Khalid Ikram, who headed the World Bank's operations in Egypt in the late 1990s, looked into the performance of Faisal Islamic Bank of Egypt (FIBE) back during the early boom days.

It turned out that, despite the bank's citing "religious fervor" to him as the reason for its growth, Coptic Christians made up about 10 per cent of the bank's clients, just as they do of the country's population. When returns dropped, so did the investment and market-share. Egyptians with foreign capital generally preferred to keep their cash overseas, even though the returns there were less than roughly 20 per cent. Returns FIBE was promising on current accounts. The greater security of foreign deposits made up for their lower rate of return. The rational profit motive never lost its place as the key factor in investor behavior.

Timur Kuran, professor of economics and law at the University of Southern California and author of *Islam and Mammon: The Economic Predicaments of Islamism*, points out that investing in sharia-compliant fashion doesn't just buy you decent returns-it can also buy political legitimacy. "Islamic finance didn't come into its own until the 1970s. Why during the oil boom? Huge amount of assets, petrodollars, were accumulating in the sheikdoms and with the Saudis. These regimes were considered quite illegitimate, and there were a lot of opposition movements, so they wanted to legitimize their regimes and invest the money at the same time.... They could claim that they were promoting Islam and avoiding interest."

Since the inception of Islamic economics as a distinct discipline in the 20th century, it has always been held up as a champion of ethical development. Islamist writers such as Sayyid Qutb and Sayyid Abul-A'la Maududi envisioned Islamic finance as the economic arm of a new, sharia-guided political order. Free of the scourge of interest, the instrument by which fat-cat colonial and imperial capitalists make money from money, Islamic financial institutions would effectively become private equity or venture capital firms, providing sorely needed investment and support for the region's economy. By investing in Islamic finance, you weren't just being pious-you were aiding development and helping the poor as well.

But the post-capitalist utopia that reliance on these instruments was meant to inaugurate was dead on arrival.

Those involved in the first wave of Islamic banks realized that equity financing does not make for a stable banking sector, and, after a series of shocks and bad investments, they became very conservative. It was a race to the loopholes-a search for means of sharia compliance less risky than straight-out equity investing.

Its big business, getting bigger, and those who hesitate to enter it now risk suffering an expertise deficit later.

The chief loophole was murabaha. Let's say that you, a small businessman, wish to go into business selling cars. A conventional bank would examine your credit history and, if all was acceptable, grant you a cash loan. You would incur an obligation to return the funds on a specific maturity date, paying interest each month along the way. When you signed the note and made the promise, you would use the proceeds to buy the cars-and meet your other expenses-yourself. But in a murabaha transaction, instead of just cutting you the check, the bank itself would buy the cars. You promise to buy them from the bank at a higher price on a future date-like a futures contract in the commodities market. The markup is justified by the fact that, for a period, the bank owns the property, thus assuming liability. At no point in the transaction is money treated as a commodity, as it is in a normal loan.

But here's the catch: most Muslim scholars agree that there is no minimum time interval for the bank to own the property before selling it to you at the markup. According to Timur Kuran, the typical interval is "under a millisecond." The bank transfers ownership of the asset to its client right away. The client still pays a fixed markup at a later date, a payment that is usually secured by some sort of collateral or by other forms of contractual coercion. Thus, in practice, murabaha is a normal loan.

Since murabaha must be asset-based, however, it can't help a small businessman who needs a working-capital loan, for example, to provide cash on hand to meet payroll or other expenses. To get such capital from an Islamic financial institution, an entrepreneur would have to sell the bank an equity interest in his business. This is far riskier for the bank and thus much harder to obtain.

The experts tell me that every Islamic bank has at least three-quarters of its investments structured as murabaha. Even the inaptly named Islamic Development Bank was, as of the mid-1980s, doing four-fifths of its business through murabaha, and only 1 per cent through equity transactions.

What the "Islamic" label might mean is left to the beholder. The sharia scholars make it their business to pronounce only upon the letter of the law. Like legal practitioners everywhere, they focus on the technicalities. The spirit, being intangible, tends not to cloud their rulings. The leading critics of this inconsistency are political Islamists themselves. Majed Jarrar, a personable young man who studies electrical engineering, wears a long beard, and is keen to discuss his faith, recently opened an account with FIBE here in Cairo, only to let it sit empty. He's been investigating whether "it's actually Islamic or not," and he doesn't like what he's finding.

Despite the zeal of purists like Jarrar, an entire banking sector without debt would be far too unstable. Such a system has never had to exist-medieval Islam had extensive regulations governing trade relations and individual contract law, but there was no banking, so there were no banking rules.

The Sharia-compliant financing directly retards economic and social development, there was agreement that it does much less than the original rhetoric claimed. Not only are working-capital loans, critical to many small businesses, rare, but also sharia-compliant transactions tend to be short-term.

Still, there's something reassuring about the way that the rational profit motive trumps strict ideology. The willingness to put profit first is, it turns out, the real shared value that links Islamic and Western civilizations.

OVERVIEW OF ISLAMIC BANKING

Islamic banking is based on the principles of Islamic economics - an economic framework in accordance with Islamic law (Sharia'h). There are two types of Islamic economics:

1. Caliphate, the Islamic form of government representing the political unity and leadership of the Muslim world (Islamic political framework), and
2. Assuming the political framework is non-Islamic, therefore, seeking to integrate some prominent Islamic tenets into a secular economic framework.

Caliphate is the absolute Islamic rule, thus the economy focuses on distribution of resources in order to meet the basic and luxurious needs of individuals in society, and the state has a clear role in policing, taxation, managing public assets, and ensuring the circulation of wealth. Such a political framework in its true form does not exist in today's world.

Assuming non-Islamic political framework simply proposes two main tenets: no interest can be earned on loans and socially responsible investing. This is the way conventional banking is Islamized-the first step towards an Islamic economic framework.

Modern day Islamic scholars and academics have developed various modes of Sharia'h complaint financing that are designed to work within the prevailing capitalist economic framework. In order to achieve this balance numerous concessions have been afforded to financial institutions that would not apply if a viable interest free economic system existed. The intention behind making these concessions is to encourage the evolution of this type of alternative system.

Islamic banking refers to a system of banking or banking activity that is consistent with Islamic law (Sharia'h) principles and guided by Islamic economics. In particular, Islamic law prohibits usury, the collection and payment of interest, also commonly called riba. Generally, Islamic law also prohibits trading in financial risk (which is seen as a form of gambling). In addition, Islamic law prohibits investing in businesses that are considered unlawful, or haraam.

Islamic finance has been gaining momentum on a global scale for the last 30 years. Many Islamic Banks have sprung up over the last few years. These changes are occurring both in Muslim and in western countries, and are driven by a global trend amongst Muslims to become more observant of their faith. It might have been the reason why Islamic Banking emerged, however, today Islamic Banking is sought by Muslims and non-Muslims due to the benefits it offers.

Industry size is currently estimated at more than $400 billion, with projected growth of 15% per annum.

Financial institutions around the globe are trying to keep pace with the growing demand for Sharia'h compliant products and services.

MODES OF ISLAMIC FINANCE

Murabaha

Literally, it means a sale on mutually agreed profit. Technically, it is a contract of sale in which the seller declares his cost and profit. Islamic banks have adopted this as a mode of financing. As a financing technique, it involves a request by the client to the bank to purchase certain goods for him. The bank does that for a definite profit over the cost, which is stipulated in advance.

Ijarah

Ijarah is a contract of a known and proposed usufruct against a specified and lawful return or consideration for the service or return for the benefit proposed to be taken, or for the effort or work proposed to be expended. In other words, Ijarah or leasing is the transfer of usufruct for a consideration which is rent in case of hiring of assets or things and wage in case of hiring of persons.

Ijarah -Wal-Iqtina

A contract under which an Islamic bank provides equipment, building or other assets to the client against an agreed rental together with a unilateral undertaking by the bank or the client that at the end of the lease period, the ownership in the asset would be transferred to the lessee. The undertaking or the promise does not become an integral part of the lease contract to make it conditional. The rentals as well as the purchase price are fixed in such manner that the bank gets back its principal sum along with profit over the period of lease.

Musharakah

Musharakah means a relationship established under a contract by the mutual consent of the parties for sharing of profits and losses in the joint business. It is an agreement under which the Islamic bank provides funds, which are mixed with the funds of the business enterprise and others. All providers of capital are entitled to participate in management, but not necessarily required to do so. The profit is distributed among the partners in pre-agreed ratios, while the loss is borne by each partner strictly in proportion to respective capital contributions.

Musawamah

Musawamah is a general and regular kind of sale in which price of the commodity to be traded is bargained between seller and the buyer without any reference to the price paid or cost incurred by the former. Thus, it is different from Murabaha in respect of pricing formula. Unlike Murabaha, seller in Musawamah is not obliged to reveal his cost. Both the parties negotiate on the price. All other conditions relevant to Murabaha are valid for Musawamah as well. Musawamah can be used where the seller is not in a position to ascertain precisely the costs of commodities that he is offering to sell.

Istisna'a

It is a contractual agreement for manufacturing goods and commodities, allowing cash payment in advance and future delivery or a future payment and future delivery. Istisna'a can be used for providing the facility of financing the manufacture or construction of houses, plants, projects and building of bridges, roads and highways.

Bai Muajjal

Literally it means a credit sale. Technically, it is a financing technique adopted by Islamic banks that takes the form of

Murabaha Muajjal. It is a contract in which the bank earns a profit margin on his purchase price and allows the buyer to pay the price of the commodity at a future date in a lump sum or in installments. It has to expressly mention cost of the commodity and the margin of profit is mutually agreed. The price fixed for the commodity in such a transaction can be the same as the spot price or higher or lower than the spot price.

Mudarabah

A form of partnership where one party provides the funds while the other provides expertise and management. The latter is referred to as the Mudarib. Any profits accrued are shared between the two parties on a pre-agreed basis, while loss is borne only by the provider of the capital.

Bai Salam

Salam means a contract in which advance payment is made for goods to be delivered later on. The seller undertakes to supply some specific goods to the buyer at a future date in exchange of an advance price fully paid at the time of contract. It is necessary that the quality of the commodity intended to be purchased is fully specified leaving no ambiguity leading to dispute. The objects of this sale are goods and cannot be gold, silver or currencies. Barring this, Bai Salam covers almost everything, which is capable of being definitely described as to quantity, quality and workmanship.

7

Issues in Islamic Banking

HUMAN RESOURCE FOR SHARIA'H COMPLIANCE

Users of Islamic financial services assign primary importance to Sharia'h compliance of the services they use. It is understandable that Sharia'h noncompliance entails a serious operational risk and can result in withdrawal of funds from and instability of an Islamic bank, irrespective of its initial financial soundness. Sharia'h compliance is hence a serious matter for an Islamic bank, in addition to its compliance with other regulatory requirements.

UNRESOLVED FIQH ISSUES

Lack of standard financial contracts and products can be a cause of ambiguity and a source of dispute and cost. In addition, without a common understanding of certain basic foundations, further development of banking products is hindered.

LEGAL FRAMEWORKS

An appropriate legal, institutional and tax framework is a basic requirement for establishing sound financial institutions and markets. Islamic jurisprudence offers its own framework for the implementation of commercial and financial contracts and transactions.

Nevertheless, commercial, banking and company laws appropriate for the enforcement of Islamic banking and financial contracts do not exist in many countries.

EXCESS LIQUIDITY

Islamic banks have over 60 % excess liquid funds which cannot be properly utilized due to non-availability of Sharia'h Compliant products and instruments.

The competitiveness and soundness of financial institutions depend on the availability of efficient financial products. Islamic banks urgently need Sharia'h compliant products to meet a number of pressing needs.

TECHNOLOGY

Designing technological solutions around a concept requires extensive knowledge of the domain. Conventional banking today is technologically advanced; however, for crafting Islamic financial solutions, considerable time and expertise are required.

ISLAMIC BANKING - POSSIBLE SOLUTIONS

1. Establishment of Shari'ah Governance Systems
2. Settling unresolved Fiqh Issues
3. A sufficient number of well-trained, competent, high-caliber Islamic finance professionals and management teams with the required expertise
4. Well-informed individual and corporate consumers, knowledgeable about Islamic banking and takaful
5. The availability of Sharia'h compliant products (Sharia'h Compliant Stocks, Sukuks, etc.)
6. Development of a Legal, Regulatory, and Institutional Framework complying with Sharia'h
7. Advanced technology solutions designed to support Islamic Finance

LENDING AND BORROWING: AN OVERVIEW

Lending and borrowing between humans has taken place since time immemorial. People borrowed and returned implements, animals, foodstuff, etc from their friends, neighbors and relations. They returned the same after use or in the case of foodstuff consumed and returned the equivalent when they came into possession of similar stuff. When money came into being people borrowed that too and returned. It was all on the basis of mutual help - the borrower today may be the lender tomorrow and vice versa. As time progressed professional moneylenders appeared on the scene, and they demanded a "fee" for the use of their money. This fee is now called interest, but till a few centuries ago it was called usury. In Islam, interest or usury, which in Arabic is called riba, is prohibited. Demanding, receiving, paying, witnessing, and anything connected with these activities are all equally prohibited. There is no controversy over this. Similar prohibitions exist also in the religious laws of Judaism and Christianity. Although other religions may not have written laws explicitly prohibiting usury, their followers do eschew the practice of usury.

Lending and Borrowing: Then and Now

In earlier times, lending and borrowing was mainly between individuals, and what was meant by usury in these transactions was commonly known and understood. In money matters, any amount over and above the lent sum was defined as usury or riba. The ill consequences of usurious lending - the ruination of individuals and families - were witnessed at the local level and therefore the community held the practitioners in contempt. But the need for capital and loans existed and, in the absence of alternative solutions, the usurious lenders became an indispensable component of the society. They also exercised invisible power over their clients' resources. If the clients happened to be in authority, the power extended to other areas as well; the greater the client's authority the extensive the power of the lender.

Kings and nobles needed money to wage war or to live extravagantly. Moneylenders were happy to oblige, not only for the profit it brought them but also for the privileges and concessions they could extract from their royal clients. Mining concessions, special trading licenses, tax exemptions, lucrative contracts for public projects, land grants, and personal privileges such as royal titles and appointments to influential positions are just a few examples. These dealings were carried out discretely and the public was generally ignorant of them. But the citizens paid the price, one way or another.

The most important concession so extracted was the passing of the Usury Law. This law introduced an innocuous term called interest and usury was defined as high rate of interest. Usury was still prohibited, in deference to the Church, but "reasonable" interest was made permissible. What is reasonable and what is high was to be determined by the parliament! Now that interest is legal, kings may lose their thrones, soldiers may lose their lives, families may lose their livelihoods, but the country must pay its debts with interest. Moneylenders extracted their pound of flesh.

In recent times, presidents and ministers have replaced kings and nobles, and corporate and international financial institutions with the individual moneylenders. The game was the same_ only new names and wider settings. It is now global, the suffering is universal, and the statistics are in the public domain. Yet, hardly anyone dares to point the finger at the real culprit - usury, whatever the legal name it may assume. Neither are the real needs objectively looked at. Consequently, no meaningful alternatives are offered.

Lender, Borrower and the Church: Different Goals

Governments, businesses and individuals need money for various purposes. The methods of catering for these needs must match the purpose for which the money was needed. A mismatch can lead to disastrous consequences, but this requires much thought and effort. Borrowing is an attractively easy solution, and this is what the moneylender would recommend for all situations, for it is the most profitable one from his point of view. When the borrower is impatient or desperate and the only game in town is the moneylender, borrowing from him is the only option and the consequences are inevitable. To avoid disasters, then, we have to first study the different purposes for which money is needed and then devise methods most appropriate to each purpose. We have to provide more alternatives. The moneylender has only one purpose and concern: his profits and benefits. But the society has more and larger concerns, for it is its responsibility to cater for and protect all its members, individually and as a whole, those living now and those still to come. In this connection, it is well to remember that all the basic rules, methods, procedures and laws relating to banking and finance were either formulated by the moneylenders themselves or they had a hand in their design and/or execution.

When the usury law was proposed, it was argued that the merchants needed financing, they made profit using the borrowed funds and, therefore, they had the ability to pay the financiers a portion of that profit_very reasonable. The trouble was that once the law was passed, it was applied to all situations - whether the borrowed funds brought about a profit or not. The Church had become too weak but still dogmatic, and the merchants and moneylenders too strong. The Church could not grasp the new need, brought about by the increased trade in Europe, and failed to provide an appropriate solution. Nor could it argue successfully to limit the application of the new law to trade financing only. Neither did it demand that the law should not be applied to non-profit-creating loans intended for basic consumption needs. It seems that the Church granted the moneylenders a blank cheque on a platter, by default - by its all or nothing insistence on a complete prohibition and by failing in this dogmatic stance.

Islamic Approach: Different Consequences

In Islam, the situation was different. First, from the beginning of the history of Islam in the seventh century, the (large-scale) merchants' need for (additional) funds was fully recognized and provided for. There were two ways in which a merchant could finance his trade. One: two or more merchants could pool their funds together and conduct the business together and share the profit or loss according to their (financial) contribution. This was called musharaka, similar to the present-day partnership company. Two: a merchant could obtain his funds from one or more financiers and share the profit with his financiers in an agreed proportion. But he has full freedom in the conduct of his business, and any genuine financial loss must be borne entirely by the financiers. This was called Mudaraba, similar to the present-day shareholder companies.

Consequently, while the riba-prohibition of Islam related to all lending and borrowing operations, it took special note of the financing needs of traders and businessmen as well as the investment and income generation needs of those who possessed extra funds. It does not mean that riba is acceptable in these cases; it is prohibited here too. But a different and equitable solution was already available in Arabia when the Qur'an was revealed; so it approved of it and went onto prohibit riba in all cases. Therefore, the merchant-need-based and return-on-investment-based arguments of Europe were not relevant or valid in the case of Islam and Muslim lands. It is necessary to recognise this fact. That is, the all-embracing usury-prohibition law of the Church and the riba-prohibition law of Islam are not exactly equivalent, despite the similarity of appearances.

Second, throughout the long history of Islam, Muslim caliphs, kings and nobles have, by and large, kept away from borrowing at interest. Even though many of them had their share of shortcomings - in common with their counterparts elsewhere - their belief in after-life and the strong words used by the Holy Book against the dealers in riba kept them away from it. The same applied to all would-be moneylenders as well. This saved the Muslim masses and the society from many of the ills experienced by other societies, even though this blessing goes generally unrecognised and unappreciated. Even under colonialism they have enjoyed this benefit. However, it would be naïve to believe that there existed absolutely no riba-based lending and borrowing, but it certainly was personal, local, small, isolated, discrete and unorganised.

Only in the second half of the twentieth century, especially after many countries became independent, established their own governments, and had to run the affairs of the country on their own, that they began to experience the claws of interest through the banking system. They needed the banking system because it provided the various services needed by the different sectors of modern society. But the moneylenders had developed it for their own benefit, based on the all-embracing usury law. It did not make the differentiation the Qur'an had made. Muslims had slumbered through the formative years of the modern world, and failed to build on the head start they had and shape a business and banking model to suit modern needs. Yet their desire to comply with the commandments of their Creator did not die. Their leaders and intellectuals have awoken to the demands of their constituents, experiments with Islamic banking have begun, but there is still a long road to travel.

Lending with and without Interest

Before we travel further, let us state clearly what we mean by interest and riba and then note the difference between lending/borrowing with and without interest, usury or riba. Limiting ourselves to monetary dealings only, any benefit demanded or received by a lender in addition to the sum he lent is termed riba. This would, however, include both monetary and non-monetary benefits. Interest, on the other hand, would legally limit itself to monetary benefits only. It is useful not to forget this difference and its significance.

When a person lends without any benefits to himself, he is bound to assess the ability of the borrower to pay back the capital as well as to ensure that the capital is to be used for a purpose that he approves of. It is also a condition of such borrowing that the lender and the borrower are known to each other or that a reliable mutual friend/ relative/ acquaintance has introduced them. In such a situation, there is an unspoken moral/ethical responsibility (and a sense of shame and reluctance, otherwise) in asking, recommending or granting such a loan.

All these restraints are absent when the lending is done at interest. The lender assesses only the borrower's ability to (or the means to) repay the capital and the interest. Collateral is usually demanded, and by the very nature of interest - its dependence on time - the lender expects that he would eventually be able to acquire the collateral at a favourable price. Both the interest and the possibility of acquiring property at very low cost drive the moneylender to readily accede to request for loans, as well as to encourage such requests. Thus, when riba or interest enters the picture, the attitudes of both the lender and the borrower head in a direction directly opposed to the one prevalent in its absence. This riba-induced change of attitude is remarkable, as are the opposing characteristics of the two attitudes. One discourages debt, and the other encourages it. One restrains expenditure on morally or ethically unacceptable items and purposes; the other places no such restrains. One is open to social control, the other not. One limits both the size of borrowing and its frequency; the other encourages increase in both. One encourages short-term loans; the other thrives on long-term arrangements.

The last two are very interesting. For, since more and larger loans would bring more profit to the lender, he would try to acquire more funds.This eventually led the moneylender to borrow from others at low rates of interest and use the same funds to lend at higher rates, as if it were his own. The bank's credit-creation technique was also developed for the same end. Furthermore, long-term loans provide a stable and steady source of income to the moneylender. This and the availability of increased funds led the banks to widen their reach and, in recent times, to enter previously untapped areas such as housing finance and student loans.

NEED FOR MONEY

To begin with, there are purposes that bring profit, and others that do not. Within these two categories there are necessary, unnecessary and harmful purposes. In the modern world one has to also make a difference between the needs of individuals, business organisations and governments. Let us take them in turn.

Extravaganza and Vanity

When the borrowing is for extravaganza or vanity, the borrowed fund produces no profit. Therefore, if the borrower is unable to repay the loan and interest from his other income sources, the interest would keep on mounting and the moneylender would eventually confiscate the collateral. All religions and sages throughout the ages have condemned extravaganza and vanity, and have advised against it. The Qur'an has specifically prohibited spending in vanity. Here the reference is to one's spending froM own resources, and the onus is on the individual. As such, if one engages in such spending using borrowed money, he is seeking his own doom. Yet, by making the riba-prohibition applicable to both the lender and the borrower, Islam seeks to protect people against their own selves. If there is no borrower there will be no lender; if there is no lender there will be no borrower. This closes all doors to doom. Thus there is no need to find any other solutions to the apparent need of the extravagant.

Housing and Education Loans

Housing and education are real needs, and therefore their financing deserves close attention. Building or purchasing a house is obviously a capital acquisition. So is education, though it does not seem that obvious. Capital acquisition has always been done using one's own savings or wealth. It should continue to be so. House-owning leads to individual and collective independence. In turn they add to national wealth and well-being. This fact is recognised by wise governments and they actively encourage private initiatives. Free education has produced wonderful results in the twentieth century.

However, the modern trend, especially in the developed world, is to have them financed by long-term bank loans. But unlike the loans for commercial purposes these loans produce no immediate profit to the borrower. Yet, to a moneylender a loan is a loan, and from his point of view these have some attractive advantages, including a secured regular return guaranteed for a long period. In many developed countries the fiscal laws encourage borrowing and discourage saving/

investment/capital acquisition by taxing the interest/dividend received from the latter and granting tax exemption to the interest paid on loans. These laws enable the banks to price the products very attractively and encourage mortgages, but the subsequent experience of the borrower and the effect on the nation are different.

For example, a house-owner who bought it on mortgage remains a debtor for practically the rest of his working life and he ends up paying several times the original price. On the other hand, if he fails to pay his instalments on time, he is kicked out as if he were only a tenant. A student forced to take a loan for his education leaves college/university with a certificate and a millstone round his neck. He may become a government administrator, business executive, politician or any other, but he is still a bonded man. And a bonded person cannot think or act independently. Anyone whose parents is too poor or unwilling to pay for his education, and himself refuses to be bonded, is denied higher education. It is a national tragedy. These characteristics of housing and education set them apart from other needs. Therefore these require special treatment.

War

Wars, in general, bring only death and destruction to people and property - never any profit. The winner and the loser are both losers in the end. If a war is fought by borrowing money at interest, win or lose the country will have to pay the debt with interest, and borrow again to rebuild. Whether the war was an offensive one or a defensive one, in the end, only the moneylenders celebrate - on both sides. Consequently, in history as well as in the present time moneylenders have played an important behind-the-scenes role in both beginning and prolonging wars. Only a total prohibition of riba on both the lenders and borrowers and its adherence at all levels, especially at the highest levels, could eliminate this factor in the war equation. Since everyone is a loser in a war, it is in everybody's interest to avoid any war; eliminating its financing by funds borrowed at interest will go a long way in this effort.

Therefore we need not seek any other solution to this contingency.

Government expenditure

Government expenditure consists of two types: capital and current. The funds for both are expected to come from taxation. So a government's ability to acquire capital goods - to buy equipment and material and to build roads, bridges, schools, hospitals, communication infrastructure, etc - are dependent on, and limited by, the tax revenue. However, the current expenditure, such as salaries of government officers, supplies and maintenance, has priority over capital expenditure. Often, like in the case of an individual, little is left over from the tax revenue for capital expenditure. Consequently, since all capital expenditure cannot be postponed indefinitely, there arises a budget deficit. A budget deficit is financed by printing money, borrowing, or both. Printing money leads to inflation, which is a tacit form of taxing the population. Borrowing increases national debt and interest payment. Credit creation by banks based on the new money (printed or borrowed) increases inflation even further.

Government bonds

Government bonds are one of the instruments used for borrowing money. Since capital expenditure on infrastructure does not produce any profit, borrowing at interest leads to additional current expenditure in the form of interest payments. This in turn requires curtailment of other current expenditure or further borrowing. Government bonds is big business, it provides those who have money to spare with a great source of guaranteed return. But the public debt it creates keeps mounting. So does the interest on it. And the inflation generated by money-printing and credit creation add onto the interest rate and lead to further increase of the public debt.

Thus once a government begins to spend more than its tax income, or fails to tax sufficiently to cover its essential expenditures, it gets into a vicious cycle of borrowing to spend and spending to borrow. To tax sufficiently the country must produce enough, and taxes are always unpopular. Borrowing is the easy way out and the country finally ends up in the grip of the moneylenders - national and international - no matter which party or person runs the government. The debt is open and legally binding but the grip - do this or return the loan, do that or no more loans - is unseen, undeclared and least understood, and hence more hideous. It is a great mystery, though, that developed countries with very large national debts keep on prospering, while underdeveloped countries with much smaller debt burdens crumble under it. However, this is no place to probe into that mystery.

Treasury bills

It is a time-honoured practice of any individual to spend on his needs from what he has earned. If there is no more money left, he either curtails his spending or postpones it till he comes into sufficient funds. If his income is fixed and regular, such as that of a salaried employee, and he finds himself short of money at the end of the month, he must curtail his expenditure. Otherwise he will find himself at a worse position next month because his income is not going to increase next month, but the gap would have doubled. If, instead, he borrows to bridge the gap he will have to borrow the next month and the following month too - an increasing amount every subsequent month. Eventually he will have to borrow to eat, and pay the loan as soon as he receives the salary and then borrow again for the expenses of the next month. Suppose he borrows at interest, then he will be bankrupt very soon on account of the interest payments, even though he continued to work and earn. One could get out of this situation only by earning more or selling some property and paying off all the debts and begin to live within the income and spend only from already earned income. Or by severely curtailing his expenditure, save and pay off the debts, and by living within one's means from then on.

In the case of government current expenditure too, somewhere along the line, they threw away the time-honoured practice of spending from realised earning (collected tax) and began to borrow and spend, expecting to repay when the tax revenue came in. This committed them to an interest payment cycle. An instrument called the Treasury Bill was developed for this purpose. This, in effect, is a three-month loan, interest paid in advance. The funds are used to pay the current expenditure for the next three months and the loan is paid from the taxes collected at the end of the quarter. New treasury bills are issued every quarter, month or week. The cycle goes on. An elabourate set of financial tools and markets are built around this. So elabourate that no one remembers when, how or why it started in the first place, or how it keeps perpetuating itself. It is a given in Finance and Government, and theory and practice have canonised it. Moneylenders (private individuals, banks, financial institutions, insurance companies, pension funds, etc) thrive on it, and a whole army of professionals service it. But the general public pays for it, suffers the consequences, and is blissfully unaware of what is happening to it. Enlightening the public further on this point is not within the purview of this essay.

ISLAMIC BANKING CONFUSION

Islamic banking is rooted in the facts that riba is prohibited and trade is permitted, and the profit resulting from trade is permissible income. By extension, it was argued that interest, which is equated to riba, must be replaced by profit. To achieve this, lending transactions must be replaced by trading transactions. This simple concept is religiously applied to all situations. Where the difference was not clear, legal devices were adopted to dress it up as trade and profit. One may cheat himself, but can you fool God? He may be amused by our poor attempts, but does He approve of it? Whatever God does or does not, others are laughing at us. Sincerity is supposed to be the bedrock of our relationship with God. If we are sincere in our efforts to obey His commands, He will certainly show us the right way.

When the commands were issued 1400 years ago, they were directly understood in the context of the social and economic environment then prevailing, and their application was easily achieved. Today, the environment has changed and that makes the application seem difficult. But the solution is not through legal devices, but through our studying and understanding the new environment and sincerely seeking to apply the commands without any adulteration. Trade and profit have their place, but it is not appropriate for all occasions. We have to explore other options. If our intention is sincere, He will certainly guide us to the right solution.

SOLUTIONS

By looking at the needs of society, we can identify three different kinds of needs - investment and finance, banking and loans, and charity - and they each need be handled using a different technique. Moneylenders offered one solution for all three needs because it was to their advantage, but the society has to cater for larger concerns and therefore must offer more appropriate solutions. The Qur'an points out these different needs and presents us with different techniques to suit each need. It is for us to translate them into present-day "language" and set up appropriate institutions. Outlines of such institutions are presented in another essay (see, *Meeting the Financial Needs of Muslims: A comprehensive scheme*). Other essays elsewhere expand on these outlines.

Properly dealing with lending and borrowing transactions requires an understanding of the meaning of modern bank interests in relation to usury and riba. In an essay entitled, *Interest, Usury,* Riba, *and the Operational Costs of a Bank,* the history of interest, its relation to usury and riba, the origins of dogmas and theories that prohibit or justify its practice, and the meaning of interest in the modern setting of banking are explored. It also presents a general model of interest in which several scenarios - from person-to-person lending to modern commercial bank lending - become sub-models. This enables one to separate riba from the operational costs of a bank and thus to devise a riba-free system of commercial banking that is both viable and compatible with the conventional one.

Inflation has become a fact of life; it erodes the value of capital - depositors' savings, banks' loans, and cash-in-hand.

It has also been offered as an excuse for charging and accepting interest. But the main cause of modern-day inflation is not in the short-term supply-demand pull-push tensions, but in the long-term effects of increased money supply. The basic cause of this increase is the de-linking of the currency-gold relationship. It occurred gradually over time, but the final blow was dealt in 1971 when the US dollar was de-linked from gold and the promise to redeem every dollar for $1/35^{th}$ of an ounce of fine gold was withdrawn, reneging on the Bretton Woods Agreement of 1945. US dollar was allowed to float (meaning more dollars were printed without the constraint of the 35 dollars per ounce of gold ratio), and the other currencies, which were all linked to gold through the dollar, also started their free-floats, each in its own pace. Today, at 350 dollars an ounce, gold is ten times more costly. It is said that the price of gold has gone up; but the reality is that the currency has depreciated that much. Re-linking all currencies directly to gold, and strictly adhering to the agreed currency-gold ratio, is the proper solution to this problem. But a global agreement on this is not going to occur anytime soon. In the meantime savings, loans and cash-in-hand are going to lose their purchasing power.To neutralise the effect of inflation (due to currency depreciation) on capital, without recourse to increasing the interest rate, a new mechanism is necessary. Such a mechanism is presented in a book entitled, Commercial Banking in the presence of Inflation. This mechanism is applicable in person-to-person lending-borrowing transactions as well. It is straightforward and not difficult to implement.

RIBA FREE COMMERCIAL BANKING

Commercial banking has become an essential sector of the modern economy. While it may be smaller in some countries than in others, rarely a country can do without its complete services. In the advanced economies, practically every government department, business organisation, institution and private individual needs, and has, a bank account. In the developing countries too the trend is in this direction. Muslims, who follow the religion of Islam, and who form nearly one fifth of the world's population and live in all parts of the world, are no exception to this trend. However the Muslim community has a problem with the banking system as it exists today and this essay aims to address their concerns. But before we do so, let us briefly examine the services banks provide and how they do it, so that we can determine exactly where the problems lie. Then we can devise solutions to address the specific issues that concern Muslims.

CONVENTIONAL COMMERCIAL BANKING

The main functions of modern conventional commercial banks as they exist today include providing what is called current account facilities, money transfer services, accepting funds into savings accounts, granting loans and advances, facilitating import-export transactions, and buying and selling foreign currency.

Current account facilities include accepting cash deposits into your account and allowing you to withdraw from it as when you require the whole of it or a portion. You can also use a cheque to instruct the bank to pay another person or entity a stated amount of money and debit the same from your deposit in the bank. Similarly, you can receive payments made by others into your account. This ability to pay and receive without having to personally carry notes and coins is a great boon to transacting business - personal and institutional. Private individuals use the current account to receive their salaries and wages and to pay their bills. Businesses and institutions use the current account to make payments for the goods and services received and to receive payments for the goods and services provided. It saves time, and is safe and less expensive. The transactions through cheques can be made whether the payer and the receiver use the same bank or different banks, and whether the concerned banks are miles away in the same country or continents away in different countries.

Money can also be transferred from one person to another, even without having a current account with a bank, through the banks' money transfer arrangements - money orders, pay orders, bank drafts, mail and telegraphic transfers, electronic transfers, etc. - both within and outside the country. There are also other bank guaranteed payment facilities, especially the letters of credit and bills of exchange, which greatly facilitate import-export trade. In fact such trade is practically impossible without this facility.

Banks also accept funds from the public and institutions into savings accounts, keep them safe, and pay interest on such funds. In turn, they use these funds to grant loans and advances to borrowers, to whom the bank charges interest. This service provides the savers with a known income, while their capital remains intact. On the other side, it provides the borrowers access to funds, which they would otherwise not have. The borrowed funds may be used for setting up a new business, to expand existing business, to provide working capital for a running business, or for consumption purposes including buying consumer durables, to ride through a difficult period and to meet unexpected expenditure.

They also provide many other services including agency services, business introduc-tions and credit reports. Another important service is in the foreign currency field - buying and selling foreign currency, issuing travellers cheques and credit cards.

Some of the above are paid services, others are not. Some involve paying or receiving interest, others not. But the commercial banks (henceforth the 'banks') and their services have become an integral part of the present-day world.

THE NEEDS AND CONCERNS OF MUSLIMS

The nearly 1.2 billion Muslims in the world are scattered all over the planet. There are 56 member-countries in the Organisation of Islamic Conference, and there are Muslim minorities, large and small, in almost all countries. There are over 100 million Muslims in India, an amount similar to that of all the Middle-eastern countries put together, though they are a minority in that country of over one billion people. The countries and people are also at various different stages of development and advancement. A major characteristic of the

Muslim population distribution is that the majority are in the developing countries, with all the associated infrastructure deficiencies, including low levels of literacy. Many of them need modern banking facilities, and most of them have a common concern - avoiding riba (interest) in their dealings. A banking system designed to address their concerns has to take into account this main concern as well as the other factors.

Inflation

In common with most developing countries, the Muslim countries also face extreme levels of inflation. Conventional banking deals with the inflation problem tacitly – by incorporating it into the interest rate. Since that is not possible in a riba-free system, we have to address the problem explicitly.

The riba limitation

The main concern of the Muslim community is its desire to avoid dealing in riba, because riba is strictly prohibited in their religion - Islam. As far as money is concerned, riba is loosely translated as interest. Whether this translation is accurate or not - whether the Arabic word riba and the English word interest mean the same thing - is the subject of a long-standing debate. This question needs to be satisfactorily resolved in order to find a proper solution to the problem. In the meantime, one comprehensive and commonly accepted definition of riba (in matters of money) is that when money is lent, if the lender demands more than his principal to be returned, the excess amount so demanded is riba. Islam strictly prohibits demanding and/or receiving riba, paying riba, witnessing or writing such a transaction.

In the context of modern banking, the depositors receive interest, borrowers pay interest, and the bank both pays and receives interest, writes and perhaps also witnesses the transaction as well as keeping account of it. It is on this basis that modern banking is repugnant to the Muslims. Their dilemma is that it is difficult to be part of today's world without the medium of modern banking. Hence the search for a riba free alternative.

We can begin by asking whether all the operations of a commercial bank are unacceptable to the Muslims on account of the riba prohibition. Can they make use of some and seek alternatives for others? To do that, we need to look first at the working of a conventional bank in some detail.

SOME DISSECTION AND ANALYSIS

The sources of funds available in a bank can be categorised by the type of deposit account in which it is held as well as by the purpose for which it is held.

The first source is the current account deposit. They are held in the bank for the purposes of safety and ready availability and for transaction convenience, which has become almost a necessity in modern life. We have already seen the working of a current account.

The second source is the ordinary savings deposit. Banks pay interest on savings deposits in order to attract more funds, but the primary concern of the depositor in an ordinary savings account is the safety of his/her savings and its easy availability when needed. It is usually a temporary holding and the paid interest is expected to cover the value loss due to inflation. In less developed countries, many people have no need or access to current accounts, for various reasons, and therefore they resort to ordinary savings accounts. Whatever the intentions of the depositors the banks use the funds to grant loans and advances to clients and borrowers.

The third source of funds is the fixed deposits. Here the main consideration of the depositor is the fixed and assured interest (or return) he receives from the bank. Safety and compensation for inflation are also considerations but they are part of the package. The bank uses the funds from this source to grant long-term and large-size loans.

INVESTMENT AND FINANCE

The fixed deposits are investments from the point of view of the depositors, and the loans granted, using this source of funds, are financed from the point of view of the entrepreneur-borrowers. Since the fixed return paid to the depositor will fall under the category of riba, Muslims depositors cannot accept the paid return. The loans are also given on fixed-return basis. This too is riba and therefore Muslim entrepreneurs cannot make use of such finance. Hence a riba-free bank cannot provide such an account. Islamic bankers came up with the idea of converting this account into an investment account and using the funds to finance borrowers' projects under a profit-and-loss-sharing scheme whereby the investment of account holders too will receive a share, which will not be a pre-fixed amount and it may well be a loss. But this scheme has not proved viable and has in fact created more difficulties.

In order to deal with these difficulties, which are peculiar to Muslims and therefore have not been taken into consideration by the conventional banking system, Muslims will have to develop their own institutions. A suitable proposal has been made elsewhere. It is suggested that the funds from the third source be handled by an entirely separate institution operating under the rules of Mudaraba.

CHARITABLE LOANS

The Islamic banking movement has introduced another category to the use of funds. This is called by various names such as *qard hassan*, (sometimes transliterated as *gharz-al-hasaneh* and *qard-e-hasana*). The important requirement here is that if the borrower is unable to repay the loan at the agreed time, further time should be allowed for repayment or the loan should be written off and regarded as charity. But it begs a reasonable question: does an entity that holds other peoples' money in trust have any right to give charity out of it? Furthermore, it will undermine the promise to return the full amount to the depositors. How is the shortfall to be made up? Besides, imagine the branch manager of a chain of banks being given the authority to determine who of his borrowers is under dire circumstances and the power to write off his loan. It is an open invitation to corruption and fraud. Therefore we will leave the charitable loans to private individuals and charity organisations.

Then we will have a bank that is free of the encumbrances of the charitable loans, but it will also be without the benefit of a large source of funds - the fixed deposits. Yet this bank will be able to provide all the services generally required of a commercial bank and the resulting bank the riba-free commercial bank.

THE RIBA-FREE COMMERCIAL BANK

The bank under consideration is a commercial entity that provides services for a payment. It accepts deposits, guarantees their safety and full return, and provides all current account facilities - such as cash receipts, cheque collection and payment, electronic and other types of fund transfers, etc. - currently provided by conventional commercial banks. Depositors explicitly or implicitly agree to their funds being used to grant loans to borrowers, but the bank guarantees the full return of their deposits as and when required or as agreed. The depositors do not demand nor are they paid any financial returns on their deposits. As such, the depositors deal in no riba.

The borrowers are granted loans on condition that the capital, which belongs to the depositors, is returned in full, whatever their financial circumstances, and they pay the bank a fee for making the funds available to them. The fee includes all the costs incurred by the bank and a remuneration (or profit) for providing the service. This service can be likened to the services provided by a courier who carries the money from the depositor (the real owner-lender of the money) to the borrower. At the end of term, the courier carries the money back to the owner. The courier is also responsible for the security of the money while in his possession. Since the owner-lender does not demand any extra amount (which would be riba) therefore the borrower does not pay any extra amount (to the owner-lender) beyond the principal. Since no riba was demanded or paid, the courier does not carry witness or keep account of any riba. Therefore the bank's "lending" operation is free of riba. The bank makes sure that the borrower has the ability to repay the capital and the fees.

At this point, it is worthwhile to emphasize two basic assumptions in the concept of this riba-free bank. One, riba is what is demanded and/or received by the capital-owner (who is the real lender) over and above the capital he lends; and two, the payment made by the borrower to the courier for his services is not riba. It is necessary that these two crucial points are fully understood and accepted as correct under Islamic law before we proceed with further discussions.

There is also another important aspect: the perception of a bank as a money-lender. True, banks originated from the moneylender who lent his own money on interest. But the modern banks no longer do that (even though some of the shareholders' money may also be used). It is mainly the depositors' money that they lend to the borrowers. In this sense they are couriers of money as described above. They are also couriers of money when they carry payers' money to the receivers (which is the main current account operation). Therefore, we have to take account of present-day realities and change our traditional perception of banks as moneylenders to one of couriers of money. This changed perception will free Muslims of many difficulties, which arise as a consequence of equating banking with money lending, and the banks with moneylenders. In any case, our riba-free commercial bank is designed strictly as a courier of money - it is a service provider in the field of banking and finance. Seen in this light, this bank's operations are all riba-free and the fees it charges for its services have nothing to do with riba.

Requiring the bank to write off the loans of persons who are unable to repay, and to consider these as charity, it is also a consequence of equating a bank to a moneylender who lends his own money. One is free to do what he wants with his own money but a courier who carries someone else's money has no right to give it away in charity. As such, our bank, being a courier of other people's money, does not get involved in charitable loans. Consequently, there is no "leakage" to its funds.

Compatibility with conventional banking is one of the desired goals in devising this riba-free bank. As mentioned above, we have also eliminated the possibility of a leakage and that should find favour with the banking authorities. But the riba-free limitations have made it a smaller bank and now examine the positive aspects of these features.

The Smaller-size and its implications

The commercial bank envisaged here is a much smaller one than a standard conventional bank.This is a consequence of accommodating the riba-prohibition rule of Islam and hence a built-in feature.Therefore we need to examine the implications of this necessarily smaller size.

It came about because we spilt the deposit base of the conventional bank into two parts: demand deposits and ordinary savings deposits on the one hand and the fixed deposits on the other. The latter is generally much larger in size, and therefore what is leftover is at most only one-half of the standard size of a conventional bank.

On account of the smaller size and its composition, this bank cannot grant long-term and large-size loans; it is limited mostly to advancing short-term and small-size loans, although some medium-term and medium-size loans may be accommodated.

On account of these term and size limitations, this bank is much less exposed to business-failure risks. That gives more stability to this bank and to the banking system as a whole.

The smaller deposit-base and the larger reserve requirement on these deposits also result in much reduced bank-created credit. It does not negate the bank's credit-creating ability, and thus deny the economy of the benefits of this facility, but it limits its size. Thus, it reduces the risk of bank failures and, adds to the stability of the banking system. Furthermore, it restrains money supply expansion and hence helps to hold down inflation.

If the equity capital required to set up a bank is based on the size of the bank, this smaller-size bank, with much reduced failure-risk, will entail a smaller equity capital. This will enable the establishment of more commercial banks, resulting in increased competition, which, in turn, should result in better service and efficiency.

The reduced capital requirement will also help to take banking facilities to remoter areas. People residing in areas away from the main cities hold their monetary capital in the form of cash (notes and coins) for want of a bank in the neighbourhood. This is the case in many developing countries and hence a considerable portion of the available monetary capital remains outside the banking system. If this cash both idle and active could be brought into the banking system more funds from domestic sources will become available for business purposes.

Compatibility with conventional banking

Our bank satisfies the basic requirements of a deposit-taking bank. One, it guarantees the depositor's capital; two, the bank contracts to pay a non-negative return; three, its assets are assessable; and four, its income is also assessable and sufficient to maintain the bank. The banking authorities, who are more concerned with the maintenance of capital certainty than with the rate at which interest is paid, should to this extent be satisfied. There are also no built-in leakages due to charitable loans.Other formal legal requirements are easily met. Thus our bank qualifies to be registered as a deposit-taking bank with the central bank under conventional banking laws. This authorisation to set up and operate as a commercial bank under conventional laws has several advantages.

- One, it will ensure proper auditing and monitoring, which will in turn inspire public confidence in the bank. This is vital.
- Two, it will enable riba-free commercial banks to be set up in *all* countries of the world, Muslim and non-Muslim. This will greatly facilitate international export-import trade without the fear of being involved in any riba dealings.
- Three, since this bank can be set up in non-Muslim countries as well and it will offer all conventional commercial banking services, its clientele need not be

limited to the Muslims. Therefore, it has as good a chance of survival as any other bank.

- Four, the considerable number of Muslims living in non-Muslim countries will have the possibility to bank with a riba-free bank which is competitive and offers all the generally-used facilities of a conventional bank.
- Five, since all religions prohibit interest earnings, and even where it is not explicitly prohibited people do look down upon those who lend on interest, some people will appreciate the chance to bank without interest provided the value erosion of their capital due to inflation is compensated and all other banking facilities are offered. There are also people who eschew interest for reasons other than religious belief. They too will appreciate the opportunity given by this bank.
- Six, this bank can hire officers who have already had training and experience in conventional banking, and they can get to work practically straightaway without having to undergo further training in an entirely new system. This is a very big advantage, and is cost-wise and time-wise efficient. It will minimise any gestation period and reduce teething troubles.
- Seven, the compatibility with conventional banking makes the conversion of a conventional bank into a riba-free one easy and quick.
- Eight, from the customers' point of view too, it is easier to understand and follow the procedures since they are not very different from the ones the customers are already used to in dealing with the conventional banks.
- Finally, these banks, being compatible with the conventional system, will be able to easily communicate and deal with other banks, within and outside their own country.

The Islamic banks as they operate today do not offer these advantages, even within the few Muslim countries where they are permitted to operate on their own terms. As such it is worth giving some serious thought to the proposed riba-free bank.

Transparency

Transparency is absent in both the conventional and the Islamic forms of banking. But it is the foundation of the proposed riba-free commercial banking. In the first place, transparency tells both the bank itself and the supervising authorities what the real costs are, how they are distributed, and what the profits are. Secondly, in dealing with inflation, it enables one to know exactly what the loss of value of capital due to inflation was and how it was compensated. Both the depositors and the borrowers too know what they are being charged or paid, and for what reason.

This transparency comes about on account of the model we are using in computing the fees charged by the bank. In conventional banking this fee is a single item, called interest, and it is calculated as a per centage of the principal and depends on the duration of the deposit or loan. In Islamic banking as practised today, in most cases, it is also a single item called profit (or mark up) though it may or may not depend on the size and duration of the "loan". In the model used here this single item is considered as consisting of six components: interest paid to the depositor (which is identified with riba), the cost of specific services provided to the borrower on account of the current loan, cost of overheads of the bank (which includes the costs of general services provided to the depositors and borrowers), bank's profit, a premium to the loan default insurance, and compensation for the loss of value of capital due to inflation.

From the borrower's point of view "interest" charged by the bank is the cost of borrowing, and it has now been shown to consist of six components, only one of which is real interest (identified with riba). The first component (interest) is present in conventional banking and absent in riba-free banking; the next three components cover the fee charged by the bank; the insurance premium goes to a separate fund; and, if inflation is taken into consideration, the last component (compensation for inflation) is recovered from the borrower and passed onto the depositor. Unlike in the computation of conventional interest, each one of these components is computed in a different way and posted to its own separate account. This may seem much additional work, but in this computer age it is not. The result, however, is a positive gain. Let us take a closer look.

Compensation for inflation is the same for all loans in all the banks because it is computed using the same data and formula. The loan default insurance is expected to be run by a single body (or several bodies operating under the same rules) and therefore the premium should be the same for any given borrower in any bank.

Within the fees charged by the bank, the first component is the cost of services procured in the course of processing the loan application. This is specific to the particular loan under consideration, and often consists of charges paid to outside agencies (such as to a lawyer for title checking of the collateral, stamp duties to the government, etc.) and is a one-time cost. The second is the cost of overheads. This is a generalised cost estimated using total annual average *net* overheads cost of the bank (consisting of staff salaries, buildings, supplies, maintenance, etc. *less* income from paid services using the same facilities) divided by the total annual average loans granted by the bank during the same period. Thus it is the bank's cost in obtaining and sustaining loanable funds. This is a per-dollar-per-day cost, equally applicable to all loans and advances. This cost, being expenses minus incomes of the bank, will depend on the efficiency of the bank. Hence it is subject to market forces. It is continuously monitored, and may vary from year to year, but is kept fixed during the year. The third component, bank's profit, is a per centage of the first two components. This per centage may vary from bank to bank, but since this system is transparent, under normal circumstances market competition will determine its size.

The fact that all of this information is routinely available to the borrowers gives them the necessary information to shop around to their advantage, creating competitive market conditions. This management information is also very useful to the bank supervising authorities, who will then have a good overview of general trends in the whole sector.

This detailed transparency, which is not available under the current practices, is a major characteristic of the proposed system. Furthermore, since all the components (of the bank charges) are subject to market forces, and none to arbitrary fixation, and the results are transparent, it is a truly free-market system. Consequently, it reaps the benefits of that system efficiency and lower costs.

MISCONCEPTIONS ABOUT LOSS AND GAIN IN RIBA-FREE BANK

Frankly speaking, when one talks of Islamic banking there seem to be two expectations - expressed and unexpressed - in the minds of people. Those who expect to borrow seem to feel that they would get loans on which they need not pay any interest - they need to repay only the capital. On the other side, those who have capital seem to feel that they would get a return on their capital that would be higher than if they used a fixed-deposit account in a conventional bank. And, the bankers are afraid that no one will deposit in a no-interest account, and that a no-interest loan is simply impossible. These are valid concerns and expectations. But, it should be pointed out and emphasised that, they relate to the savings accounts, especially the fixed deposit accounts; and our scaled-down commercial bank does not deal in this type of deposit, neither in medium in long-term loans granted using such funds. As such they are beyond our scope here. Our bank deals only in current and ordinary savings account deposits and in loans and advances granted using funds from these deposits. Yet it would be useful to examine the validity of these expecta-tions and reservations in the case of our bank, *vis-à-vis* the conventional banks.

First the current (or demand deposit) accounts. Conventional banks do not pay any interest on current account deposits. Our bank also does not. So there is no difference between the two banks in this area. This leaves us with only the ordinary savings accounts and the short- and medium-term loans.

An ordinary savings account in a conventional bank stands somewhere between a current account and a fixed-deposit (or time-fixed) savings account, both in terms of interest received and facilities provided. An ordinary savings account holder has the advantage of withdrawing his deposit (fully or partially) practically at any time (or at very short notice). In this he is nearly akin to one having a demand deposit account, but without the other facilities of the latter (mainly transactions using cheques). A depositor holds his funds in such an account because he is not sure when he may need his funds back or how much at any given time. Here he has the advantage of taking out what he needs when he needs, but what is not withdrawn earns interest, *albeit* at a reduced rate compared to a fixed deposit but better than the zero interest of a current account deposit. The main concern of such a depositor is the safety of his funds. In developing countries, for various reasons, some people are unable to have a current account and therefore they use a savings account instead. These latter are not concerned about the interest. Some others use this account to build up a certain amount for future use (such as to buy property, durable goods, or invest in a business) by depositing their extra earnings as and when they receive it. These and such others consider any interest received as compensation for loss of value suffered by their capital due to inflation. But the interest on these deposits is computed on the minimum balance held during a calendar period, such as a quarter or month.

When there is high inflation the lower rate paid on ordinary savings accounts hardly covers the capital loss due to inflation. Further, when the minimum balance and calendar period criterion are taken together, many depositors miss out on their interests. For example, if one deposited 5000 on 5 January and withdrew it on 27 June, given a minimum period of three months, he would have missed the first quarter by four days and the second quarter by three days and would receive no interest whatsoever, even though his money was available to the bank for a full five months and more. As another example, suppose a person deposits 5000 on 15

December, withdraws 4000 for an emergency on 20 March and deposits it back five days later on 25 March, and finally withdraws the whole amount on 15 April. He will receive interest only on the 1000 minimum balance held during the first quarter, on account of that withdrawal for five days. This happens all too often in practice, and therefore the perceived loss to ordinary savings depositors is in reality minimal. If compensation for inflation loss can be arranged, as is proposed in this system, then such fears will have no basis.

The expectation of cost-free loans from a bank is simply wishful thinking. It is both unrealistic and impractical. Unfortunately it is the result of a narrow, out of context, interpretation of a Qur'anic verse. The verse is addressed to a lender who lends his own money to a known person, in a person-to-person context. The lender is asked not to demand anything more than his capital from the borrower.The additional amount is called riba and prohibited, but the capital is his due. Even here, if the borrower had to incur expenses in travelling to meet the lender, the lender is not expected to pay the travel expenses of the borrower, and the travel expense is obviously not riba. If he sent a courier instead and the courier asked for the same travel expenses, and his wages in addition, these will have to be paid by the borrower and not by the lender, and this expense is not riba. Obviously, it is ridiculous to expect the courier, who provides a tangible service to the borrower spending his own time and effort, to do it free and also to incur the travel expenses without any benefit. Yet, this is exactly what some seem to expect when they demand interest-free loans from a bank. That a modern bank incurs a lot of expenses - in collecting funds from depositors, keeping them safe, scrutinising the loan applications of the borrowers, disbursing the loans, re-collecting them and repaying the depositors, and in keeping accounts and records of all these - is for all to see. Riba-free loans are possible, when the capital owners do not demand it, but cost-free loans are a fantasy, except when it is a person-to-person transaction in the same locality.

What the proposed riba-free bank promises is exactly what it says - banking facilities without involving in riba. The small reduction in the charges the borrower pays this bank (as compared with those paid to a conventional bank), because it does not include the riba component, is incidental. So is the minimal loss an ordinary savings account depositor may suffer. The yardstick of success is whether the bank operates riba-free or not - not whether the loss or gain is more or less when compared with a conventional bank.

However, the transparency we discussed earlier will bring about reductions to the cost of borrowing, compared to a non-transparent conventional bank. Additionally, the compensation for inflation provided for in this system will safeguard the depositor from real loss to his capital without recourse to riba.

OPERATIONS OF THE BANK

The compatibility of this bank with conventional banking procedures facilitates its integration into an existing banking system. For all the tried-and-trusted methods of the conventional banks can be readily used by this bank, except that the cost of borrowing as explained above will replace bank interest in all calculations, and the deposit interest rate will be set equal to zero. Where relevant, compensation for inflation will be computed as explained in Gafoor (1999) and will be collected from the borrowers and paid to the depositors, as appropriateand briefly sketch the main operations of the bank.

Deposit accounts

This bank will have two kinds of deposit accounts: demand and savings. Demand deposits will earn neither riba nor any compensation for inflation. Savings deposits too will not earn any riba but they will be paid compensation for inflation on minimum balances held, say, for a minimum of three calendar months.

Loans

It will provide short-term advances, and short-term and medium-term loans, which can be for durations of less than a month, less than a year and less than three years, respectively. Borrowers will pay the cost of borrowing on all loans and advances. However, one or more components of the cost of borrowing may become zero, depending on the type of loan. For example, compensation for inflation will be collected from all loans of three months or more duration but this component will be zero in shorter-term loans; short-term advances will not have the service cost component; and inter-bank loans will entail only the overheads charge, all others being zero. Islamic banks as they operate today find it difficult to provide needed services in many important areas. These include short-term advances to see through liquidity problems, medium-term loans to set up small businesses, short-term loans (or working capital) to running businesses, and consumer credit, on a viable commercial basis. But these are among the most important banking services required in any economy. Inter-bank credit is also another necessity in a conventional banking system, but Islamic banks are unable to provide it. Under the proposed riba-free bank these loans and advances can be provided very easily.

Bills of exchange

Other important areas include treasury bills, bills of exchange, and any financing connected with letters of credit. These too present no problems, since they can be treated as short-term loans (of generally less than three months) and charged accordingly.

Government bonds

Another important area is government bonds. The suggested solution to this is to denominate these bonds in units of gold. Then they will be sold at the current price of gold and will be bought back at the price current at the time of maturity. Thus the government will not pay any riba and the bond-holders will not demand or receive any riba, but the real loss of value of their capital due to inflation will be automati-cally and very transparently compensated. This, however, will require new govern-ment legislation. Governments of high inflation countries should consider this course of action seriously. Banks come into the picture only after government action.

Other services

All other normal commercial banking operations will take place as in a conventional bank.

BANK'S SERVICES TO THE DEPOSITORS

Depositors, both current and savings account holders, receive several types of services from the bank. These include accepting deposits whenever they are brought in, keeping them safe, returning them fully or in part when requested, keeping account of all these, accepting cheques drawn in favour of an account-holder and presenting it to the drawer's bank and collecting the proceeds and crediting it to the payee, paying cheques drawn by an account-holder, honouring standing orders for regular payments, electronic transfer of funds, cash dispensing from automatic teller machines, and so on. Most of these are offered free of charge though the bank incurs a lot of expense in providing them. They are offered to the depositors free only because their money, while held in the bank, is used by it to lend to borrowers and thereby earn an income. These services are needed by the depositors, and they should pay for them in cash if obtained from any other source. But the bank provides them free in order to induce them to keep their money with the bank. This service in kind is offered and received only because the depositor has given (or lent) some money to the bank; otherwise it would require payment in cash. Seen in this light, is it riba?

The Islamic banking literature seems to be largely silent on this question. But it is necessary to raise the question, even though we do not propose to answer it. It is for the *Shari'a* experts to enlighten us on this. All that we can say here is that the bank as proposed above can accommodate both yes and no answers. If the answer is no, then nothing in the present state of affairs need to change. If yes, then the depositors will have to pay a fee for the services they receive and it will become an income to the bank, reducing its *net* overheads cost. Consequently the cost of borrowing will become cheaper.

DISCUSSION AND CONCLUSION

In the foregoing paragraphs we have taken a conventional bank and divided it into two sectors, one that provides a banking service and the other that caters to investment and finance. Our essay here was concerned with the former and the latter has been dealt with in a companion article. The sector that is under consideration here plays an important and essential role in conducting the businesses of individuals, organisations, businesses and the government, and touches the lives of practically everyone. Most of the daily activities in a bank, including almost all the transactions, take place in this sector. Comparatively speaking, the number of people involved and the number of transactions taking place in the other sector is much smaller even though each transaction may involve huge sums of money.

In the history of banking, the origins of the first sector goes back to the goldsmiths and their receipts confirming the deposit of gold by a client and its availability to the bearer, and the second sector goes back to the moneylender who lent his own money on interest. Later on these two were combined to form the progenitors of the modern bank. The activities in the first sector provide the modern bank with the ability to create bank credit, and the second the bulk of the monetary basis for this creation (using depositors' money). Thus this combination enables the modern bank to lend huge sums of money. In turn, this enables the debt-based financing of enterprises, large and small. This contributes to a greatly accelerated economic activity, using a relatively small monetary base; but it also has its negative side. Business cycles are traced back to speculation and excessive bank credit. Beyond a certain limit, unstable banks, bank failures, and the consequent economic chaos are the results.

By separating the two sectors, this chain of events can be eliminated at source without losing the benefits of either. The commercial bank can still create credit and help cash flow and provide financing, but on a smaller scale and on shorter terms, using the funds in current and savings accounts. This would practically eliminate risks of bank failures. And, the funds that would otherwise go into time-deposits will be used by investment companies and investment banks to equity-finance enterprises, giving stability to the economy. But both will have to go together to create a comprehensive banking and finance system.

Unfortunately, Islamic banking has come to be associated with the investment and finance sector, and has practically ignored the other sector, except in a few countries such as Iran and Pakistan where it has been compelled to accommodate it. There is a historical background for this situation.

In the Middle-east, Islamic banks came into being consequent to the oil price hike of 1973 and the resultant flow of huge amounts of money into the oil producing countries. When the new money flowed in the only income-earning investment options available were those offered by the conventional banks, based on interest. This pricked the Muslim religious conscience, and they searched for interest-free alternatives. Dubai Islamic Bank, the DMI (Darul Maal Islami) group with banking subsidiaries such as Faisal Islamic Bank, the Dallah Al-Barakah group and the Kuwait Finance House, these are some of the first fruits of this search. They came into being beginning 1975.

What was required here was an agent to find *opportunities for the direct employment of new money*. The ancient concept of Mudaraba suited this situation best, and the investment accounts of these banks and the mark-up trade financing model served the purpose well. Some of the new money began to be deposited in the investment accounts of these banks, and the banks used it to finance the imports required for public and private development projects and consumption needs. The size of both the deposits and the transactions were large, and the profits were good. There was also enough new money in private hands providing sufficient liquidity in the economy. The conventional banks continued to operate in these countries side by side with the new banks. Large Western banks provided all the conventional facilities, both nationally and internationally, and dominated the field. Since the current account operations of the conventional banks were considered riba-free, the need for a fully riba-free system was not acutely felt.

When it was sought to establish Islamic banks in Western countries, based on this model, their conventional central bank regulatory authorities refused permission. Therefore financial institutions, which are governed by a different set of rules, were set up in these countries, and they targeted high net-worth individuals and large ticket trade items. They concentrated on short-term trade financing and generally avoided long-term commitments. Reputed Western banks joined in the bonanza, and Islamic banking came to be identified with this model.

In Iran and Pakistan, Islamic banks were established (beginning 1981) for a different reason - religion and politics. It was by government initiative and the aim was to completely rid the economy of riba, and they began with the banking system. The needs and circumstances of these countries are different. Unlike in the oil producing countries of the Middle-east, there is no (or very little) inflow of new (oil-bonanza) money here. Most of the money comes from normal economic activities, except for any outside loans and aid. There are few high net-worth individuals. The deposits come mainly from a large number of small depositors. There are also few large ticket items of import. The economies of these countries are dominated by a large number of small and medium size businesses which need temporary advances to tide over short-term liquidity problems, and loans to set up new enterprises and to expand existing ones. Inflation and liquidity are also acute problems. The situation is similar in most of the other Muslim countries too. The existing Islamic banking models do not suit this situation. Therefore their search for a riba-free alternative continues.

The profit-and loss-sharing (PLS) concept of the Islamic banks seems to work when it comes to financing one-time trade contracts (even though such activity gives rise to questions of economic morality), but has proven itself difficult to implement in the financing of enterprises on a medium or long-term basis. We have dealt with this aspect and provided a viable solution in the companion article mentioned earlier.

The PLS scheme is also unsuited to catering for the short-term liquidity needs of businesses, individuals and the government, nor can it provide short- and medium-term loans to set up new small enterprises and working capital for existing businesses. Furthermore, it is unsuitable for providing consumer loans on a commercially viable basis. Inter-bank credit is another difficult area.

In this article we have tried to rectify this lacuna by establishing a riba-free commercial bank that uses conventional banking methods and operates under conventional banking laws. This bank provides all current account services, and makes use of the riba-free demand and savings deposits to provide riba-free - but not cost-free - loans and advances. It can also create bank credit to meet the credit needs of its clients, and provide inter-bank loans.

There is a need for riba-free banks in all countries where Muslims live. But most countries operate under conventional banking laws, and it is futile to expect the situation to change. Neither need it change. Given also the generally tight monetary situation in countries other than the oil producing ones, we have to look for a solution within the conventional model. The model presented above is designed to work within the conventional laws. Under this model converting an existing bank into a riba-free one, as well as setting up a new bank, is relatively easy.

Now it is up to the Muslim bankers and others to take steps to establish such riba-free commercial banks in all countries of the world, and pave the way for riba-free economies in Muslim countries.

MEETING THE FINANCIAL NEEDS OF MUSLIMS

Today, a fixed deposit in a bank is considered an investment because it earns a return, and a loan is considered an asset by the bank for the same reason. But they are both interest-earning loans. Whatever the purpose, money is available only as a loan at interest. The lenders (both the depositors and the bank) are not really concerned about whether the money was invested in a productive activity or consumed; neither is their return related to the result of any productive activity in which their capital was used. Even when the loan was intended for consumption, or the investment resulted in loss, the pre-determined interest must be paid. In contrast to this, in the Islamic tradition, the distinction between investment and lending had been clearly recognised and provided for, but unfortunately, in modern times, its importance does not seem to have been fully appreciated and acted upon.

The Qur'an recognises two different sets of purposes for which money is needed, and notes the two techniques used by capital-owners to cater for these needs. But the techniques must match the purposes. The need of entrepreneurs for capital is recognised, and in order to cater to this need investment of capital in productive employment is encouraged, but it must be done on a profit and loss sharing basis. Borrowing and lending (for productive or non-productive purposes) are also recognised as legitimate need and technique, but they should be done on the basis of mutual help - without loss or profit to either party. The need of entrepreneurs for short-term (couple of weeks to couple of months) advances and loans (to overcome cash flow difficulties, for unspecified purchases, miscellaneous expenses, bridging loans, import/export credit, letters of credit, etc, etc.) fall within the latter category. This is a very important type of financing need for all running enterprises, but especially critical for small businesses, which are the backbones of all developing economies, to which category most of the populous Muslim countries belong. Conventional banking deals with it very effectively by advancing short-term loans, at interest. But Islamic banking and finance as practised today has great difficulty in dealing with this need; in fact, it is one of its major shortcomings.

The Qur'an also recognises a set of circumstances in which one may find himself/herself - circumstances which warranted leniency or pure charity. A borrower, who borrowed with the intention of repaying the loan, hoping on better future circumstances, may find that hope remaining unrealised within the expected timeframe. He needs leniency until better times return. Others may find themselves in circumstances where they could not even promise to repay. They deserve charity. The Qur'an encourages leniency on the part of lenders, and recommends voluntary charity to those who posses the means.

By recognising the different types of needs and circumstances which naturally occur in any human society and dealing with them using suitably different techniques, the Qur'an seeks to prevent unpleasant consequences, rather than seeking to find solutions after the damage is done. In this essay we propose to explore the specifics of this comprehensive approach in the context of the present-day world.

The circumstances, in which man lives, change with time and space. But there seem to be also some inherent characteristics that remain constant. It is necessary to distinguish the latter from the former, and to devise new methods and institutions that address the needs of these inherent characteristics when circumstances change. The inherent characteristics that remain constant are: 1) the need of capital-holders to earn an income using their capital; the need of traders, merchants and entrepreneurs for such capital; the latter's ability to use that capital to earn a profit doing their business; and hence their ability to reward the capital-providers for their contribution, 2) the need for loans (for business and personal use), and 3) the need for charity.

How do we address the above needs and characteristics in the circumstances of our day? Many of the verses of the Qur'an were revealed to address specific questions or situations that arose during the lifetime of the Prophet (peace be upon him) but the general guidance contained therein is independent of time and place. The messages should be understood in the context in which they were revealed but the resulting guidance is for all time and place. The Qur'an is no cookery book; it leaves the details to the humans, giving them enough latitude to devise their own solutions according the circumstances in which they happen to live in time and location. In our present-day circumstances, we need to realise that there are subdivisions within these major categories and that these need be dealt with appropriately.

Investment and finance

This falls under the first category. To illustrate the position of the Qur'an in this case, let us take an example. Suppose a person at the time of the Prophet (peace be upon him) in Mecca had some capital. He could earn an income from it in one of two ways: by engaging in trade (buying and selling) or by lending at interest. The Qur'an said: do the former and avoid the latter, for they are not the same though some do argue so.

At this point, it is necessary to note that trade was the main occupation of the Meccans at the time. But the principles involved are applicable to all enterprises. Trade was practised either individually or in partnership. Partnership was on the basis of either musharaka or Mudaraba. Musharaka is where both partners invested capital in a business (trade) and jointly ran the business, and shared the resulting profit or loss. A capital-holder who did not wish to engage himself directly in the business opted for *mudarab*, where he teamed up with an entrepreneur (trader), provided him with all the necessary capital and shared in the profit of enterprise at a pre-agreed ratio (or absorbed the full loss if and when that occurred) in effect, a sleeping partnership. So a capital-owner who wished to earn an income using his capital but without directly engaging himself in an enterprise was given only one option: go into partnership with an entrepreneur on the basis of Mudaraba (profit sharing and loss absorbing).

It is remarkable that the same choices exist even today: a) put your money in a partnership company (with you as the sleeping partner) or buy shares in a shareholder company; b) deposit in a bank or buy bonds and securities. In the former you share in the profit and loss, and in the latter you receive an interest income.

In the circumstances of the present-day world, investment and finance can be dealt with efficiently by recognising the subcategories within this main head and adopting appropriate techniques.

Shareholder companies

The first need is easily addressed in the form of sleeping partners and shareholders in modern companies. Unfortunately, this type of modern company is rather rare in the Muslim world, though it is actually the modern version of the ancient practice of Mudaraba. On the contrary, they play a major role in the economies of the developed countries. Large-scale industries and trading concerns, contributing to the real economy, were established using such investment and finance. What exist in the Muslim world are the one-person-owned-and-operated businesses and enterprises. These are, of course, necessary but they have their limitations. To advance, Muslims will have to follow the example of others. The idea of sleeping partner and shareholder companies should be promoted among Muslim financiers and entrepreneurs and such enterprises should be set up and professionally run in all sectors of the real economy. There is no choice, even though, in doing so, they will be only regaining their lost heritage of 1400 years ago.

Participatory financing

Another complementary form of investment option, also based on the Mudaraba principle, which caters to small capital-holders who would otherwise resort to bank deposits and/or bonds, is presented in Gafoor (1996). This can be operated by investment companies and investment banks, and provides the investors with a unit-trust/unit-share type of investment and will finance enterprises that are currently financed by bank loans. This is a new concept and a comprehensive project proposal is available at the author's website. This was developed as a riba-free alternative to fixed deposit accounts and medium- and long-term loans in order to address the concerns of Muslims. But the resulting product does not require the participants to be Muslims. It is simply a responsible form of financing, operating under conventional business laws. Hence it can be practised by anyone in any country. This should go a long way in preventing businesses and enterprises going bankrupt due to their inability to service bank loans. And thereby provide stability to all economies.

Mudaraba partnerships

Pure Mudaraba partnerships between known parties at the local level also should be promoted and popularised. This will help both the small capital-holders and budding entrepreneurs, and will contribute to the development of the local economy. This is another lost heritage that Muslims should revive at the earliest opportunity. It requires trust, honesty, integrity and professionalism. But advice and intermediation by independent accounting professionals and bookkeepers should be used to substantiate such trust by verifiable documentation.

Banking and loans

This falls under category of lending and borrowing. Here too, by recognising the subcategories within this head and adopting appropriate techniques, we can deal with the needs very efficiently.

COMMERCIAL BANKING

The first thing that comes to mind when one thinks of a bank is bank loans. But the bulk of the work that goes on within a commercial bank (retail bank, deposit bank) is transfer of funds, from one account to another - within the same branch, between branches of the same bank, between different banks, between different countries, etc. Individuals use their demand deposit (current) accounts to pay their bills and receive their salaries/wages/pensions; businesses use current accounts to make and receive payments for the goods and services supplied; government and other entities use them to pay and receive their dues. This has become a basic necessity in practically all countries, a backbone of all modern economies and societies - the more advanced a country the more essential this service. It saves tremendous amounts of time and effort for individuals and organisations in travelling and carrying the necessary cash to and from *each* of their creditors and debtors. Thus its contribution to the national economy and its efficient running is immeasurable.

Yet, this important service is provided by the banks, in large measure, free of charge. Why free, and how is the operational costs of this services met by the bank? For, on the one hand, this transfer of funds from account to account without actual movement of funds makes possible what is called bank credit creation (that is, the act of lending more money than that available in the vaults of the bank). Therefore, the bank encourages the public to use its services to transfer funds by providing the service free. On the other hand, the cost of the operation is recovered from the borrowers as part of the interest. Thus, in conventional banking this essential service has become intertwined with riba, in the form of interest charged on bank loans and interest paid on bank deposits (which is the major source of funds for the loans). This is unacceptable to the Muslims, yet they too need the banking services (transfer of funds as well as loans) just like everyone else.

Islamic banking theory sought to resolve the problem by offering the loans completely free of interest (or grudgingly with some service charge) and meeting the costs of the services from earnings made elsewhere (profits made from buying and selling, and other forms of trade) using funds in the investment accounts. This has led to several complications. A major problem is that this form of banking is not workable under conventional banking laws and therefore cannot be implemented, except in a few Muslim countries where special laws have been enacted. In all other countries, banking services and loans have been left to the conventional banks and Islamic banking has limited itself to financing, tacitly calling itself Islamic Finance. Thus a riba-free (retail) banking system is still to be designed and implemented.

The question of providing loans and all other banking services without involving in riba is addressed in Gafoor (1995). This uses a general model of the cost of borrowing and a courier-bank concept. A detailed discussion of this is available as an article at the author's website. A comprehensive project proposal is also available at the author's website.

The proposed banks will provide all banking services and are designed to operate under the conventional banking laws and regulations. They will accept demand deposits and ordinary savings deposits, and will use the funds in these deposits to provide short-term and (some) medium-term loans and advances. To be sure, this is only "half" of a modern bank, the other "half"- consisting of the fixed deposits and the long- and medium-term loans - being given over to the participatory financing companies and banks mentioned earlier. The need for and the advantages of such a division and separation are given in the project proposal referred to above.

Again, though the system was developed in order to address the riba concern of Muslims, the resulting product does not require the clientele to be Muslims. It has been shown that when the bank is constituted as envisaged here, the riba involvement becomes insignificant and its removal will be hardly noticed by the clients. It becomes simply a transparent form of banking that can be implemented in any country, without any changes to the present banking laws. This should be of special interest to Muslim communities living in non-Muslim countries.

Savings and loans at community level

Historically, all banks have generally served governments, businesses, and the well-to do. For good collateral and guaranteed revenue to service the loan are essential considerations in granting a loan. As time passed on, the banking business expanded into the newly developing middle class that had gradually acquired savings, properties and stable incomes. Their savings made them welcome, and their properties and stable (mainly wage) income made some of them eligible for small loans. Legislation has been passed to safeguard the interests of both parties, though by now the banks have emerged as the stronger of the two. This is the case in the developed countries. In the developing countries, with their low levels of literacy and economic development, participation of the majority in the banking sector is very limited. They have a long way to go. Yet, they too have need for credit, *albeit* in small measure. But the conventional banks are not designed to cater to them. Neither will the riba-free commercial bank we have presented above be able to act differently. One little appreciated reason is that the modern banks are not like their forerunners, the moneylenders of old who lent their own funds. The modern banks handle, borrow and lend other peoples' money and are managed by professional executives who are governed and constrained by legally binding rules and regulations. They have very little personal discretion.

That leaves a large section of the population in the developing countries, and many small communities in the developed countries, outside the banking system. This is where the private moneylenders come in. They are still alive and well, and ready to pounce. They usually know their clients, live in the same locality, are very reasonable as to collateral, and are quite accommodating - no lengthy approval procedures either - provided the "risk premium" is set suitably high. It is difficult to beat them - they have survived many attempts - but a try is still worth it. Massive efforts at education and economic development at grassroots level are still necessary to keep the unfortunate out of their clutches.

In the meantime and beyond, there is a need for institutions between the type of commercial banks described above and the others to be described below. It is possible to set up savings and loans societies at the local community level to serve the needs of those not served by the commercial banks. They can be organised and run along the lines of the non-profit community lending discussed in the article, *"Interest, Usury,* Riba *and the Operational Costs of a Bank"*, mentioned earlier. Community leaders can play a major role in this project, and religious leaders should promote and support it, because, being an alternative to private riba-based money lending, it is an effective preventive strategy.

GRAMEEN BANK

There is still another section of the population - the unbankable, who are either fully avoided by the moneylenders or mercilessly exploited. These are the ones living on the fringes of the society; their concern is daily subsistence. They are not beggars, neither are they unwilling or unable to work. They often have a useful locally marketable skill. They simply lack that very small capital which can enable them to own the tools and the small stock of raw materials necessary for their trade. In dollar terms, the capital they need is often less than the cost of a meal in New York or London.

The Grameen bank movement in Bangladesh has proved that such people are bankable and that with very little help they can be put on their own two feet and enabled to regain their place in society with dignity. It has a twenty-five year successful history, and its methodology has been adopted in many countries around the world. So the tools are already there. What is necessary in any community is to examine whether the concerned community needs such a bank, and then to set about it. It needs dedicated workers, but the results can be very satisfying.

Private lending

Private person-to-person lending at interest is, and has always been, the primary focus of all religious and social prohibitions. But the need for such personal lending has always been there and will continue to be there for all times. Often it is mutual (borrower today, lender tomorrow, etc.) between known persons - friends, family, colleagues, etc. Sometimes, one may need to go outside this small circle, to wealthier persons who are in no need of the supplicant's help in money matters. It is in these cases that the lender tries to derive some benefit from the borrower's need, by charging interest. The ill effects of interest in this transaction can be removed only by personal refrain by the lender. This can be attained only by personal enlightenment or the fear of accounting on the Day of Judgement. The revulsion of society to such an act is also an effective restrainer. The work is cut out in this area for the religious leaders and teachers of morality.

The leniency and charity recommended in the Qur'an, when the borrower is in straitened circumstances, can be practised only in the case of private lending. For a person can exercise such personal judgement and authority only on his or her own possessions. All other cases considered above relate to people handling other people's property.

The fact that private money lenders were the forerunners of conventional banks, and that no banking institutions comparable to the modern ones existed in Muslim history, seem to have led today's Muslims to apply the *Shari'a* rules relating to private lending to bank lending as well. However, not recognising the difference between a private lender lending his own funds and a bank lending other peoples' money, has created much confusion, false expectations and some misuse by borrowers. Islamic scholars and banking institutions could spare a lot of trouble by recognising this difference, declaring it and advising the borrowers and the general public *beforehand* that no leniency or charity of this kind is to be expected from banking institutions.

Charity

The money-related needs discussed in the previous section (Banking and loans) concern a section of the population that is able and expects to repay their debts, as well as any expenses incurred in the process. But there is always, in any society, another section of the population which simply cannot even expect to pay their debts. They are poor, unemployed or unemployable and have no or small and uncertain income; most often they will not be given any loans and therefore will not even dare to ask for one, small as it may be. They are the ones the society as a whole, and the able in particular, are obliged to look after by means of charity. But this is the area of private individuals and not of banking institutions.

Conventional banking wisely kept out of it; but Islamic banking, in its enthusiasm to solve all problems with one tool, tried to deal with it too and got itself into trouble. Like personal lending, charity too should be left to individuals. They only have full authority over their own funds to use it as they see fit.

Charity is the third category of needs, and here too we find subcategories that need be dealt with using different techniques.

Personal charity

The third need is recognised and charity is recommended in several places in the Qur'an. (Here we are not talking of the obligatory alms-giving called *zakaat* but of optional charity, which is called *sadaqa*.) This is a personal affair. Those who have extra funds may give any amount they wish to whomever they wish. This does exist and will continue to exist, but people must be continuously reminded of its necessity and merit. Personal charity should be encouraged at all levels. This is a task especially of social and religious workers at the personal and community levels.

Institutional charity

However, in the present crowded world where fewer and fewer people know others at a personal level, there is also a need for organised charity. Therefore, charity organisations catering to specific needs, purposes, places or communities should be set up and run, perhaps on the lines of modern Western ones.

The Qur'an talks of two types among the poor, the needy and the beggar *miskin* and *fakir*. The needy are generally not known to the others because they do not ask, but they may be in more straightened circumstances than the beggar. This is one area where an organised charity may be of great relevance on account of the (donor and receiver) anonymity it can provide. Social and religious workers along with like-minded professionals should give some thought to this.

In the above paragraphs, we saw the Qur'an guiding us to recognise the existence of three different needs in any society - investment and finance, banking and loans, and charity - and pointing to the proper techniques for dealing with each of them. The guidance is applicable to our present-day world too and the techniques are already available. We need not re-invent the wheel. We need to only recognise them and make use of them. It is hoped that our small exercise in the foregoing pages has enabled us to identify the necessary components of a comprehensive financial system for an Islamic economy in today's context, and has placed them in perspective.

CURRENCY DEPRECIATION: ESTIMATION AND APPLICATIONS

In another work (Gafoor, 1999) we looked at inflation and its measurement in some detail. In it we also developed a new method appropriate for the measurement of inflation on capital, and we used it to compensate capital erosion due to inflation in lending and borrowing transactions as well as in investment and finance. It was necessary to develop a new measure because it was found that the existing measures of inflation (such as the consumer price index) were not appropriate for the measurement of inflation on capital.

In another work on money (Gafoor, 2001), the history of money was traced from antiquity to the present and its transformation from gold coins and gold-backed paper currency to the present fiduciary currency, whose value is dependent on market forces. Currency depreciation is defined as the value depreciation of currency relative to gold; that is, how much less gold a given amount of the currency would buy from one point in time to another point in time. For example, if 1000 units of currency bought one gram of fine gold last year and 1100 units of currency were needed this year to buy the same amount of the same quality of gold, then the currency has depreciated by 100 units during the year. This is also the magnitude of the value erosion of capital due to inflation during the year, and it may also be called the inflation on capital. Consequently, the new measure (or index) developed to measure inflation on capital is also the same as currency depreciation.

This measure is based on the market price of gold. Very briefly defined, the price of gold for the current week is the average open market price of gold in the local (meaning national) market, for the past thirteen consecutive weeks. Thus it is the 13-week moving (or rolling) average price.

In this essay we propose to demonstrate how this measure (or index) is computed using real-life data. The procedure explained below could then be used to compute the magnitude of the value erosion of capital due to inflation in any given country in any given time period.

Data

The data necessary for the exercise is the daily price of gold (of a specified quality and quantity) in terms of the national currency at the local (meaning national) open market, collected and collated consistently and continuously by an independent body (or authority) using predetermined and documented transparent procedures and a single national price determined and reported daily, and published in the official and public media. Each of the adjectives and adverbs used in the last sentence are of high importance for the success of the procedure and the systems that use the results – daily price, specified quality, local open market, consistently and continuously, predetermined and documented transparent procedures, single national price, daily reporting, public media, etc. This is to ensure that no room is left for any manipulation of the data or the results before, during or after their collection, collation, computing and reporting. Once published in the media the raw data is in the public domain, and any manipulation afterwards can be checked and challenged.

In practice the price can be defined as "the price of one ounce (or gram) of fine gold in the national currency in the local open market". The competent body could be the central bank of the country, the national statistics bureau or any other competent public or private organisation. It is important that the methods of collection, collation and computation are well documented and published and that the procedures are transparent. It is also important that the price data are collected and collated each working day and the single realised market price computed, recorded and published the very following day.

Data collection and price determination

The competent body mentioned earlier is entrusted with the data collection, collation and estimation process. These are statistical procedures and we have to leave it to the competent authority to decide on the parameters and to the statisticians of the authority to devise a sample survey plan. The parameters include the required accuracy, coverage, time frame and cost considerations. This exercise will result in the publication of a single national price of gold that was realised in the market during the previous day.

Computations

The daily price data is arranged in weekly blocks. Generally a week consists of five working days but in some weeks one or more holidays may occur making it a 4- or 3-workday week. Therefore the average daily price for the week is obtained by dividing the total in each block by the number of working days in that week (data points in that block). We may call this the weekly average price or the average price for the week.

Next, the 13-weeks average price is obtained by computing the average of the weekly average prices of 13 consecutive weeks. This will be the operative price for the next consecutive week – the 14th week. This price will be used for all transactions during the 14th week.

The operative price for the 15th week is obtained as follows. During the 14th week, enter the daily price for each day as it is published. At the end of the week, the weekly average for the 14th week is computed and recorded. Now, add the 14th week average price to the total of the 13 consecutive preceding weekly averages computed earlier, and drop (subtract) the 1st week's average price from the new total. This gives the total of the 13 consecutive weeks immediately preceding the 15th week (i.e. 2nd to 14th weeks). Divide the total by 13 to obtain the 13-weeks average price, and this will be the operative price for the 15th week. Similarly, the operative price for the 16th week is obtained by computing the average of the 13 weeks immediately preceding the 16th week (i.e. 3rd to 15th weeks).

Operative price and its operation

At this point we need to explain what is meant by operative price (for the week). Keeping it short (refer to Gafoor, 1999 for details), though deposits and loans of a duration longer than 13 weeks (3 months) will be accepted and granted, respectively, in terms of the local currency the accounts will be kept in terms of gold units – say, so many grams of fine gold. When the depositor wishes to withdraw it the same amount as was recorded in terms of gold units will be returned to him, even though he may receive more (than he deposited) in terms of currency units. In theory, this is exactly as if he deposited a certain amount of gold at the bank and later retrieved the same without any loss or gain – absolutely riba-free. In the case of loans, the borrower is obliged to return the same amount of gold units as was recorded in the books when he borrowed, but this amount of gold may now cost more in terms of currency and consequently he may have to pay more than he received in terms of currency. The conversion factor used – to convert currency units to gold units and vice versa – is the operative price of gold. If the week's operative price is denoted as "wop" (i.e. say, 1 gram of gold is wop units of the local currency), then when 1000 units of local currency is deposited it will be recorded as 1000/wop units of gold.

In order to fix the idea firmly, let us take an example. Suppose a deposit of 1000 units of currency was made in a certain week, and the wop in that week was 50. Then this is equivalent to (1000/50 =) 20 units of gold. Say, the depositor returned after 40 weeks asked for his deposit, and the wop in that week was 55. His deposit in the bank's records is still 20 units of gold, but since the wop this week is 55 he will be given (20x55 =) 1100 units of currency. The extra 100 he receives is compensation for the value loss his capital suffered during the 40 weeks it was with the bank.

This means that he could go out to the open market and buy the same amount of gold today that he was able to buy 40 weeks ago – that his depositing the money with the bank (or lending it) has not eroded the purchasing power of his money in terms of gold, a basic metal with an intrinsic value, which used to be the universal currency from antiquity till very recent times. The fiat money (paper currency) can still perform the functions of unit of account and medium of exchange, but the function of store of wealth, which it had lost in recent times, has now been restored to it through this devise. Thus this method builds a bridge between the two extremes of going back to the gold coins as currency and the inevitable collapse of the monetary system if the present state of the un-anchored fiat currency (at the mercy of currency traders, government printing and bank credit creation) is allowed to continue. It will retain the convenience of the paper currency, which is more convenient to carry than bags of gold, on account of which the paper currency was originally invented, without losing the currency's function as a store of wealth.

In private person-to-person lending or borrowing transactions too the same method could be used. Again, the idea is that the same amount of gold is borrowed and returned without any addition or subtraction – an absolutely riba-free transaction as it would have been in the time of the Prophet (pbuh) and until recently. Any additional amount the lender may receive in terms of paper currency is the loss his capital suffered while in the hands of the borrower due to currency depreciation. In this method of transaction the lender does not suffer real loss of value in his capital, nor does the borrower gain any advantage due to currency depreciation. Hence this additional amount is definitely not riba, but an accommodation necessary to adjust to the peculiar circumstance of our time. Hopefully this is a temporary step until such time as better counsel prevails and paper currency is again pegged to solid gold. Perhaps this effort will help bring to a halt the present slide towards chaos and initiate the journey back towards gold-based paper currency.

(This method is equally applicable when the currency appreciates – a phenomenon rarely seen in recent times – and in that case too the lender will not gain any advantage and the borrower will not lose.)

Applications

In conventional banking too, currency depreciation is taken into account, but tacitly, and it is included in the all-inclusive interest rate as compensation for value loss of capital due to inflation. In the case of deposits it is always seen to that the interest rate is set higher than the inflation rate and therefore the real interest rate is always positive or seems to be positive. However, there are three difficulties in this concept; two are common to everybody and one is specific to the Muslims.

1. The measure of inflation used (or assumed to be used) is inappropriate for measuring inflation on capital.
2. An estimation of inflation is made by the bank right at the beginning of the transaction (deposit or loan) and is effective (generally) for the total duration of the deposit or loan – three months, one year, three years or more. But there are no measures of inflation that could predict inflation of the future with any accuracy – the further the future the wider off the mark the prediction.

   Taking the above two difficulties together, the inflation estimation is both inappropriate and widely off the mark. In order to be on the safe side the bank always uses the lowest estimate (whatever the measure used) in setting the deposit rate, and the highest estimate in setting the loan rate. Since in most of the transactions the bank is an overwhelmingly powerful party, what the bank says goes. Hence both the above difficulties are used in favour of the bank and to the disadvantage of the customer.
3. Interest has always been considered a single entity, both in theory and practice. But in reality, several factors are

taken into consideration by the bank in fixing this single entity. For example, the deposit interest consists of both compensation for inflation and real interest (or usury, riba). (And the loan interest consists of these as well as the operational costs of the bank, its profit, etc.). This has consequences for a conscientious Muslim. For when he rejects interest on his deposit considering all of it as riba he also throws away the compensation for inflation part. The latter is his due since his capital lost part of its value through no fault of his. But he has no option since he cannot separate one from the other.

In the method presented in the foregoing paragraphs, we have provided a theory and procedure by which all the above three difficulties are overcome – a measure of inflation appropriate to the measurement of inflation on capital; a procedure that estimates and compensates the realised (and therefore accurate) loss of value suffered by capital, thereby protecting both the lender and the borrower (and this both transparently and equitably); and a method to separate riba from interest and thereby help Muslims to keep away from riba without suffering loss to their capital. The last helps those Muslims who live in both Muslim and non-Muslim countries, where fixed deposits in conventional banks is the only option to keep their monetary wealth safe, to keep away from riba (by throwing away the riba component) and still protect their capital from any value loss.

In short, we have now come into possession of a method and procedure that helps us keep capital counted in currency units to be coupled to gold so that the real value of capital is not eroded by inflation (due to currency depreciation). This method can be applied to protect capital in all kinds of situations, such as, in bank deposits and bank loans, investment and finance, and in person-to-person lending or borrowing.

Index

A

Accounts, 23, 26, 27, 32, 35, 44, 48, 50, 54, 55, 65, 81, 179, 256, 277, 278, 280, 289, 290, 291, 292, 293, 296, 297, 303
Advance Purchase, 43
Advisory Services, 57
Amanah, 18, 36, 37, 53, 140, 141, 217, 218, 220
Assigning of the Lease, 149

B

Bai Muajjal, 148, 246
Bai Salam, 148, 247
Bai-Al-Dain, 91
Bills of Exchange, 23, 56, 91, 265, 280

C

Cancellation of Contract, 150
Capital and Return, 201
Capital Guarantee, 205, 206, 207
Charitable Loans, 268, 269, 270, 272
Charity, 3, 4, 16, 81, 83, 86, 108, 156, 221, 268, 275, 277, 293, 294, 301, 302, 303
Commercial Banking, 29, 30, 31, 201, 205, 206, 217, 262, 272, 274, 281
Commercial Interest, 138, 142, 143
Commodity Fund, 89, 90
Compound Interest, 140, 144, 145
Computations, 299
Conventional Banking, 25, 30, 39, 51, 53, 192, 210, 213, 217, 226, 231, 244, 268, 270, 272, 273, 274, 279, 280, 285, 291, 292, 302
Currency Depreciation, 263, 298, 301, 302, 303

D

Data Collection, 299
Debt Instruments, 216
Deposit, 18, 23, 26, 27, 33, 41, 48, 50, 51, 53, 54, 55, 58, 59, 65, 81, 140, 165, 172, 275, 277, 278, 280, 283, 286, 290, 291, 301, 303

Deposit Accounts, 27, 48, 50, 207, 209, 276, 279, 289
Diminishing Musharakah, 179, 181, 185, 186, 187
Dispute Resolution, 174

E

Equity Fund, 80, 86
Equity Instruments, 215
Excess Liquidity, 36, 37, 50, 192, 198
Export Financing, 73, 159, 165
Extravaganza and Vanity, 257

F

Financing Contracts, 41
Five Khiyars, 187

G

Generic Ijarah process, 218
Generic Murabahah Process, 219
Government Bonds, 259, 280
Government Borrowing, 35, 191
Government Expenditure, 259
Grameen Bank, 294

H

House Financing, 152, 180, 185, 187

I

Ijara Contract, 43
Ijara Muntahia bi at-tamleek, 43
Ijarah Fund, 88
Ijarah -Wal-Iqtina, 245
Import Financing, 72
Inflation, 259, 263, 266, 267, 271, 273, 274, 275, 277, 278, 279, 280, 297, 298, 302, 303
Inheritance Under Debt, 97
Institutional Charity, 296
Interest-free Banking, 28, 38, 44, 45, 46, 47, 195, 210, 211, 228
Investment Financing, 49
IPO Services, 56
Islamic banking, 17, 18, 19, 22, 23, 25, 27, 28, 29, 30, 31, 295, 300, 303
Istijrar, 156, 157, 158

J

Joint Stock, 23, 26, 28, 80, 82, 93, 97, 156, 234

L

Liquidity of Capital, 176
Loans, 19, 21, 26, 28, 30, 34, 38, 50, 51, 55, 96, 139, 140, 270, 271, 272, 275, 276, 292, 293, 295, 297, 300
Long-term Projects, 191

M

Mudarabah, 58, 59, 60, 61, 65, 66, 67, 72, 73, 74, 89, 157,

159, 160, 161, 162, 163, 164, 165, 172, 211, 247
Musawamah, 148, 246
Musharaka, 41, 42, 49, 212, 234, 288
Musharaka Partnerships, 42
Musharakah, 55, 56, 58, 59, 60, 61, 62, 63, 64, 65, 66, 171, 172, 173, 174, 175, 185, 186, 187, 194, 246
Musharakah, 175, 196, 200
Muslim Countries, 1, 17, 29, 43, 46, 92, 137, 195, 198, 201, 204, 207, 210, 212, 216, 217, 238, 266, 272, 273, 284, 285, 286, 291, 292, 303

N

Nasiyah, 5, 8, 9, 10, 13, 143, 145

P

Parallel Salam, 155, 156
Personal Charity, 296
Price Determination, 299
Profit-sharing Agreements, 233
Prohibition of Riba, 16, 17

R

Riba, 2, 3, 4, 5, 6, 8, 9, 10, 11, 12, 13, 16, 17, 40, 41, 47, 76, 131, 132, 137, 138, 142, 143, 145, 153, 158, 165, 231, 262, 263, 269, 276, 278, 293

S

Securitization of Ijarah, 78
Securitization of Murabahah, 78, 158
Securitization of Musharakah, 75
Shareholder Companies, 254, 289
Shirkat-ul-wujooh, 167
Single Transaction, 67, 160
Sub-Lease, 149

T

Tenure of Musharakah, 179
Termination of Mudarabah, 164
Trade Financing, 49
trade financing, 25, 39, 41, 51, 195, 204, 253, 283, 284
Transaction Processes, 218
Transparency, 274
transparency, 274, 276, 279
Treasury bills, 260
treasury bills, 37, 261, 280
Trust, 29, 41, 53, 54, 80, 140, 172, 193, 268, 289, 290
Two-tiered Mudabara, 234

W

Waqf, 95, 96
Working capital financing, 68, 165